"Should be one of the first books a family buys after a diagnosis . . . it will be invaluable to so many children and their families."
—CLAIRE LaZEBNIK, coauthor of *Overcoming Autism* and *Growing Up on the Spectrum*

"Honest, kid-friendly . . . with an upbeat 'can do' spirit that never feels phony or pretentious. It's this constant current of ability, rather than disability, that sets this book apart from others geared to spectrum kids."
—VERONICA ZYSK, coauthor of *1001 Great Ideas for Teaching and Raising Children with Autism or Asperger's*

"This book will give kids and parents reason for hope."
—KIMBERLY KLEIN, PH.D., pediatric neuropsychologist with Fraser Child and Family Center

"An excellent resource, and it's also a survival guide for parents!"
—MARY STEFANSKI, parent of a son with autism

The Survival Guide for Kids with Autism Spectrum Disorders

(And Their Parents)

Elizabeth Verdick & Elizabeth Reeve, M.D.

Illustrated by Nick Kobyluch

free spirit
PUBLISHING®

Library of Congress Cataloging-in-Publication Data
Verdick, Elizabeth.
 The survival guide for kids with autism spectrum disorders (and their parents) / by Elizabeth Verdick & Elizabeth Reeve ; illustrated by Nick Kobyluch.
  p. cm.
  ISBN 978-1-57542-385-2 (pbk.)—ISBN 978-1-57542-674-7 (ebook) 1. Children with autism spectrum disorders—Juvenile literature. 2. Autistic children—Family relationships—Juvenile literature. 3. Parents of autistic children—Juvenile literature. I. Reeve, Elizabeth. II. Kobyluch, Nick, ill. III. Title.
  RJ506.A9V466 2012
  618.92'85882—dc23
                                                            2011046520

eBook ISBN: 978-1-57542-674-7

Note: The names of some children described in this book have been changed to protect their privacy.

Reading Level Grades 4–5; Interest Level Ages 8–13; Fountas & Pinnell Guided Reading Level T

Edited by Marjorie Lisovskis
Cover and interior design by Michelle Lee
All illustrations by Nick Kobyluch, except illustrations on pages 11 (rainbow), 34, 45, 61, 62, 67 (calendar), 70, 77, 99, 100, 141, 145 (pencil and books), 158, 160, 222 by Michelle Lee
Photo on page 32 © istockphoto.com / Leontura
Photo on page 33 © Rosalie Winard

10 9 8 7 6 5 4 3 2 1
Printed in the United States of America
B10950212

Free Spirit Publishing Inc.
Minneapolis, MN
(612) 338-2068
help4kids@freespirit.com
www.freespirit.com

Dedication

To Nancy, Cara, and Trish: You were there in the beginning and you helped bring us further than we imagined possible. Forever grateful, EV

To all the patients and families I have worked with over the past 20 years. You have each taught me something! ER

Acknowledgments

For their careful and thoughtful reviews of the manuscript for this book, thanks go to Cindy Kaldor, autism behavior consultant for the Osseo School District; Kim Klein, Ph.D., pediatric neuropsychologist with Fraser Child and Family Center; Amy Nygaard, attending child and adolescent psychiatrist at Regions Behavioral Health, Woodbury, Minnesota; Pat Pulice, director of Fraser Autism Services; Linda Sieford, Ph.D., family and educational consultant and adjunct faculty in psychology; Angela Henchen; Mary Stefanski; and Daniel Stefanski.

We also send out a huge thank you to all the kids, teens, moms, and dads who took the time to tell us their thoughts about life on the spectrum.

Contents

Introduction for Kids

Have you ever sensed you're different somehow? Maybe you don't seem to fit in with the kids at school or in your neighborhood. You look around and see them talking, laughing, texting, and living life at a different speed than you are. Perhaps you even feel out of step within your own family.

Or, maybe you don't feel so different but other kids treat you as if you are. They may tease you, stare, shy away from you, or tell on you for behaving in ways you didn't even know were "wrong." What's going on? You're special in some way, but how?

This book is about discovering why you're different. Like many people, you have some special skills and gifts. But you also have some special needs. More specifically, you have a condition known as autism spectrum disorder, or ASD. The definition on the next page will explain it more.

1

ASD—What Do These Initials Mean?

ASD is the short and simple way to say **autism spectrum disorder.** But ASD is far from simple.

You probably noticed that the word *autism* is part of ASD. So, what is autism? Doctors and other professionals use this word to describe brain disorders that affect how you think, learn, communicate, and behave.

Autism is part of a diagnosis known as PDD (more initials!). **PDD** stands for **pervasive developmental disorders.** *Pervasive*, in this case, means that something affects your body, mind, and overall health. The word *developmental* describes how you grow over time. *Disorder* means a difference in how you function. Having PDD or PDD-NOS (not otherwise specified) means your development will be different from that of many other kids. **Asperger's syndrome (AS)** is also a form of autism. Whether your medical charts and school records say autism, AS, PDD, PDD-NOS, or ASD, this book can help you.

Some experts use the term **high-functioning autism (HFA)** as well. Someone with HFA can learn and communicate to a higher degree than someone with **low-functioning autism (LFA).**

Throughout the book, we mainly use the terms **autism spectrum disorder** and **ASD.**

(Hope that's A-OK with you.)

Learning that you have ASD can be a confusing experience—and we'd like to make it easier for you. We want to tell you "It's going to be okay." And it *is.* That doesn't mean it's going to be "super simple" or "problem free," though. We wish it could be. But life is hardly ever super simple and problem free.

We wrote this book to help you better understand your needs and differences. We hope it will help you with daily issues, such as your feelings, behavior, and communication with other people. We recommend that you read the book with an adult, even if you're already a strong reader. Why? Because reading with a parent or another grown-up who cares about you is an important way to get support. An adult can answer your questions and help you try out the ideas and tips.

Another reason we wrote this book is because we have a special place in our hearts for kids who have ASD. Both of us are mothers whose sons are "on the spectrum," which is another way of saying they have autism spectrum disorder. While raising our sons, we've heard comments like:

"People with autism can't live in the 'real' world—
they're in their own little world."

or

"People with Asperger's never have many friends
or want to be social."

We don't believe in **can't** or **never.** If you have ASD, there are some differences between you and other people. But your life can be about *can.* You *can*

- make friends
- succeed to the best of your ability in school
- be an awesome son, daughter, sister, brother, or friend
- learn, grow, and connect with others

Never say **never.** Life is about trying your best and learning from each new experience. We believe in you! As authors of this survival guide, our wish is for you to grow up healthy, strong, and proud of who you are. We think the power to do that is in your hands—with help from your family, your school, and the experts you work with.

Let this book help you along the way. We know it's a long book. But we also know that learning about ASD and facing its challenges can be a long process—one that takes time and effort. The book is not meant to be read all at once. Use it in whatever way works for you, focusing on chapters or sections that are useful at a given time. Think of it as a handbook you can go to when you need help with a certain issue or have a question about ASD. You and your parents can turn to it again and again over the years.

The table of contents (page iv) and the index (page 230) can guide you to topics of interest. Take a look at the stories of kids with autism and Asperger's—you may find inspiration or shared experiences. Try some of the book's tips to see what helps you right now—but don't attempt to do everything at once. Learning new skills takes time, patience, and practice. Give yourself the time you need.

You might have questions that the book doesn't answer. If you do, or if there's something you want to tell us about yourself, write to us at:

Elizabeth Verdick and Elizabeth Reeve, M.D. • c/o Free Spirit Publishing
217 Fifth Avenue North, Suite 200 • Minneapolis, MN 55401-1299

You can email us at: help4kids@freespirit.com

We can't wait to hear from you!

Elizabeth & Elizabeth

P.S.   On the next page is a section for adults, written especially for any of the grown-ups who are reading this book with you. If you'd like, you can go straight to Chapter 1 (page 10) to find out more about the question "What Is ASD?"

Introduction for Adults

*"If you've met one person with autism,
you've met one person with autism."*

What a great quote. It's often repeated, and for good reason—people with autism spectrum disorders are complex and unique. They're *individuals.* They can't all be lumped together, because there are vast differences in how they think, learn, feel, behave, and communicate. It's why this popular quote is important for parents, educators, doctors, and experts to always keep in mind.

Sometimes autism is referred to as an invisible disability. In other words, the person isn't in a wheelchair or may not have an obvious physical impairment—so people might assume there's nothing different, nothing "wrong." But autism does affect how someone communicates, socializes, and learns. People with autism spectrum disorders (ASD) behave differently from what is considered "typical" or *neurotypical* (a term sometimes preferred by the autism community; it means "neurologically normal"). A person with autism isn't typical, yet he or she cannot be defined only in terms of the diagnosis.

You're probably reading this book because someone you love (or teach) has autism spectrum disorder. You want to help. Chances are, this young person in your life is now old enough to begin learning about the diagnosis. *The Survival Guide for Kids with Autism Spectrum Disorders (And Their Parents)* is a handbook to help children through the questions, challenges, frustrations, tears, mysteries, successes—the journey. We recommend this book mainly for kids ages eight to thirteen, although older kids may also find it useful. Depending on age and ability, some children may be able to read the book independently. However, we suggest that you and the child share and discuss it together. Even a child who is an adept reader will benefit from having a grown-up read alongside for support, empathy, and further explanation of the issues discussed. As a parent, you may also find that reading together is a chance to strengthen your relationship with your child and keep the door open to questions and issues that arise.

This book is designed to help a child with ASD through many ages and stages, from learning about the diagnosis to facing physical and emotional challenges to improving communication and social skills at home, at school, and in the wider world. Use the book as an everyday tool or guide, or as a way to introduce a new topic or skill. You may find it helpful to come back to the book during times when the child is asking questions, facing changes at home or school, reaching a milestone, or struggling. Because children grow and change—and because their ASD changes, too—they need a book that keeps them informed and helps them achieve to the best of their abilities and at their own pace.

As you may know, the autism community is growing larger by the day. More kids are being diagnosed, more parents are becoming advocates, and more educators are being trained to understand the autism spectrum. There are many voices, many points of view—so many stories of hardship and hope. And we've been a part of the story ourselves. Both of us are mothers of sons who have autism, and one of us is a doctor who works with children and adults with autism spectrum disorders. At times, the two of us wondered how this one book could possibly meet the needs of such a wide and varied audience of passionate, questioning advocates.

In the end, we kept coming back to these questions: What do the *kids* need? What are *their* issues, questions, and experiences? We wrote this book to help kids with autism spectrum disorders get answers to the questions that are important to them, learn more about issues they struggle with, and find out what it's like for other kids who have ASD.

The Survival Guide is divided into three parts:

- **Part 1: A Look into Autism Spectrum Disorders** is a kids' primer on the symptoms, the sensory issues, famous people with the condition, questions that arise, and building a team of helpers.

- **Part 2: Home, School, Community** is about improving daily life at home, at school, and in the wider world. We want kids and families to know that *everything you do can make a difference.* Some days, you may want to give up, or you'll think "This is just too hard" and "Why even try?" Daily life with ASD can be frustrating—but it also can be full of great humor, acceptance, and gratitude for the little things. Part 2 offers tips for making everyday life easier, as well as for setting short- and long-term goals for improving social skills or school performance. What you do for your child matters. Our aim with Part 2 is to help both your child and you keep moving forward, even when it's hard to do.

- **Part 3: Body and Brain Basics** looks into the physical and emotional issues that are such a big part of life with ASD. Readers will learn about exercise, nutrition, sleep, relaxation, handling intense emotions, and more. Here we emphasize the importance of good self-care—because it's a huge step toward better health and greater confidence.

All three parts of the book contain real-life stories of kids with autism spectrum disorders (names and details have been changed to protect their privacy). These stories give a glimpse into the range of challenges our children face each day. The book also includes quotes from real kids who have shared thoughts and insights that may help others with ASD realize they're not alone.

After Part 3, you'll find additional information for you and your child, including a section for parents and caregivers called "Sharing the Diagnosis with Your Child." We hope it helps you feel more confident about—and ready for—this special conversation.

Your role as a parent is unique and complex, just as your child is unique and complex. You need added support from relatives, friends, neighbors, teachers, therapists, doctors, experts, and local organizations focused on autism spectrum disorders. If you're struggling to juggle all that's required of you, ask for help. Even if you're not struggling, ask for help. Reaching out can be an enlightening, rewarding experience. You'll likely find a community of people with amazing stories, invaluable knowledge, strong bonds, and exceptional openness and tolerance.

Being a parent to a special-needs child takes a unique kind of knowledge, courage, and dedication. There's no map to point the way—no expert who can tell you exactly what's best for your child now or in the future. You'll learn by trying new things, seeing what works and what doesn't, and gathering all the support and resources you can. Autism spectrum disorders teach you. Your child teaches you. Other families living with ASD teach you. Together, you and your child grow stronger with every new challenge you face.

We wrote this book because we care a lot about young people on the spectrum. We believe they can succeed at home, at school, and in their communities. We want them to enjoy life, set goals within their reach, make friends, *keep* friends, learn, grow, achieve, know who they are, and feel a sense of belonging in the world. We hope to give readers (both young and not so young) a sense of optimism and positive direction. However, we're not suggesting that you should be relentlessly upbeat about your child's condition or expect miracles—after all, autism spectrum disorder is a very real and challenging condition. Let's put it this way: Don't think of ASD as a life sentence . . . it's a life difference. People with autism spectrum disorders can have rich, fulfilling lives.

You teach them how. You lead the way. Let this book be one of the many tools you turn to for help on the journey.

Part 1

A Look into Autism Spectrum Disorders

Chapter 1

What Is ASD?

ASD stands for autism spectrum disorder. But *disorder* isn't a very friendly word. If you want, you can think of ASD as a brain difference.

Because the difference starts in the brain, ASD has an effect on your body, too. Your brain is like your command center. It sends billions of messages 24/7 to all areas of your body. Messages like:

"Legs, run!"   "Hey, what's that noise?"

"Ouch, that bright sun hurts my eyes."

"Mmmm, I smell lunch. Time to eat."

Your brain plays an important role in three areas having to do with autism spectrum disorder:

1. **Communication:** This is about how you listen, speak, write, or get messages across to others.

2. **Socialization:** *Socializing* is doing things with other people. Your brain affects how you socialize with others and how much you *want* to socialize with them. It affects how you fit into a group, like your family, friends, or community.

3. **Interests and behaviors:** Interests are the things you think about and the activities you enjoy. Behaviors are the things you do and how you act. Your brain plays a role in how often you think or do things, and how much you enjoy them.

If you have ASD, your brain has to work harder when it comes to communicating and socializing. All this hard work might make you feel tired or frustrated, but you can do it! This book will tell you how.

On pages 15–24, you'll learn more about each of the three key areas mentioned above. But first, a word about rainbows . . .

The Many Colors of ASD

Rainbows? What do rainbows have to do with the autism spectrum? You might have seen the word *spectrum* if you've read about rainbows. The spectrum refers to the colors of light in a rainbow (red, orange, yellow, green, blue, indigo, and violet). Just like the rainbow, autism comes in many colors, including your special color! The "spectrum" part of ASD means that each and every person with this condition is different and unique.

ASD and Y-O-U

Even though this book uses the term *autism spectrum disorder,* or ASD, your doctor and the other people in your life may use the words *autism* or *Asperger's*. All these words look and sound different, but their meanings are similar.

Maybe your doctor and parents (or caregivers) have explained your condition to you already. Or maybe they're still in the process of figuring things out. Coming up with the diagnosis of ASD takes time.

To do so, your doctor looks at your medical history, your habits and behaviors, and information about you from your school. Lots of questions come up, like:

- How do you communicate?
- What are your interests?
- How do you play?
- Do you have friends? How do you get along together?

- How do you do in school?
- What do you like to eat?
- What are your sleeping habits?
- Do you have trouble handling your feelings?

To understand you even better, the doctor takes your answers to the questions and compares them to the list of autism symptoms (problems) in a special book*. This can be tricky because every person with autism is so unique. The "magic number" of symptoms the doctor looks for is six. A person with ASD must have at least six symptoms that include difficulties with:

- communication
- socialization
- limited interests and/or repetitive behaviors

You might have more than six symptoms— that's okay, too.

Your doctor will also take a look at your childhood history, especially at what age you learned to speak. Most kids who have a diagnosis of autism had a hard time learning to talk when they were young. They may have been late to start talking, and might have needed speech therapy to start getting the words out. Some people with autism never learn how to speak. They may use special communication tools.

---

*The book is called *The Diagnostic and Statistical Manual of Mental Disorders,* or *The DSM*.

Sam's Story

Sam is 10 years old and has autism. He looks like any other 10-year-old boy—unless something exciting is happening. Then Sam starts rocking back and forth in his chair and flapping his arms like a baby bird ready for its first flight. This is one of the things Sam doesn't like about his autism—he can't keep himself from "flapping" when he's happy or excited.

When Sam was younger, the kids at school didn't seem to mind his flapping. But now that he's older, the kids don't seem as accepting of his behaviors. These days, he feels really embarrassed when he flaps.

Another problem for Sam at school is his voice. People say he talks too loud. His teacher reminds him to use his "indoor voice." Sam tries to talk more softly, but this only lasts a short time. Pretty soon he's speaking loudly again, and he gets the same reminder about using his indoor voice.

Sometimes Sam feels sad or frustrated about what's hard for him. Then he tries to stop and think about the good things in his life. Sam is the best speller in his class, and he has lots of energy and enthusiasm. He loves to learn new things, and he knows more knock-knock jokes than anyone else in his whole school! Many kids at school and in Sam's neighborhood know him, and they always say hello. All of this makes Sam feel better about himself.

For now, he thinks, maybe a little flapping and loud talking aren't so bad—especially when he thinks of all the good things in his life.

Asperger's syndrome is similar to autism, which can be confusing for doctors, teachers, parents, kids, and anyone else learning about the "spectrum." But the key difference has to do with when you began to talk and learn. If you were talking by age 3—and you didn't have difficulty learning language—your doctor may suggest a diagnosis of

Asperger's. With Asperger's, you may have as few as four symptoms from the special book (instead of six).

Some people think Asperger's is a milder form of autism or a "better" diagnosis than autism. This just adds to the confusion. The difference between autism and Asperger's is related to when you learned to talk and began to develop your other learning skills. Even though Asperger's has fewer symptoms, those symptoms are still part of ASD and may not be mild at all.

ASD Is Not . . .

- your fault
- something you "caught" like a germ
- something you can "give others" (autism is not contagious)
- a sign that you are stupid, bad, sick, crazy, lazy, flawed, or weird

ASD Is . . .

A medical condition. You have symptoms, but with help from experts, family members, and teachers, you can work on improving those symptoms. ASD is also a way of being—it's how you experience the world.

You may have ASD, but you're still **you.** You're a whole person, head to toe, inside and out. You have the potential to live a healthy, unique, and remarkable life.

I have what some people would call a disability but I call a gift—Asperger syndrome. . . . I am not your average child. I like to think of myself as the 'new and improved model.'

—Luke Jackson, from his book *Freaks, Geeks & Asperger Syndrome*

Chapter 2

Symptoms of ASD

In many ways, autism spectrum disorders are a mystery. There's no simple test (like a blood test) to show that a person has autism or Asperger's. Instead, it's a matter of looking for symptoms and seeing whether they match up with the diagnosis of ASD.

This chapter is all about understanding the symptoms you may have. You can imagine that you're a detective, looking for clues to the mystery. Detectives almost always have partners. Ask a parent or another adult you trust to study the clues with you, so you can figure out things together.

Detectives take good notes. Get a pen or pencil and some paper. Whenever you read about a symptom that sounds familiar, write it down. These notes are clues about areas you might need help with.

Symptom 1:
Communication Difficulties

Most people with autism spectrum disorder can talk, although it may be hard for them to find the right words to express what they want to say. Do you ever feel like other people are watching you too closely or hurrying you to say something? Or do you sometimes use words that are correct but sound odd to your friends? Sometimes, you might have trouble understanding what others are saying. Maybe it seems like they talk too fast. Perhaps they tell jokes that don't seem funny to you, or use slang words you haven't heard before.

Some people who have ASD may misunderstand common expressions. For example, you might hear your mom say she's "fed up" and think she's full from eating too much. But what "fed up" really means is *frustrated.* Or, someone might say "Take a hike." You might think the person means "Put on some hiking boots and find the nearest trail." The expression "Take a hike" said in an annoyed tone of voice usually means "Go away!"

Understanding words that you read may also be hard, even if you love reading! Some people with ASD are super spellers and fast readers but may have trouble making sense of the story or information. Do you sometimes read a section nearly perfectly, even when it's full of long words? And then find that you're unable to explain to someone else what you just read? If so, this is because your brain is good at decoding (figuring out) the *sounds* of words, but not their *meanings.*

Problems understanding the meaning of language happen when parts of your brain don't communicate with each other. Think of it this way: Part of your brain has the job of making words. Another part has the job of understanding feelings. Both parts of your brain may be doing their jobs—but they're not talking to each other! Messages are lost along the way or take a while to get there.

Because of your ASD, your brain tends to focus on one thing at a time. For example, imagine someone is angry at you. That person may look something like this:

Your brain might not see the "whole picture" that someone without ASD sees. What do you see instead? *Pieces* of the picture. You may hear an angry voice but not be able to focus on what the words mean. You may see an angry face but not notice the person shaking her foot. You may be focused on listening for words, and then miss the person's facial expression.

People use a combination of words, actions, and facial expressions to let others know what they think and feel. For you, it's harder to see, hear, and understand that combination.

When your brain doesn't see the whole picture right away, you have to put the pieces together bit by bit. You might not realize at first that the person is angry at you. Or you may notice the person is mad but not understand why. It's almost like someone is talking to you in a different language. You hear the words and you see the person's mouth move, but it takes you longer to figure out what's being said.

Then there's the communication that happens without any words. You might not notice people's gestures: like when they wave, wink, roll their eyes, or tap their foot. Or you might misunderstand someone's body language. For example, if someone elbows you in the ribs, you might think, "Hey, he's bothering me!" But maybe the person didn't mean to bother you at all. Maybe he was trying, without words, to get you to notice something interesting or funny.

Having ASD might mean your brain has a slower "processing speed." So, you can think interesting thoughts, but then have a hard time putting them into words. You might not be able to answer a question as quickly as you'd like. Or, you might have trouble organizing your thoughts when you have to write. These communication problems slow you down, but they don't mean you're not smart!

Sometimes you might get stuck on words. Maybe certain ones are special to you, and you repeat them again and again. Other times, you may feel the need to ask the same question over and over. You might do this even though you know the answer and the person has already replied to you lots of times. It's almost as if your brain has a hiccup. You can't control these brain hiccups, just like you can't control regular hiccups.

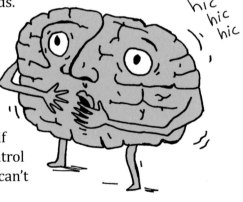

Take a Look!
This chapter is all about the three main types of symptoms of ASD. You'll find help for coping with all these symptoms later in the book, especially in chapters 10, 11, and 12.

Most likely, your family and friends get annoyed when you're repeating words or questions—even though you can't help it. This urge to repeat yourself just feels right to you, the same way it feels satisfying to scratch an itch. Then, just as suddenly as the urge started, it stops. It can feel like a big relief to you when you finally quit repeating yourself.

All sorts of communication issues come up with ASD. You may have some of the ones discussed here or other ones unique to you.

Symptom 2:
Problems with Social Skills

Social skills are something everyone has to learn within their own family, culture, and community. We're not born knowing exactly how to be social. But most people are born with a built-in ability to watch and copy the people around them.

Maybe you've seen how babies look closely at their parents and imitate motions like waving or clapping. Toddlers learn to nod their head for yes and shake their head for no. As they grow, young children learn other social skills. They learn to do things like say "please" and "thank you," or apologize if they've hurt someone.

Having ASD makes it harder to learn these everyday skills. Imitation doesn't come as easily to you. Remember, your brain tends to focus on one thing at a time. This affects your social skills because you don't always see the "whole picture" at once.

Experts have discovered that people with autism spectrum disorders may have problems in the *mirror neurons* of their brain. (They're called mirror neurons because their job is to act like a mirror and "reflect" what they observe back into the brain. The brain then stores the reflection into memory, to be used later.) From the time when you were a baby, your mirror neurons may not have worked properly, making it more difficult for you to learn how to interact with people. Your brain had to figure out other ways to take in the information, store it, and use it day to day.

Because of your ASD, it might be hard for you to look people in the eye or to look at their faces when you talk. At times, you might try to look them in the eye and then forget what you wanted to say.

The back-and-forth of conversation is probably difficult for you, too. For example, you may find it fairly easy to talk about what interests you. But then you might forget to give the other person a chance to speak. Maybe you forget to ask questions, or find them hard to ask. Perhaps you have trouble following other people's conversations. Or maybe people tell you not to interrupt. Because of these difficulties, social situations are tougher for you. You might feel shy or misunderstood.

For everyone, a big part of being social is using their face, hands, or body to express themselves. ASD makes these things hard to do. You may not be able to easily understand the expression on someone's face, especially if it doesn't seem to match what the person is saying.

Take teasing as an example. Someone might say to you, "Nice job!" right after you spilled milk all over the table. This phrase could mean two very different things, depending on *how* the person said it and the *expression* on the person's face. Someone could say it in a gently teasing way. The person might smile, grab a napkin, and use a friendly tone of voice. These things would let you know that "Nice job!" actually means "We all make mistakes, and I'm here to help." On the other hand, the person could say "Nice job!" in a mean tone of voice with a rude look as a way to make fun of you.

 Sometimes eye contact is hard. It's really easy to lose focus when I look people in the eye.

—12-year-old boy with Asperger's

This difficulty with gestures and facial expressions might mean that you don't use much body language. Have people ever told you that you seem "like a robot" or have an odd tone of voice? Maybe you don't use your arms and hands much when you speak—instead, you stay still. Or maybe the expression on your face stays flat, not changing into a smile, a frown, or an angry look very often. You might speak in a *monotone*, meaning your tone doesn't change to show the feelings behind your words. You might not nod your head when you're listening to others speak. (Nodding can be a clue to tell others "I hear and understand you.")

These differences in how you interact with other people might confuse them. The good news is you can learn to use more gestures and expressions if you want to. The more you practice, the better you'll get at it.

Symptom 3:
Intense Interests and Repetitive Behaviors

If you have ASD, you probably also have some cool hobbies and interests. Kids with autism spectrum disorders often have intense interests, fascinations, and obsessions.

Maybe you know nearly everything there is to know about dinosaurs, presidents, or the planets in the solar system. When you're fascinated by something, you want to learn as much as you can about it. What's wrong with that? Nothing! Hobbies and activities give you something to do and help you discover more about the world.

It's great when your interests fit the interests of your friends and other people your age. Maybe you love video games that are popular with other kids, or you enjoy movies, collector cards, chess, or math. These activities give you an opportunity to make friends with people who share your interests. But sometimes, ASD leads to interests that are unusual and make it harder to have friends.

For example, what if you're fascinated by bus schedules or phone numbers? Or what if you have an obsession with sports statistics, even though you don't actually care much about the sport itself? Interests like these aren't bad—but you do them alone. They often involve a lot of memorizing, which you're probably good at, but they don't give you a way to relate to other people.

Maybe family members and friends often ask you to stop talking about a certain topic or to get a new activity. That's not easy to hear. You may be happy talking about the same thing or playing the same game for hours. But people who don't have ASD usually don't have your level of intensity. They like to talk about lots of different things. Sometimes

DeShawn's Story

DeShawn, who's 12, *loves* to take apart anything electronic. His friends gave him the nickname "Garbage Guy" just for fun, because his favorite activity is going to the junk store to buy old stuff to take apart. DeShawn spends hours each day looking through websites that sell electronics. He makes lists of all the things he wants to buy. He even has a special box in his room to store his favorite creations—things he's made from junk. He put a lock on the box so his younger brother can't get into the stuff and break it.

Sometimes DeShawn gets in trouble at home because he doesn't do his homework when he's supposed to. He forgets all about his homework when he's busy doing his electronics projects. And he's not that into homework anyway. To him, junk is much more interesting. DeShawn's mom says his family can't afford to keep buying all the junk he wants. Sometimes she complains that DeShawn's autism is "driving her crazy."

But DeShawn loves his autism. He thinks it makes him smart in science. Plus, the other kids in the neighborhood think that the stuff DeShawn builds is really cool. DeShawn wants to be an inventor when he grows up. He has big plans, and he doesn't want homework or other people to get in his way.

they like to talk more than play. That's a social difference between people who have autism spectrum disorder and those who don't.

Chances are, you feel more comfortable when things in your life are the same: your clothes, the food you eat, the activities you do. If things change, you might get upset. Even so-called simple things, like wearing a different kind of pants or getting a new bedspread, might make you nervous. You probably like routines so life is easier to predict.

Talia's Story

Talia is a fifth grader with Asperger's. She never really knew she had a "problem" until this year. At school, she started going to a special classroom once a week to learn social skills. Talia doesn't understand why she has to leave language arts, her favorite subject, to go to the other classroom. It isn't fair.

In the social skills room, she meets with a social worker and three other students to practice looking at each other's faces and asking each other questions. They also talk about how to make friends. But Talia doesn't think she needs to make friends. After all, she's friendly with everyone. Sometimes people think she's *too* friendly.

She'll talk about her favorite things with anyone who listens. And she loves explaining about all her stuffed animals—their names, how they look, and the magical world she's created for them. Lately, some adults have been telling Talia that other kids her age aren't that interested in stuffed animals anymore. These adults want Talia to learn to talk about other things. Talia wonders, "How could anyone *not* be interested in stuffed animals?"

At night when Talia goes to bed, she takes all of her stuffed animals and organizes them on her bookshelf. They each have to be in the exact right spot in order for Talia to feel happy and ready to sleep. One night she couldn't find Lennon, her stuffed turtle, and that meant she couldn't go to sleep. Talia's mom and dad got frustrated. Her parents love her. But they don't love her Asperger's because it makes her get "stuck" on things.

Now Talia wonders what all the fuss about Asperger's is. Is she really so different? Are people always going to be frustrated with her? Does being friends *have* to be hard? Talia knows she has lots to think about. In some ways, she's glad she can go to the social worker to ask all the questions that are on her mind. Talia's parents say they'll always be there to talk with, too.

Sometimes, people with ASD have repetitive behaviors that calm or soothe them. Maybe they rock back and forth, pace, spin in a circle, hum, or flick their hands. Maybe you have habits like these that you hardly notice, just like some people bite their fingernails when they're nervous or fiddle with a pen when they're bored. It may even come as a surprise to you when other people point out what you're doing and ask you to stop. (By the way, these movements are called *stims,* and you can read more about them in Chapter 16.)

A Word About "Differences"

It can be a real challenge to have ASD. There are differences in how you communicate, socialize, and behave. This doesn't mean you *can't* communicate, make friends, or get along at home. You just have your own unique style in these areas.

When you read the stories about Talia and DeShawn, did you notice that other people sometimes were frustrated about these kids' behaviors and challenges? Family members and friends don't always understand what it means to have autism spectrum disorder. There are things these people need to learn, too!

You can help the people in your life by saying:

"Having ASD means I act differently sometimes."

"Everyone has challenges—this is one of mine."

"I'm doing the best I can."

"Sometimes I need extra help."

"I'm just being myself!"

Or:

"I have ASD, but I can still learn and grow. And this means *you* can, too."

Chapter 3

ASD and the Senses

Chapter 2 explained the three main symptoms of ASD: difficulties with communication, social skills, or behavior. Lots of people with ASD also have differences in how their senses (like hearing and taste) do their jobs.* These differences, called *sensory issues,* are another symptom of ASD.

As soon as you arrived in the world, your senses began to shape your experiences. It's through the senses that you learn to understand yourself, other people, and your environment. When your senses work differently, the way you experience the world is very unique.

This has its ups and downs. On the upside, you have *intensity*. When you love something, you really, *really* love it. You might have laser-like focus. You probably notice details that no one else in your family or classroom is aware of. Autism spectrum disorder is a special way of perceiving the world and living in it. This way may not be typical, but it's *yours*.

On the downside, the world is often noisy, bright, busy, messy, social, and full of chaos. All kinds of input is coming at you: voices, movement, faces, textures, sounds. That's a lot to take in, especially if your processing speed is slower or your senses are different from many people's.

How Some People with ASD Explain It

Temple Grandin is a famous doctor of animal science, a professor, and an author. She also has autism. Successful today, she faced many challenges growing up with ASD. Thanks to her books and lectures, the world understands more about the experience of autism and how it may affect someone's life.

*The chart on page 29 describes the senses.

Temple says she was overwhelmed by her senses as a child. Loud noises were terribly painful to her ears. Her underwear felt like sandpaper against her skin. She would flinch if the teacher touched her. She says that being hugged by her heavy, affectionate aunt was "like being suffocated by a mountain of marshmallows."

So Temple spent her days dreaming up comfort machines in her mind. One idea was a suit that inflated like a plastic beach toy. The suit would apply comforting pressure to her body. Another idea was to build a special heated enclosure "about three feet wide and three feet tall—just big enough so I could get into it and close the door." There she'd feel safe and secure.

Do you sometimes get overwhelmed by all that's going on around you—the sights, smells, and sounds? Maybe you sometimes long for a dark, quiet place where you can be away from the world and feel peaceful.

Or maybe you have the opposite problem: You need *more* input from your eyes, ears, and body to get your senses working better. This is another common experience for people with ASD.

Donna Williams, an artist and a writer with autism, has said her sensory experience is "like having a brain without a sieve." *Sieves* are tools with tiny holes for straining liquids or collecting the finest bits of sand. You could say that a sieve *sorts* the liquids and solids that are poured into it. When your brain has trouble sorting information, the world can be a very confusing place with lots of distractions.

For example, when you're sitting in a classroom trying to listen to your teacher, it's easy to get distracted by:

- bright fluorescent lights that "hum"
- other students moving, talking, or whispering
- noises from the hallway or the ticking clock
- what your teacher *says* versus what he *writes* on the board
- how hard your chair is, or how close your desk is to another student's

With all that going on, no wonder it's challenging to pay attention to the lesson!

Then there's what's happening inside you. Hungry stomach? Nervousness? Sore fingers from writing? A sickening feeling because of the weird smells drifting from the cafeteria? Distracting!

And what about what's going on in your *brain*? (Another inside part.)

At times, your brain might unexpectedly get locked onto one of your special interests or fascinations. Suddenly you're thinking about your favorite video game . . .

or model cars

or card collection

or princess movies

or weather patterns

Luke Jackson, a young author who's written about his Asperger's, says his obsessions creep up on him like a thief in the night. "One minute I am just very interested in a topic and the next it seems as if my mind has been infiltrated by an army that stamps around and eradicates [erases] my everyday thoughts, replacing them with thoughts of computers."

Does that ever happen to you? Throughout the day, your brain might leap to thoughts about your favorite subject. This may be in response to "sensory overload"—or that feeling of being overwhelmed by what's going on both inside and outside of you. Is it "bad" that your brain and body may get distracted in unexpected ways? No. It's just part of ASD and a unique part of who you are.

When you have ASD, you need to find ways to help your senses work better for you. Take Temple Grandin as an example. As a young woman, she spent time working on a cattle ranch. There she watched as nervous, twitchy calves were put into a device called a "squeeze chute," which provided gentle pressure. The chute calmed them down. She became a bit obsessed with that device!

So, what did she do? She built a squeeze machine for *herself.* Inside this device, she felt calmer. She could control the amount of pressure on her body and relax. This was just one step on her long journey to understanding herself and her autism.

For Donna Williams, art became a way of expressing her sensory experience of color, texture, and pattern. She calls her work "ARTism." Maybe you too can find new ways of expressing yourself through paint and clay.

Both of these women grew up during a time when not much was known about ASD. But now, lots of experts are paying attention to the sensory needs of people with autism. This means you don't have to figure out on your own what might help you feel better. That's good news.

You might want to take a close look at the chart on page 29 and think about your own senses. Are some of the sensory issues listed familiar to you? Are there other ones that you've experienced? Write them down if you'd like. The list you create can help the adults in your life figure out whether certain types of therapy and activities might help you.

Making Sense of the Senses

This chart shows seven senses that can play a role in how you feel:

Sense	Where it comes through	What happens
Sight	**Eyes**	Light may be too bright and disturbing. Or you might have difficulty "tracking" moving objects with your eyes.
Hearing	**Ears**	Loud noises may be painful, or you may not be able to tune out background noises. Maybe you react strongly to sharp, high-pitched sounds.
Smell	**Nose**	Some smells might make you gag or feel sick. Or you may tend to sniff objects to get information to your brain.
Taste	**Mouth**	You might love some tastes (like salty) but hate others, and avoid certain food textures (like crunchy or mushy). Or, you might enjoy licking objects to discover their taste and the sensation in your mouth.
Touch	**Skin**	Certain fabrics might feel unusually itchy or scratchy to you. Sometimes a light touch feels like a push. Maybe you resist touch—or perhaps you crave it. You might enjoy the pressure of tight clothing and tight hugs.
Balance (also called *vestibular*)	**Inner ear**	You might have difficulty balancing, riding a two-wheeler, walking on uneven surfaces, or using stairs. Maybe you feel stressed out when your feet leave the ground. You may hate or love spinning.
Body awareness (also called *proprioception*)	**Muscles and joints**	It might be hard for you to understand where your body is in space. Do you tend to bump into people or objects? Or do you like to flop onto soft furniture and snuggle under heavy blankets? Coordinating your body's movements can be difficult. So can figuring out the steps you need to do for certain tasks.

> I have 'artillery'! Earplugs are a must—when I'm walking around, when I'm in the shop, when I'm in the car . . . I always have sunglasses and gloves for touch issues.
>
> —Rudy Simone, author of *Aspergirls: Empowering Females with Asperger's Syndrome*

Want a fun way to keep your senses engaged? Or to take your mind off something that's stressing you out? Ask a parent to stock up on sensory items. There are all sorts of stress balls you can squeeze or bounce. You can also try colorful items like pinwheels, balloons, Chinese yo-yos, or even a lava lamp. Get some whistles or a harmonica. Chew sugarless bubblegum. Make or buy some Play-Doh to squish and squash. Buy lots of bubble stuff to blow and pop. Or how about a mini trampoline to bounce on? Everyday items like these help keep your mouth, body, eyes, ears, and hands busy.

Chapter 4

Well-Known People with ASD

For many years, very little was known about autism. Today, all sorts of books, magazines, and websites talk about the condition. It's common to hear about ASD on the news and TV talk shows. Television programs now feature characters with ASD, too.

Some people have been looking back in history to imagine whether anybody famous had autism. For example, researchers at Cambridge and Oxford Universities in England say that two of the world's most famous scientists may have had ASD:

Brilliant Albert Einstein developed the theory of relativity. But as a child, he was a loner. He had an obsessive way of repeating sentences until he was seven years old. Is this proof of ASD? Maybe.

Sir Isaac Newton discovered the laws of gravity (when an apple fell on his head, according to a long-standing story). He often got so interested in his work, he'd forget to eat. He had few friends and had a hard time socializing with them. Is this evidence of autism, or simply high intelligence?

Some people suggest that musical genius Wolfgang Amadeus Mozart had traits of autism. Others think the talented artist Andy Warhol, known for his famous paintings of Campbell's soup cans, had signs of ASD. Because these men are no longer alive, it's impossible know the truth.

Autism and Talent

When it's said that famous people in history may have had autism, good and bad things happen. What's good is that people start talking about ASD. They take notice. They get curious. They realize ASD is a big part of many people's lives. Also, as a person with ASD, you realize that some of the most talented people on Earth may have had it, too. That can inspire you.

What's *not* so good about all that talk of geniuses and autism? It leads people to think this: ASD = Genius. People might find out you have ASD and then expect you to be a "walking calculator." Or to have the ability to put 1,000-piece puzzles together as easy as one, two, three. The truth is, being a genius is uncommon for anyone, whether the person has ASD or not. It's also unusual to have an extraordinary talent that leads to fame and fortune.

Maybe you've heard of the movie *Rain Man* from 1988, about a man who was a genius in counting but couldn't take care of himself. The story was based on a real-life man named Kim Peek. Kim actually was born with damage to his brain, but he also had unique and incredible memorization skills. This condition made him seem like an "autistic savant." Because of the popularity of the movie, people still think of *Rain Man* whenever they hear the word *autism*. But being a savant is really rare, whether someone has autism or not.

Another famous savant is Stephen Wiltshire, an artist with autism. He's been nicknamed "The Human Camera" because he can study a building for several minutes and then go to his desk and draw it from memory. Once, he flew over an area of London in a helicopter. Afterward he drew what he saw. He created a perfectly scaled drawing of a four-square-mile area of the city with 12 historic landmarks and 200 other structures. Now that's amazing!

Many people love stories like this. We enjoy discovering the potential of the human mind and finding unlikely heroes. Yet, most people

with autism or Asperger's *don't* have a special talent. Maybe you do, and maybe you don't.

Like anyone else, you have a set of strengths and weaknesses. For example, you might do well in certain subjects in school and not so well in others. You could be into sports or music or theater, just like anybody. You might be good at "regular stuff" like collecting trading cards or reading comic books, like many people your age.

On the other hand, you might have a fascination or special hobby that someday leads to a talent or even a career.

Remember reading about Temple Grandin in Chapter 3? (See pages 25–26.) All her life she was interested in constructing things, in her mind and with her hands. She also had a special bond with animals. She somehow understood them more deeply than others could. Her job now combines both of those interests. Today, she is Dr. Temple Grandin, known for designing more humane ways to handle livestock (like cattle and pigs) at meatprocessing plants.

Talent helped her—but *hard work* was a huge part of her success. The same is true with Stephen Wiltshire. He's been drawing steadily since he was 7 years old. His work is part of who he is, like his autism.

Young People with ASD Today

Have you heard of Jason McElwain—better known by the nickname J-Mac? In 2006, he was just a regular guy, a young man with autism, living in Rochester, New York. Jason loved basketball. He had earned the job of team manager for his high school's basketball team, but he wasn't a player. Still, he was a familiar face at every game—the boy who helped run the clock, fill the team water bottles, and pass out towels to players as they came off the court.

During the Senior Night game that winter, his school's varsity team had a comfortable lead. With a little over four minutes left on the clock, the coach decided to put Jason in the game to reward him for his dedication to the team. The crowd was waiting for this moment. To show their support of Jason on this big night, many of them held up photos of him. They cheered "J-Mac!" *Clap, clap.* "J-Mac!" *Clap, clap.* Their feet thundered in the stands. Everyone was excited, but no one could have imagined what happened next.

In just a few short minutes, Jason hit *six* three-point shots and a two-pointer. He had tied the school record for the most three-pointers in a game! J-Mac was carried off the court on his teammates' shoulders, the crowd screaming. All of it was captured on student video, and that video was sent to a local news station. Before long, all the TV networks had picked up the story. J-Mac was a hero.

How did J-Mac sink those amazing shots? Well, he'd been obsessed with basketball from the time he was a young kid. He watched it on TV. He followed his NBA heroes in the newspaper and in sports magazines. And he spent hours and hours on his driveway shooting hoops with his brother Josh. Jason McElwain may not have had the size and skill to play varsity, but he was dedicated to the team and his sport. When it was his turn to shine, he was prepared—and maybe luck was with him, too.

After his moment as a basketball hero, J-Mac coauthored a book about his life and sold the movie rights to his story. He became an assistant coach for the school's junior varsity team and got a job at a grocery store. Today, he's still just a guy who loves basketball.

As a result of his fame, Jason helped draw attention to autism. His book gave him a chance to tell his story. In it he says, "Just because you have autism, it doesn't mean you can't do certain things, or that you can't practice certain things and get better at certain things. It doesn't mean that you have to be one way for the rest of your life. . . . Never give up. Never give in."

James Durbin is another famous guy you might have heard of. He was the Top 4 contestant on the TV show *American Idol* Season 10. Onstage, James was known for his "rocker" hair, sideburns, and "tails" made out of scarves hanging from his pants. Fans grew to love his unique voice and intense devotion to rock and roll.

But there was another side to James, one that made his life difficult while growing up in Santa Cruz, California. By the time he was in middle school, he had been diagnosed with both Asperger's syndrome and Tourette syndrome. Tourette causes him to have facial tics (muscle movements he can't control). His face twitches, but he can't make it stop. When he auditioned for *Idol* he told the producers, "As I was getting older, at school, people would tell me, 'Cut that out, stop that.' I was like, 'I can't.' I always got made fun of and beat up. I was just lost." James also talked about being bullied during his teen years and how hurt and angry he felt.

Music, he says, is what saved him. He got involved in community theater and starred in musicals such as *Grease, West Side Story,* and *Beauty and the Beast*. Later on, he became the lead singer in a heavy-metal band. Performing on *American Idol* helped him win fans around the world.

Although Asperger's is a condition that causes difficulty in social situations, James Durbin stood up before large crowds to share his talent. He interacted with screaming fans and gave interviews to reporters. After being voted off *Idol,* James returned to Santa Cruz for what was called "Durbin Day." He also made appearances on *The Tonight Show with Jay Leno* and *The Ellen DeGeneres Show.* He has said that he's now so busy that he hardly has time to think about his Asperger's or Tourette syndrome!

Actress Holly Robinson Peete and her husband, Rodney Peete, a former NFL quarterback, have a son with autism. His name is RJ, and he has a twin sister, Ryan, who helped their mom write a children's book about autism. *My Brother Charlie* was created with the goal of letting "kids and their parents in on a little secret: Kids with autism are valuable human beings with real feelings, even though they can't always express them." Ryan and her mom based the story on events that happened in their family.

These young people with ASD have been in the spotlight. That means their stories and voices are being heard. They're part of the autism community, like **you** are. Each day, that community gets a little bigger and a lot stronger.

Your voice—your words and thoughts—are important, too. Write down these thoughts in your journal or on a piece of paper, if you'd like. Here are some ideas to get you started:

Now that I know I have ASD, I feel . . .

My "ASD Heroes" could be . . .

The activity that I really *love* is . . .

When I do this activity, I feel . . .

Chapter 5

The "Big" Questions

Learning you have ASD isn't something that happens all at once. It takes time to understand what the diagnosis means. You may be thinking about yourself and your life differently than you did before. Most likely, you have questions that need answering.

This chapter gives you a Q&A (Question and Answer) of some of the hardest ASD questions. It doesn't have all the answers, but it's a starting point. If you have other questions, write them down. You can go to a parent, a teacher, or another trusted adult for answers.

Why Do Some People Have Autism?

(That's the million-dollar question!)

ANSWER: Doctors want to know what causes autism. So do families affected by ASD. Researchers are trying to find out. But, as of now, the answers just aren't clear. Experts *do* know that autism is partly genetic—meaning it starts in the *genes.*

What are genes? Every living organism has genes, which are like a set of instructions telling what the life form is like, how it survives, and how it behaves in its environment. Humans have thousands of genes. Think of genes as the computer program that makes each one of us what we are.

A number of genes play a role in autism. Some of these genes make a child more likely to have ASD. Other genes affect how a baby's brain develops. Still other genes determine how the brain cells communicate with each other.

Genes also play a part in how severe someone's symptoms of ASD may be. Some of these genes might be passed down from the parents. But other gene problems happen spontaneously (all of a sudden on their own).

How did experts find out that autism is partly genetic? They studied twins.

Researchers learned this: In identical twins, if one twin has autism there is a very good chance that the other will have it as well. However, if the twins are not identical (called *fraternal*), the chance is less than 10 percent that both twins will develop autism. Why this difference? Identical twins share more genes in common—that's what makes them identical! So the more genes the twins share in common, the more likely it is that they'll both have autism.

Environment plays an important role, too. (We know this from the twins study as well.) Researchers want to know: Does a virus trigger autism? Are air pollutants involved? What about toxins in our environment? Just what *is* the cause of autism?

Experts have looked into whether vaccines might cause autism, or if reactions to certain foods and drinks have something to do with ASD. In fact, people often have very strong opinions about the possibility of vaccines or diet being a cause. This book doesn't focus on the vaccine and diet issue. This is because medical professionals, scientists, and parents of children with autism may have widely differing viewpoints. (Entire books have been written on those issues!)

The focus here is on *you* and questions you might have about ASD. Right now, the world of science doesn't yet understand what causes autism. Maybe by the time you're grown up, more will be known. New research is being done every day.

Why Me?

ANSWER: It's not easy to hear about your diagnosis and learn that your ASD will have a big effect on your life. One of the first questions that might come to mind is: "Why me? Why do *I* have to have ASD when other people don't?"

It's a good question, but there's no simple answer. Nobody gets to choose their genes. If we *could* choose them, we'd probably all choose to be incredibly intelligent, good-looking, athletic, and talented. We'd pick never having any kind of problem in life. If only that could happen . . .

But the reality is we all have a genetic code that determines how we look and grow. Think of all the characteristics that make you **you.** Your eye color, skin color, and hair color, for example, are a basic part of you. They were determined before you were born. Your height is already set in your genes, even though you aren't done growing yet. In the same way, certain things about your brain were preset as part of your genetic code. It's just what makes you who you are.

Will I Always Have Autism?

ANSWER: The short answer is yes—but there's more to it than that.

Sometimes people get an illness like a cold or virus, and it goes away after a few days or weeks. The symptoms lessen over time and eventually disappear. When you have a cold, you probably lie in bed, get lots of extra sleep, and drink liquids. Once your body has had enough time to fight the germ or virus, you get out of bed and back to your life.

Other illnesses are more serious and need medical attention. For example, you might have had strep throat before. Your doctor probably tested you for strep and then gave you an *antibiotic*—a medication that helps fight infection. In this case, the "cure" is an infection-fighting medication and lots of rest.

Then there are medical conditions that require ongoing treatment, like asthma. This lung condition causes coughing, wheezing, and difficult breathing. Maybe you know kids with asthma or have it yourself. Usually, the treatment includes breathing medications, such as an inhaler or pills. Having asthma means making some adjustments in life. For example, the person may get sick more often and need to see a doctor more frequently than other people do. But people with asthma still lead normal lives.

Take a Look!

It may help to know that *lots* of people have ASD:

- According to the Centers for Disease Control, an average of 1 in 110 children in the United States have autism spectrum disorder.

- Autism is more common than Down's syndrome, childhood diabetes, and childhood cancer combined.

- According to the White House: "With autism spectrum disorders affecting nearly 1 percent of children in the United States, autism is an urgent public health issue with a profound impact on millions of Americans." In 2011, President Barack Obama proclaimed April 2 of each year as World Autism Awareness Day, writing: "I call upon the people of the United States to learn more about autism and what they can do to support individuals on the autism spectrum and their families."

You are not alone!

Autism spectrum disorders are different from the types of illnesses and conditions just described. Why? For one thing, your body doesn't fight your ASD like an infection. For another thing, autism doesn't concern only one part of the body (like the lungs). ASD affects your brain, body, and development.

Remember that part about genes on page 38? You are born with your autism, and it stays with you for life. Your symptoms aren't necessarily a sign of something that needs to be "cured." They're a part of you, just like your autism.

However, your symptoms may change as you change, learn, and grow. Many people with ASD leave some of their old behaviors behind. For instance, they may "flap" a lot as kids, but then do it less when they're older. They may learn to try new foods, instead of sticking with the same ones every day. They may find ways to become better sleepers or to make more friends. The changes don't happen automatically—they take some effort.

Just know this: As you grow and change, so will your ASD!

> [My] autism has gotten way better over the years. Only some parts aren't as good. When I feel upset, I feel as though I don't want to have autism anymore. When I do talented things like [my] art, it makes me feel as though autism is a good thing in some ways.
>
> **—Max LaZebnik, from his article "A Journey Through Autism"
> in *The Autism Perspective (TAP)* Magazine**

Long ago, doctors used to think of autism as a lifelong disability, one that made the person unable to learn or change. Back then, doctors had some low expectations for people with autism. But now with so many parents, educators, and experts trying to understand ASD and help kids, the view of autism is changing for the better.

Still, many ASD experts are careful about using the term *cure*. They don't want to suggest that autism is curable because it's not a disease or an illness. Some people are more comfortable with the word *recover*. They say that a person can recover from some of the most challenging symptoms and feel better.

Other people, many of whom have ASD, don't like all this talk about cures and recovery. They want the world to know that autism isn't something negative. They don't like being thought of as "broken" or "in need of fixing." They're proud to be different, proud of who they are. They work to let people know that having ASD isn't about being a misfit, a genius, or someone to pity.

You are Someone with ASD—an individual. This means you have the right to think about autism in **your own unique way,** whatever that way may be.

Don't feel sorry for me. I have autism, but I'm cool with who I am. I love lots of things about my life. . . . I will always have autism, but that doesn't mean my future won't be great.

—**Daniel Stefanski, from his book** *How to Talk to an Autistic Kid*

Chapter 6

Think About It, Talk About It

Right now, you might feel confused about your ASD and what it means for your future. It's okay to feel that way. Give it time. Your feelings will change as you learn more about yourself and living with ASD.

 To *me*, autism is 'normal.'
—16-year-old boy with autism

Everybody has personal stuff they need to work on. Everyone has things to celebrate about themselves, too. In that way, we're all alike.

This chapter is about taking time to think and talk about what you've learned so far.

43

> ### *Note for Adults*
> The Introduction for Adults (page 5) and Sharing the Diagnosis with Your Child (page 227) contain information that may be helpful as you talk with a child about questions, worries, feelings, and coping strategies.

Ask questions. It's likely you have lots of questions about your ASD and how it will affect your life. Who can you ask? Make a list of your helpers: a parent, your doctor, a therapist or counselor, a social worker, a teacher, a school counselor, and other adults you trust. (Chapter 7 is all about helpers.) Maybe your dad or mom can find a support group for kids and families affected by ASD. A group like this can be a great place to share questions and learn more.

Talk about your feelings. You probably have mixed feelings about all you're learning about ASD. Talking about feelings can help. You can go to a parent or relative, an older sibling, or another adult you trust. These people may not have all the answers, but they can listen. And they might be able to find other people who can support you.

Draw or write about your feelings. Everyone has strong emotions that need to be expressed. Why not keep a feelings journal? Journals come in all shapes and sizes. There are big ones with fancy covers, little diaries with a lock and key, or plain old spiral-bound notebooks. You can also keep a journal on a computer at home, if you prefer.

Journals are for your own private words, so write anything you want. Don't worry about whether the handwriting looks sloppy or whether your punctuation is correct. You can also sketch in your journal, paint in it, draw comic strips, or make collages.

Express your feelings in healthy ways. Many people with ASD have difficulty handling their feelings and managing strong emotions like anger, fear, and frustration. You might struggle to hold your temper or have frequent meltdowns when your days are rough. Over time, you can learn to handle those feelings more successfully. (See Chapter 15 for more on that.) Meanwhile, there are healthy ways to express strong feelings without hurting yourself or others. Try running around, swinging, dancing, or bouncing on a mini trampoline. You could scribble, pound a hunk of clay, or bang on a drum.

Get to know your ASD community. Your family can look for a social skills group for you. Or they can seek out other people with ASD in your town or city. See "Where to Go for More Info" on page 224 for a list of organizations that can help.

A Message for You

There's a commercial on TV and the Web where the people push a big red button to make everything easier. It's called the Easy Button. The idea is that you push it and—*poof!*—you get just what you need when you need it, and life is *goooood*.

Well, there's no Easy Button when it comes to ASD. But some things do get easier.

Over time, you'll learn ways to manage your symptoms and handle your feelings. Your body will get stronger, and you'll most likely become better able to do things that seem hard right now. With practice, communication can get easier and so can being social. You'll find friends, and these buddies will help make life more fun.

You have some challenges ahead, but you've got what it takes to meet them. Instead of an Easy Button, how about an "I Can Do It!" Button?

Kayla's Story

Kayla is quirky—at least that's what her mom always tells her. Her mom says that quirky means "special and unique, like no one else." Kayla already knows that every person is special and different from everyone else, so she doesn't spend much time thinking about being quirky. But now that she's in sixth grade, Kayla is starting to look back. Maybe there's more to being special and unique than she realized.

When Kayla was 3 years old, her family sometimes called her "Quiet One." Although she could speak very well, she rarely said a word when she was at preschool or in a group. The preschool teacher told Kayla's mom, "Don't worry, Kayla is just shy." In kindergarten, Kayla had trouble in the mornings. She was always sad when her mom dropped her off for the day, and sometimes Kayla cried. The kindergarten teacher said Kayla was a little anxious.

In third grade, the lunch servers said Kayla was a picky eater because she always chose exactly the same foods in the cafeteria each day. And in fifth grade, some of the other girls called Kayla a tomboy. This was because she always wore pants to school (never a dress or skirt), and she preferred to run and swing at recess rather than talk with the other girls. Kayla wished she could swing all day long. She loved the feeling of flying in the air. And she felt so much calmer after a few minutes of swinging. Because of what other people said about her, Kayla started to think of herself as a quiet, shy, picky-eater tomboy.

Kayla is a good student, and her best class is spelling. The other kids in school often come up to her and ask her to spell words. It almost feels like they think she's a trained animal in the circus performing tricks. The kids try to stump her by giving her hard words to spell, but Kayla has no trouble! Spelling just comes easily to her.

Kayla likes being smart, and she loves learning at school. But she often feels lonely. Other kids talk to her—but they don't invite her over or ask her to come to their birthday parties. Kayla has some friends, but not as many as other people do. When she tells her mom about her worries, her mom usually says, "Don't worry, Kayla, you're just a little quirky."

As a sixth grader, Kayla has an important job at school: being a helper for the first graders learning to spell. It's fun, but when the social worker at school first told Kayla about the special job, he mentioned it would help Kayla build her social skills. "What?" she thought. "Why do I need to learn social skills?" She knew she needed to talk to her mom to get some answers.

Kayla got up the courage to ask her mom an important question: "*Why* am I quirky?"

They talked for a long time. Kayla's mom told her she has Asperger's syndrome, which affects her ability to be social. The Asperger's, Mom explained, is a part of Kayla, but it's not *all* she is.

Kayla started to understand why she preferred the same foods every day, and why she only felt comfortable in certain clothes. It was almost a relief to finally understand more about herself. She had lots of questions over the next few days, and her mom did her best to answer them. Kayla and her mom went to the bookstore to get a book about Asperger's so Kayla could read more about it.

Now Kayla has a deeper understanding about the things that made her different when she was younger—things that continue to make her unique. This doesn't mean she understands everything about herself or about Asperger's, but that's okay. Kayla now knows she isn't just a quiet, shy, picky-eater tomboy who can spell really well.

Tonight, as her mom sits with her before bedtime, Kayla says: "Asperger's—I can spell that, Mom. Q-U-I-R-K-Y. Goodnight!"

Chapter 7

Your Team of Helpers

During the process of getting a diagnosis for ASD and being treated, you'll probably meet lots of different experts. Think of these people as your personal helpers. Autism spectrum disorders are conditions that affect the brain *and* body. Because of this, you might need to see experts who have knowledge of both. This chapter tells you "Who's Who."

Neurologist: A neurologist is a doctor who studies the brain and brain disorders. He or she may see you to decide if you need special tests of your brain—such as an EEG to measure brain waves, or an MRI or CT scan of your head to take pictures of your brain. Some people with ASD have other medical problems such as seizures. A neurologist helps treat those issues.

Pediatrician: Pediatricians are doctors who take care of children and teens. A pediatrician can provide checkups and give you medications when you're sick with an infection or a virus. You've probably been seeing a pediatrician since you were a baby. This doctor may have been the first to notice your signs of autism. If so, he or she probably sent you to a **developmental pediatrician** for further tests.

Psychiatrist: Psychiatrists are doctors who help with behavior and emotional problems. They do this by teaching you and your family new ways to manage and cope. Psychiatrists may also prescribe medications to help with difficulties such as attention span, moodiness, sleep problems, hard-to-handle feelings, or meltdowns.

Psychologist: A psychologist works with people to understand emotional issues and solve problems. A psychologist may give you special tests to help understand your learning levels. (This can help you do better at school.) Psychologists also help families learn to handle living with autism or Asperger's. Or, a psychologist may help with communication and social skills.

Occupational therapist (OT): OTs do tests to check your body coordination compared to other people your age. Based on the results, the OT comes up with a plan to help you develop more strength and coordination. Occupational therapists may also look at how you react to light, sound, taste, smell, and touch so you can get help with sensory issues. (See Chapter 3 for more on that.) You may go to an OT if you need help with daily activities like buttoning, tying shoes, or writing.

Physical therapist (PT): PTs are experts in muscle strength and development. They can measure the range of motion in your joints. They can help you with mobility (how you move). And they can show you exercises that may improve the way your body works. When you have physical therapy, you might work on riding a bike or gaining more strength and balance.

 My advice is . . . to follow the advice your parents and doctors give you.

—14-year-old boy with autism

Speech therapist: A speech therapist helps with communication—mainly, your ability to speak and use language. People with ASD almost always need to see a speech therapist because communication problems are a main symptom. At speech therapy, you may learn to pronounce words more clearly or practice conversation skills. Or you might learn to use a special communication system instead of words.

Special education teacher: This is an expert at your school who observes how you learn and interact with others. A special ed teacher notes whether you can pay attention in class and how well you learn reading, math, and other subjects. This teacher also notices how you get along with other kids your age. Special ed teachers are trained to spot behavior issues and help kids learn new ways to manage.

The list of experts doesn't stop there. Other helpers may include a **behavioral therapist** who can help you improve how you behave at home with your family. Or, you might visit with a **nutritionist** to get information on eating healthy foods or taking vitamins. At school, you might see the **social worker, school counselor,** or **reading specialist.** You may also have a **classroom aide** or **paraprofessional.**

Some kids with autism even get a **service dog.** These dogs are specially trained to help a child stay calmer at home and in public places, for example. Many families have found that having a dog helps a child with ASD feel more comfortable in social situations, too.

> [My dog] Henry was just really gentle, friendly, and sociable. I liked that he had a wise look on his face and I always trusted him, which made me feel very comfortable with him. . . . It made me feel good when people admired him and would talk to me about him.
>
> —Dale, a boy with autism, from the book *A Friend Like Henry: The Remarkable Story of an Autistic Boy and the Dog That Unlocked His World*

After reading this chapter about getting a team of helpers, you may think "Well, that's a *lot* of helpers for just one person!" True. And if you have this many helpers, it means you also have a lot of new faces and places to deal with. Autism spectrum disorders are complicated. Whether you have a few helpers or a lot, each one is an expert in certain areas of autism. Together, this team of helpers can advise you, teach you new skills, and make sure you stay healthy.

This book can be a part of *your* team. If you'd like, you can come up with a team name. A strong team:

- listens
- shares information
- adjusts to change
- keeps trying, even when the going gets tough!

You are the heart of this team. The things you do to help yourself will make life with ASD easier for you.

Although your team may be full of experts, they will probably tell you this: You and your family are truly the experts when it comes to YOU. None of the experts live with you around the clock. They can't observe your every strength and challenge. That's why it's so important for you and your family to learn what works well for you and what you might need to change. Then you can go to your helpers with lots of information, ideas, and questions (not just once but at each new appointment).

Over time, as you learn more about your ASD and yourself, you'll become your own expert—with a little help from your family and team.

Part 2 Home, School, Community

Chapter 8

Family Matters

Have you heard of a safe harbor? A safe harbor is a place boats set out from and return to after going to sea. The waters in the harbor are calm, and the boats are protected from the wind and waves. A family is a kind of safe harbor, too. It's the place we leave and come home to. It's where we can feel comfortable and safe. In the best of worlds, families provide not only shelter but also love, support, and acceptance. Home needs to be a place where people understand your quirks and differences, and love you no matter what.

Maybe your home fits this description. Maybe not. Not all homes do. Some aren't places where kids feel cared for and accepted. When this happens, other people can step in to help: grandparents, aunts, uncles, cousins, older siblings, other relatives, or family friends. Whoever takes care of you—whoever acts as your safe harbor—is *family* in the best sense of the word. They're the people who can help you figure out your ASD, your strengths, your challenges, and your path in life.

In this chapter, we talk about ways that families can support your social growth. You and the adults who read this *Survival Guide* with you will learn about four social skills that start at home:

1. using manners

2. playing fair

3. handling conflict

4. doing your share

These skills not only improve your communication, but also build your confidence. And there's an added benefit: They can help strengthen family bonds.

Skill #1: Using Manners

Manners are rules to help people understand how to behave in social settings. When you have manners, you have a better idea of how to act around others. That builds your confidence and improves your social skills. People notice when you're polite. They'll be more likely to see you as thoughtful and nice to be around.

There are a few important "manners words" you can use every day to improve your communication. Practice them as much as you can with your family. The more you use these words at home, the more you'll use them *away* from home, too.

You can download the "Manners Words" list at www.freespirit.com/SGforASD and put it someplace handy. The more you practice using manners words, the more they'll come to you automatically—without your having to think about what to say.

Manners Words

What to say	When to say it
"Hello" (or "Hi")	When you first see someone
"Good-bye" (or "Bye")	When you or someone else is leaving
"Please"	When you want something
"Thank you"	When someone gives you what you want
"You're welcome"	When someone says "Thank you"
"Excuse me"	Whenever you bump into someone, need to get by people, or have to interrupt someone who's talking
"Yes, please"	When you want something being offered to you
"No, thank you"	When you don't want what's being offered
"I'm sorry"	When you hurt someone or make a mistake

There is one thing you and your family can get to work on right away: using manners words—and other manners—at mealtime. Mealtime tends to be a stressful time for someone who has ASD—and that means it's stressful for the whole family. For example:

Mali hated dinnertime because she didn't like all the waiting: Waiting for everyone to get to the table. Waiting for food. Waiting for everyone to finish. In her opinion, dinner took way too much time. She'd rather eat by herself in a separate room, where it was quiet and she could go at her own pace (fast!). She knew it was polite to wait and to share mealtime with her family, but it was hard for her to do those things.

Zach knew that sitting at the table with his family meant *conversation*. His mom explained that talking together at mealtime was courteous. But it was hard for him to figure out what to say and when to say it. Sometimes his mom asked him not to interrupt so much, and his sister said he was too loud. Zach thought dinner was a big pain. He didn't like having to be a part of the conversation. Questions like "How was your day?" annoyed him. It was better on weekends when his family sometimes ate in front of the TV.

J.J. didn't like people watching him while he ate. They wanted him to be polite and use a fork and spoon, but J.J. liked to use his fingers. His parents told him to use his napkin, not his shirt, to wipe his hands. It seemed he was always making a mess somehow, by spilling or dropping stuff. Sometimes, food disgusted him, especially if it touched any other food on the plate.

It might seem as if everything goes wrong at mealtime. It's supposed to be a time for a family to gather, share a meal, and talk. But people sometimes end up forgetting their manners. They complain about the food, get into arguments, or stomp away from the table in a huff.

To make mealtime better, your family can set *positive* goals—goals that tell you what *to* do instead of what *not* to do. Here are examples of what other families have done:

Mali's parents used a visual timer to keep her at the dinner table longer. The first night, they only made her stay five minutes. But each night, they added one minute more. It wasn't long before Mali got used to staying at the table for as long as dinner lasted. The timer helped her see that it wasn't as hard to wait as she'd thought.

Zach's family turned dinnertime into "game time." It was easier for Zach to sit with his family if they talked about familiar things. One made-up game they played was "Animals That Start With." A family member picked a letter, and each player took turns naming a mammal, reptile, or fish that started with that letter. They did this until no one could think of another animal. Thinking ahead and wondering what people would say kept Zach at the table longer. In between turns, the family could work on other skills, such as manners for eating or trying new foods. Not every night was game night, though. On some nights they practiced polite conversation. That was okay with Zach because now dinnertime had become more enjoyable overall.

J.J.'s mom got him a special plate that had dividers on it, so each food could stay in its own section. She also took J.J. to a store to pick out his own utensils. He got a fork, knife, and spoon with a superhero theme. Then he found superhero napkins and a cup with a handle, which made it easier for him to hold (so he didn't spill as often). J.J. was excited to use these items at mealtime. It took some practice for him to get into the habit of using utensils and a napkin, but he did it! His dad promised him that after dinner each night, they'd do something special together: throw a ball, play with action figures, or work with tools. Having an after-dinner reward gave J.J. something to look forward to.

What could *your* mealtime goals be? Here are some ideas to pick from:

- I will try one new food.
- I will stay at the table until everyone is finished.
- I will ask each family member one question.
- I will talk about one thing that happened today.
- I will clear my plate.

Note for Adults

Mealtime goals can work for *every* child in the family, not just the one who has ASD. Often, the child with autism or Asperger's is singled out as the one who needs help—but all children benefit from working on manners and social skills.

Also, you might want to try rewards for added motivation. They give kids something concrete to look forward to and work toward. Even simple rewards—stickers, quarters, or small toys—can be inspiring.

To stay on top of your goals, it helps to have a reminder you can *see* so you know how you're doing. A behavior chart is a simple tool that lets you track your progress each day. You can photocopy the one on page 60, or download a copy at www.freespirit.com/SGforASD. You can use the Behavior Chart for other behavior issues you want to work on, too—not just for mealtime.

Make a fresh copy each week as you're working on your goals, and then fill in the chart every day. The chart includes space for up to three goals each week, but you can focus on only one or two goals if you'd like. Be sure to make your goals *positive*—write down what you *will* do, instead of what you need to stop doing. Fill in the boxes with a star, checkmark, point, or smiley face.

Skill #2: Playing Fair

Many kids who have ASD *love* games—video games, board games, in-the-car games, you name it! Games are fun, and there's another bonus—they're a social opportunity. Your family can use games to help you practice social skills, like taking turns and getting comfortable with letting others choose what *they* want to play. In turn, you can help them with their game-playing skills—because you're probably really good at remembering rules, facts, trivia, strategies, shortcuts, or whatever else comes up.

Behavior Chart

My behavior goals for the week of _____

Goal 1: _____

Sunday	Monday	Tuesday	Wednesday	Thursday	Friday	Saturday

Goal 2: _____

Sunday	Monday	Tuesday	Wednesday	Thursday	Friday	Saturday

Goal 3: _____

Sunday	Monday	Tuesday	Wednesday	Thursday	Friday	Saturday

How I will be rewarded: _____

_____   _____
        Your signature   Parent/guardian signature

But here's a question for you: Do you sometimes get so caught up in a game that you almost forget about the other players? Maybe you ignore them when they ask to switch to another game or say they want to quit. Sometimes, you might even insist they keep playing because *you're* having so much fun. Remember, other kids usually aren't as intense as you are. You might be able to stay focused for hours on an activity you love, and you might really, *really* enjoy the repetition involved. But here's the problem: "Typical" kids often don't share that ability or level of interest. You might be able to play Monopoly or Mastermind all day, but after a while your friends and family probably get bored.

One of the best social skills you can learn through games is being a good sport. That doesn't mean you play sports, necessarily. Good *sportsmanship,* as it's called, is more about positive behaviors during games. It means you play by the rules—you play fair. You show that you're a good sport by treating the other players well. You can be a good sport whether you play for a team or prefer activities like Nintendo or board games.

Being a good sport may mean working on something that's a struggle for many kids on the spectrum: *knowing it's okay to lose.* People with ASD often have a need to win. They hate to be "wrong," or they feel very strongly that losing means they've "failed." For example, do you get upset if you're losing a game? Do the other players tell you to calm down or chill out? Do you sometimes insist other players must be cheating if you're behind in the game? If so, this probably happens because you feel a need to be right or "perfect."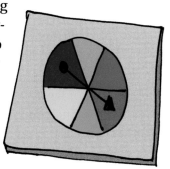

It may give you a sense of relief to know that *nobody* is perfect, and *you* don't have to be either. The point of games is to have fun and get along with other people during play. Winning really isn't as important as it seems. You may be thinking, "Oh, *yes* it is." But if you want to be social and have fun playing games with other people, everyone's enjoyment is more important than who wins.

Changing your attitude about winning takes time—and some practice. Try this: When you lose a game, instead of getting upset, take a few deep breaths. Shake your arms and legs to get rid of nervous energy and bad feelings. Turn to the other players and say "Good game" or "Nice job." Your words will help the others feel pleased and proud. *You* can feel proud, too, because you're working on being a good sport. There's another payoff for you as well: People will want to play with you again if you're a good sport and don't get upset about losing. That means more game time!

Just for fun, your family can work with you to turn *losing* into a game. Next time you play something, do your *worst*. Make all the wrong moves—be silly and don't even try to win! You'll see that the game won't have as much intensity, and maybe you'll even laugh your way through it. Afterward, reward yourself with something that makes you feel good . . . extra time on your hobby, for example. This is a fun way for your family to support you on a skill that takes time to develop. You don't have to play this way all the time, of course! Just once in a while as a reminder that games can be silly, social, and even more surprising than they usually are.

6 Tips for Being a Good Sport with Family Members

1. Can't agree on a game? Take turns playing one you like and one your sister or brother likes. Flip a coin to see who picks first.

2. Take turns going first. Do this especially with activities that include longer turns (like video games).

3. If you win the game, don't brag about it or tease the other person about losing. Just say something like "Good game—maybe you'll win next time." If you lose the game, congratulate the other player on winning. People appreciate compliments—they like to know when they've done well.

4. If you're playing an athletic game, shake hands or give high fives after it's over to show good sportsmanship.

5. Don't cheat or make up rules—play by the game rules. Cheating isn't fair. (Plus, other people don't like playing with someone who cheats.)

6. Remember, the reason people play games is to *have fun*. So, have fun! Don't worry so much about winning. Do your best and learn from your mistakes. In games, *luck* plays a part in how things turn out. If you don't win, better luck next time.

Skill #3: Handling Conflict

Your family is your training ground for getting along with other people at school, in your community, and in the wider world. At home, you probably have your share of troubles: You may disagree with a rule your parents make. You might get in fights with siblings. Maybe you feel upset about something and take out those negative feelings on everyone else. All of this is a normal part of family life, whether you have ASD or not.

> I have a 9-year-old sister. We get along sometimes, and I like to play games with her. I don't like when she sings or gets loud, which is most of the time.
>
> **—14-year-old boy with autism**

> I don't get along well with my younger brother. Sometimes we play video games together or swim, but he annoys me. I annoy him, too.
>
> **—12-year-old boy with Asperger's**

But having ASD tends to make conflict more difficult. For one thing, you probably have strong emotions that you're still figuring out how to handle. (You can read more about that in Chapter 15). For another thing, you may have sensory issues (see Chapter 3) that increase your feelings of discomfort and make it harder for you to learn self-control.

When a conflict comes up, you need a plan. This plan should be simple enough to remember and use—even in situations that upset you a lot. You know what's simple? A traffic light. Red for stop, yellow for caution, and green for go. Your plan can be as basic as STOP THINK GO.

As soon as an argument or conflict begins, and you feel yourself getting upset, STOP. Put on the brakes so you won't do something to make the situation worse.

THINK a moment before you do anything. Take a few deep, calming breaths. What's the best way to handle the situation? This isn't a time to get physical (hitting, punching) or to say something that will be hard to take back.

Next, GO ahead and act. Give your *best* response, based on the questions you've asked yourself. Be sure to choose an action that *helps*—one that won't get you into trouble or make things worse.

Imagine this happens to you: Your little brother grabs the game controller right out of your hands and starts pushing the buttons. He's totally messing up your game.

Here's how to use STOP THINK GO:

STOP. Put on those brakes—keep your hands, feet, and words to yourself. You might want to yell, but instead, try to stay as calm and cool as you can. If you start to cry, that's okay—it happens!

Pay attention to your body's signals: Do you feel hot, shaky, jumpy, or ready to burst?

These are your body's warning signs to STOP. If you have a temper and you're used to screaming and yelling, then stopping yourself is tough. But it's *really* important. Keep practicing, and over time you'll get better at it.

THINK. Consider what happened. Maybe your little brother just wants to get your attention. He might think he's being funny or that it's his turn. Ask yourself:

What do I need to do to stay calm? I can take deep breaths.

What can I do that will HELP the situation? I can keep my hands to myself. I can calmly tell my brother that I didn't like what he did.

How do I avoid doing something that might HURT me or somebody else? Instead of thinking about how mad I am, I can focus on staying calm. If my brother tries to apologize, I can listen.

GO. Walk away from your brother. Get an adult's help. If you're able to calmly explain what happened, the adult is more likely to listen and help you resolve the conflict.

STOP THINK GO is easy to remember and, over time, it becomes easier to use. But it takes practice. Some families practice together by role-playing. They act out different situations (such as conflicts about bedtime, getting dressed for school, or helping with chores). Role-playing like this helps kids understand what works well in conflict situations and what doesn't. Another option is to work with a therapist on conflict-resolution skills. You can read more about conflict and how to handle it in chapters 12 and 13.

Skill #4: Doing Your Share

Everyone in a family has jobs. Parents work outside the home or in the home. They make the food, do the laundry, and keep things clean. If no one did these tasks, your home would be a confusing place to live.

Just like adults, kids can do jobs, too. You and your siblings probably have a few chores, like feeding the pets or keeping rooms clean. Lots of kids (whether they have ASD or not) don't like chores. But chores are a "have to." When they don't get done, your home is less organized and your parents won't be too pleased.

Like other kids, you probably don't enjoy chores. In your case it may go further: maybe you *really hate doing chores*, and it's hard for you to get them done. In some families, parents avoid giving any chores to their child who has ASD because it leads to tears and angry outbursts. Does that happen in your home? Do you cry and get upset if you have to make your bed, for example? Or do you put up a fight so everyone will just leave you alone?

Maybe you don't have any chores. Or maybe you usually get out of doing them. But if that's the case, then you're not learning the skills you need to grow up and become independent someday. Other kids are learning those skills—you need them, too! You have ASD, but you can still do your share. That's part of family life.

Remember in chapters 1 and 2, when you learned that ASD is a brain difference? This difference may make it harder for you to stay organized and figure out the most efficient way to complete tasks. What does that mean? It could mean that you don't notice when your space is messy. Or that you don't remember you're supposed to clean up. Maybe you start a task but aren't sure what steps to take and in which order. Perhaps you get confused and frustrated, and you give up. What can you do?

Get an adult's help. If you're reading this book with a grown-up, you can talk together about why chores are challenging for you. Then, start small. With the adult's help, practice each step of a given chore, even the littlest steps! You can do this at home, or perhaps with an occupational therapist (OT).

If you were to break down one chore into its smallest parts, it might look something like this:

My chore: Feed the dog

When? 7 am and 6 pm EVERY DAY

How much food? 1½ cups per feeding

Step 1. Get out bag of dry food.

Step 2. Get measuring cup.

Step 3. Measure the correct amount.

Step 4. Pour it into the dog's dish.

Step 5. Check to see if dog has fresh water.
      If not, refill water dish.

Step 6. Put away dog food and measuring cup.

I rock!

You'll probably need a **chore chart** to keep track of your tasks. This way, you can see what you need to do each day. You can check off each job after it's completed. You can ask your dad or mom if there can be a reward system for doing chores, like an allowance or special treats. You can also talk together about whether there are consequences for not getting a chore done.

The key here is *practice!* It's okay if you need to be shown—again and again—how to get a task done. It's all right to break down the chore into very small steps so you get the hang of it. And it's fine to ask for help if you need it. This is all part of the learning process. Most kids who have ASD need tools to help them each day. There are many tools to try, such as calendars, visual schedules, daily planners, to-do lists, alarm clocks or timers, chore charts, bulletin boards, sticker charts, and little rewards. Experiment to see what helps you. Use whatever works!

Chapter 9

Have Fun!

Sometimes, life with ASD means a lot of therapy, and doctor's appointments, and social skills practice . . . and the list goes on. This focus on your healthcare and communication is important, but life can't be *all* work. You're still a kid! That means you like to have fun, right? You need to play, just like other kids your age. Like anyone else, you've got to find time for physical activities, a hobby, music, art, a collection, crafts, a club, or volunteering—whatever you most enjoy. That's why this chapter is focused on FUN.

Play Is Good for You

So, here's the thing about having ASD: It can affect not only how you play, but also your level of imagination. Does this mean you don't know how to play? Or that you lack imagination? Hardly! You just have your own unique style when it comes to play. And the growth of your imagination may take more time. Unlike "typical" kids, you may gain skills at a different rate, or in an unusual order.

For example, maybe you started reading at a very young age, long before your peers knew their ABCs. Perhaps when you were little, you could do simple math problems or memorize all the capital cities in North America. While other kids were doing lots of play and pretend, you were focused on other types of activities.

Or perhaps you've struggled in academic subjects. Not every child who has ASD shows an early ability in math, reading, or memorization. Maybe you're working at a different pace than other kids your age. Your brain is developing in its own way, on its own schedule.

Because of your ASD, skills such as being playful and imaginative may come more slowly for you. But they'll come, and you can help them get there.

Use Your Imagination

When you use imagination, you're able to look at the world in a different way. You can picture things that aren't there. Or pretend you're someone—or some*thing*—else. Imagination helps you be creative. It also helps you learn to solve problems.

You have imagination that you can use every day. This may mean trying new things. If you tend to do the same type of play over and over (because you like the repetition and familiarity), it's harder for family and friends to join you. Try new games or new ways of playing old favorites. For instance, change some of the rules or add a touch of humor: Monkey in the Middle is extra fun when the ball is a water balloon. Hide and Seek is spookier in the dark with flashlights.

At home, with the help of an adult, you might make a list of play activities you think you'll like. Then, over a period of time, *do* them—preferably with other people your age. This could be as simple as playing chase, kickball, tag, or four square more often. Or you could get out the board games, cards, and puzzles. Invite friends over or arrange a family game night.

You might realize you've been playing with the same toys and gadgets for a while. Are you ready for different ones? Toy and educational catalogs and websites are filled with all sorts of play materials you may not see in regular stores. Or look for toys, art supplies, or hobby materials at thrift shops and yard sales. Your dad or mom can ask friends and relatives to send along no-longer-used items that are still good. You never know what you might get: board games from the past, unique action figures or dolls, unused craft materials, and other cool stuff. Maybe you'll find something new to spark your interest and imagination.

If something you try isn't as fun as you expected, move on to the next play activity on your list. In a month or so, go back to the activity you didn't like. Give it a second chance—you might enjoy it this time.

Try Dramatic Play

One way to become more imaginative is to try dramatic play. Pretend to be a character or use an action figure or stuffed animal to act out a role. When you do this, you suddenly have to deal with *conflict*—like, the villain wants to take over the world and the hero must save the day. You have to react and be creative to keep the story alive. That's the power of play. It's practice for the real world, even if you never meet an evil villain or fly through the skies wearing a cape.

Do you spend time each day pretending or doing dramatic play? Sometimes, kids with ASD don't do enough of these activities. Maybe pretending doesn't come as naturally to you. Or perhaps you missed opportunities to be in childhood play groups where imaginary play was the main event. A need for play still lies within you. Let it out!

Max's Story

Max is 8 years old. His autism severely affects his ability to communicate and be social. One of the best ways Max's family helps him is through something they're all good at: play.

When Max was younger, his family used to set up play-dates with "typical" kids in the neighborhood. They'd play Grocery Store, using pretend food, a grocery list with PECS* pictures, and fake money. Max's job was to ask for each item on the list (to get him to talk more), pay for the food, and take it home. But for fun—and to help Max—his family would pretend that important ingredients were left off the list by mistake. Back to the grocery store Max went, over and over again, until all the ingredients were ready and it was time to "cook."

Soon Max's family decided to make the plot of the game more exciting. What might happen if a fire broke out in the store? (One of the kids became a "firefighter," with a red plastic hat, black boots, and an old kitchen-sink hose.) What if a robber held up the store? (A "police officer" with a cap and badge appeared to catch the bad guy.) What if the robber escaped from jail? (Max to the rescue!)

In a fun, creative way, Max was learning to adjust to the movement, noise, and changes that naturally happen as kids play. Best of all, he got to be part of a group of other kids his age, where he was the focus of attention. All the while, Max's family took photos of the play sessions. His mom collected them into social stories—homemade books that showed the order of what took place. Later, Max could look at the books to remember the fun he had.

Now that he's older, Max's family is working with his school to bring play and social time into his day. During one gym class per week, Max goes to a classroom with other kids who volunteer to play with him. Max's mom and the speech teacher help direct activities that teach Max social skills through play. This week the activity is about trains because Max loves trains.

Max loves the day at school. So do the other kids. They can't wait to find out what will happen next week when the social group gathers again.

*PECS stands for Picture Exchange Communication System—sets of pictures used for visual communication.

Ways to Be More Playful

- Play with a younger brother or sister, or a neighbor. Little kids love to pretend. They'll dress in costumes, make dolls "talk," build creative structures, or act out scenarios you come up with.

- Ask a parent or an older sibling to play with you for a specific length of time every day. Teens and adults may be a bit out of practice when it comes to pretend play. They still might surprise you by acting silly or telling you in an excited voice, "I remember when *I* had a robot like this!" Together, you can invent, make up stories, and discover your playful sides.

- Watch what other kids your age do for fun. Are there certain games your classmates do during recess? Do kids in the neighborhood gather at a local park or playground? Can an adult set up a play group or club for kids your age who have ASD or who share similar interests? (For more on this, see page 76.)

- Ask if you can get involved in community theater or a drama club at school. Being part of a theater group allows you to pretend in a way that's more scripted. (Having a script and a coach or director can help if you're not used to dramatic play or acting.) Along the way, you may learn about performing, building sets, putting together costumes, and even singing and dancing.

- Use play as a way to practice real-life scenarios. For

example, how would your action hero handle a bully? How would your stuffed animal throw a party? If you were a pretend teacher, how might you help your students learn about other places and cultures? When you play it, you *live* it. And that helps you make connections to the real world.

- Add imagination to everything you do. If you're sledding, pretend you're a penguin or that you're on a luge (that fast sled you see in the Winter Olympics). If you're in the pool, be a fish, a mermaid, or Aquaman. If you're giving friends piggy-back rides, make them pretend to buckle their seatbelts or give you a ticket first. Play together using funny voices. Crack jokes, put on weird costumes or outfits, sing, dance, and have a good time.

> I build with Legos. I like to construct cities.
> I like to design buildings and worlds of my own.
> I also like to make movies of them.
>
> **—14-year-old boy with autism**

Great Ways to Spend Your Time

Abby loves making friendship bracelets. She learned how to weave colorful threads into bracelets one year at a summer camp for kids with ASD. Because Abby has a good memory, she could look at a pattern and then make a bracelet without reading all the instructions. Soon she started making bracelets all the time. She gave them to her friends and classmates. This almost led to some trouble at school when Abby was making bracelets instead of doing her work. But her teacher came up with an idea. She said that if Abby agreed to make bracelets *only* at home, she could bring them in to sell at the school store. Now kids at school can buy the bracelets to give to others. Abby feels great because she's not just a bracelet maker but also a "businesswoman."

Arno realized that team sports weren't his thing. He tried activities like tennis and gymnastics, but they took a lot of coordination. He wanted an activity that got him outdoors but didn't lead to frustration. Then he remembered something he loved: *fishing*. His grandfather started taking him fishing in his boat when he was a lot younger, and Arno was good at it. He decided that fishing could be his sport. Now Arno has a journal he takes with him every time he's on the boat. He records the date, his location on the lake, and how many fish he catches. Then he leans over the side of the boat and takes a photo of the water. When other people see his photos, they see only water. But for Arno, those pictures bring back every detail—the rod and reel, the bait, the sky, the smell of the air, and most of all, the fish!

Like Abby and Arno, you might have something in your life that brings you feelings of happiness and satisfaction. Maybe it's an activity, a hobby, a collection, or a game. Having intense interests is part of your ASD—but it's also a part of *who you are.* Find ways to pursue your interests, because they give you something to *do.* They help you think, dream, relax, and express yourself.

Think of ways to include others in your special interest. Then you'll have something in common with other people. Could you:

- Teach a classmate to play the game you love?
- Find other kids who collect the same things you do?
- Invite siblings or cousins to do your hobby with you?

What if you don't have a special interest yet? Or you want new ideas for fun ways to spend your time? Try these ideas:

Sign up for an activity. Does your school offer extracurricular activities you're interested in? There might be academic clubs, band, orchestra, choir, chess club, the yearbook or newspaper, or something else. Get involved! If there isn't a club that appeals to you, what about starting a small one with a couple of friends? Some kids start book clubs or clubs based on special interests, like games or cards for collecting.

Try athletics and sports. Check out what your school has to offer, or look for programs offered at the YMCA/YWCA or your local community center. Learn skating, karate, archery, swimming, or golf. At home, stay active by playing outdoors, jumping rope, dancing, stretching, running around, or walking the dog. You can read more about the importance of physical activity in Chapter 20.

Get creative at home. Instead of spending too much time in front of the TV or computer or playing video games, do something that takes more imagination. Sketch your self-portrait. Invent a comic strip. Make collages. Write stories and poems. Teach yourself the different forms of solitaire. Take photos of family and friends, or shoot home videos. Keeping your mind and hands busy is a great way to increase your creativity.

Join the Scouts. Boy Scout and Girl Scout programs are set up to teach kids about fitness, responsibility, and good character. You'll learn to camp and hike, do fun activities with other boys or girls, and take part in volunteering. You can learn more about Scouting through your school or by going online with a parent.

Take lessons. Music, acting, singing, painting, photography, martial arts—whatever interests you, give it a try. Maybe a teacher can come to your home. Or maybe you can take lessons at a place that includes kids of different abilities. You might discover a special talent, and you'll see that building new skills can be challenging *and* fun.

> I listen to my favorite radio station and then Google the artists to learn more about them. I have a CD player and a microphone, and I deejay my 'own' station. I introduce the songs and the artists. Sometimes I do my own talk radio show where I mention stuff that happened to me at school. It's fun to include both music and talk on 'my station.'
>
> —12-year-old boy with Asperger's

Explore the arts. Attend your school's plays, and go to the plays and musicals that the local high school puts on. Show up for your school's concerts (choir, band, or orchestra). In your community, go to free concerts, shows, museums, and galleries. All of this helps create an interest in art, music, theater, and performance—works of the imagination!

Volunteer your time. Does your school have a service club? If it does, join up. School service clubs are a great way to be part of the community and help people in need. Another option is to participate in volunteer activities through a church, synagogue, mosque, or other place of worship. Does your dad or mom volunteer? Maybe you could go along to see what it's like and offer your help. When you give your time and assistance, you feel good about yourself. You see that other people have problems, too. You start to see that, as human beings, we can boost each other up and make a difference.

Act out stories. Turn your basement into Hogwarts and become characters from the Harry Potter series. Or, you can write mysteries, set up pretend crime scenes, hide some clues, and watch your friends and family become detectives on the case. Another option is to reenact famous battle scenes from history books or to pretend you're people from another place and time.

Form a social group. You'll need some help from a parent or another trusted adult to make this happen. It's worth it! Call it whatever you like—a play group, social skills club, friends club, or something you make up. The goal of each gathering should be having fun. Perhaps the group will always meet at your home, or you'll

Take a Look!
Are video and computer games the thing you love to do more than anything else? Think of ways to expand this interest beyond the screen. Can you draw the game's characters? Go outside with a friend and pretend to be the characters? Build an outdoor obstacle course that resembles the game's different levels? Use your imagination!

take turns hosting. Plan for about two hours of fun. Make sure you have games, toys, activities, and things to do. Try to organize something that involves everyone, so it truly is social time.

> Playing with other kids your age—especially in a group of three or more—helps you learn to get along with others. In group play, the rules and ideas may change quickly, and you'll learn to adjust to that. Plus, you'll keep fine-tuning social skills such as sharing and cooperation. A group like this can help you build friendships, too.

Over time, members may come and go, and you might decide to include new kids in the group. Maybe you'll meet after school once a week. Maybe you'll gather two weekends each month. See what works for everyone involved.

Summers are an especially good time to start a social group or to increase the amount of time your current group spends together. Why? Because summer days are *unstructured*—they don't have a plan the way school days do. As a person with ASD, you probably need structure to stay organized and interested. Without school, many kids with autism spectrum disorders simply don't have enough to do—they get restless and bored. Having a planned social activity written on the calendar is important!

Chapter 10

Good Communication: Body Language and Listening

One of the main symptoms of autism spectrum disorder is a difficulty with communication. You might have trouble understanding other people, reading or writing, and using language to express your feelings. This isn't because you aren't "smart"—it's a difference in how your brain is wired.

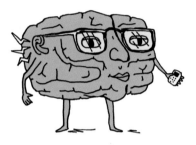

Your brain tends to see things in smaller parts, instead of being able to focus on the whole picture. Your brain may also have a slower processing speed. This means it takes you longer to gather information and put what you have learned into words. Plus, there's a difference in your *mirror neurons* that can make it hard for you to figure out what's on another person's mind. In spite of all these challenges, you can learn and practice communication skills.

Take a look at Chapter 2. It talks about these brain differences in more depth.

3 Tools for Learning Good Communication

For best results, you'll need three things: a crew (group) of communication helpers, a video camera, and time to practice every day.

Communication crew. Find an adult who can help you with the activities in this chapter: your mom or dad, a grandparent, or another caregiver. This person is like your "crew leader," who helps guide you through the activities and works with you to improve your skills.

It's also helpful to have peers you can practice with. How about brothers, sisters, cousins, neighbors, classmates, friends, or a social skills group? (Read more about social groups on pages 76–77.) Why is it important to practice with other kids? People your age have unique ways of communicating with each other. By watching other kids and doing what they do, you learn to communicate in these special ways. Plus, you get a chance to be social.

If you have a speech therapist, he or she can be part of your crew, too. Let your therapist know about what you're working on at home. Then, together, you can figure out ways to make your speech sessions even more effective.

Video camera. Does your family have a video camera or cell phone that can take videos? Or, could you borrow one from relatives? If so, you can record your practice sessions and family conversations and then watch them later. This is an excellent way to see where you need help.

Sometimes, when you start building a new skill, the other ones you've learned may fall by the wayside. For example, you might start with eye contact and make a lot of progress. But then when you move on to listening skills, you may be concentrating so hard on them that you forget to include eye contact as well. This is why it's helpful to have videos to watch. You can go back to one of your older videos and quickly see, "Oops, I forgot to *look* at the person I was listening to."

Keep the videos—don't record over them. Someday, years from now, you may want to look back to see just how far you've come.

Regular practice time. You can try working on communication skills for about a half hour each day. Or do more if you want to! The amount of time you spend is up to you and your family.

Just be sure to give yourself *plenty of time* to build each new skill. It may take weeks, months, or even years to really get the hang of using eye contact regularly or listening more closely, for example. Take the time you need—it's not a race. After all, you're working on skills to last a lifetime.

Body Language

Did you know that our bodies "talk" without saying a word? That's known as body language. Lots of things go into body language: posture, gestures, eye contact, facial expressions, and even the distance between people.

Posture and Gestures

Posture—the way we stand—"says" something. If we're standing straight and tall, this might show that we feel alert or proud. If we're slumped over, we might be bored or tired. We use our hands to make gestures: we point out sights we want others to see, or motion for someone to come closer.

We might tap our feet when we're impatient. Or shrug our shoulders when we don't know the answer to a question. Or give a huge yawn when we're sleepy. Closed fists can

Take a Look!
This chapter focuses on the *nonverbal* aspects of communication. (*Nonverbal* means *without words*.) You'll learn about body language, eye contact, and better listening. Then, in Chapter 11, you can read about another important aspect of communication: *verbal* skills, or using words.

High fives

Fist bumps and knuckle bumps ("knucks")

Pointing to something to make someone else look

Hand motions to say "Come here"

Waving hello and good-bye

Pointing to the eyes, with two fingers, to say "I'm watching you"

Thumbs up to say "Good job" or "Well done"

show anger. Folded arms can say we don't like what we're hearing. So can a stomping foot, a grunt, or a sigh of impatience.

All of these postures and gestures are forms of communication. Without saying a word, we've "told" people something about what we think or feel.

As a person with ASD, you might have trouble "reading" body-language and facial-expression clues like the ones just described.

Perhaps you don't notice the clues. Or maybe you spot them, but don't know what they mean. Sometimes, you might not be able to see the whole picture—you see "parts" of the person's body or face but can't put them together quickly or at all.

Because of your ASD, you have two communication challenges:

- reading other people's body language
- using body language yourself

Remember, practice is the key. Start by noticing the different gestures the people around you use, especially kids your age.

Sometimes, kids who have ASD have trouble with gestures. Ask someone to show you how to do the motions correctly, and practice until they look (and feel) more natural.

Then use the gestures, when appropriate. Wave to people when you say hi or bye, for example. Practice pointing with your index finger (instead of using another finger to point). Give high fives when someone wins a game or makes a great play. All of this helps you connect each skill to your daily life, which is so important!

Eye Contact

Eyes can tell a lot about what a person is feeling or thinking. Someone's eyes might have a faraway look, or be brimming with tears, or nearly "sparkle" with excitement. These clues reveal emotions that may not always come across in the person's words.

Next time you talk to someone, pay special attention to where you focus your eyes. Do you look at the person—or do you look at an object in the room? If you look at the person, which part are you focused on: Eyes? Mouth? Head? Shoulders? Another body part? Maybe you tend to look at the person's mouth. Many people with ASD look at the mouth, instead of the eyes, when people are talking.

Making eye contact is an essential communication skill. That may not seem fair to you. Why should there be some rule about looking people in the eye when it makes people on the autism spectrum so uncomfortable? But if you *don't* look at people's eyes, you miss out on a lot of nonverbal communication. The eyes can tell you about a person's emotions. They can let you know if the person is paying attention to you. And what if someone's eyes are looking in another direction, or rolling whenever you say something? That's a big clue that you don't have the person's attention.

Here are a couple tricks to use if it's hard for you to look at people's eyes:

- Look at the forehead instead. Choose a point right at the top of the person's nose, low on the forehead. Then it won't seem as if you're studying the person's hair.

- Try a technique of "brief glances." As you talk or listen, glance into the person's eyes for a second, then look away. Continue to glance and look away again. By meeting the person's eyes, even for just a moment at a time, you connect. And that's what eye contact is about—*making a connection*. In our social world, these connections are crucial.

Just to be clear, eye contact doesn't mean staring. If you stare at someone closely, that will make the person feel uncomfortable. Sometimes, staring can even be taken as a threat. It's important to practice eye contact that makes others feel comfortable. Get out the video camera and have someone record you speaking with another person. Watch the video afterward to see where your eyes were looking. Did the eye contact seem natural? Did you look at the other person frequently, without staring too hard? Did you feel yourself making a connection?

Being able to make eye contact helps you make friends. Other kids will see your interest in them and they'll take more interest in *you*. Making eye contact with your teachers will help you seem like an eager learner, or at least someone who's trying hard. Later on in life, eye contact will even help you in job interviews. It's a skill worth working on, even if it's difficult. Be patient with yourself.

Facial Expressions

Facial expressions are another form of nonverbal communication. The human face can express so many feelings: anger, fear, embarrassment, sadness, worry, joy, excitement, curiosity, boredom, satisfaction. Sometimes, a person's face can flicker from one expression to another so quickly that it's hard to keep up.

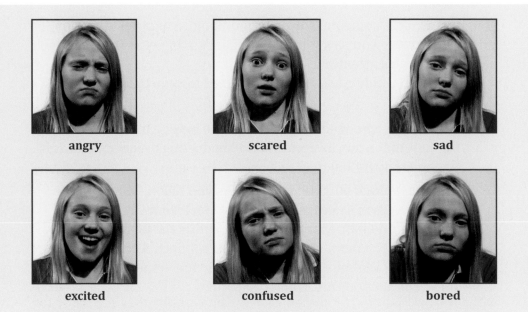

angry	**scared**	**sad**
excited	**confused**	**bored**

To make matters more confusing, the expression on someone's face can hide the person's true feelings. For example, your mom might be sad one day, but if she doesn't want you to know that, she could force herself to smile and pretend everything's okay. Or, your brother could tease you by putting a frightened expression on his face, pointing to something behind you. You might turn quickly, thinking something really awful is creeping up on you, only to discover nothing is there. Your brother's expression fooled you!

Here's an example of "misreading" body language: Suppose you have something important to tell your dad, and you find him at the kitchen table paying bills. At first, you don't notice that he has a frustrated expression on his face. He's rubbing his head. He's looking down at his calculator. You might think this is a good time to talk because your dad is quiet. But the moment you speak, your dad says, "Can't you see I'm busy here?" Chances are, you missed some important clues about his mood:

- His face was saying "I'm frustrated."
- His hands were rubbing his head. Maybe that meant he had a headache or was thinking really hard.
- His eyes were looking down, probably because he was concentrating and didn't expect to be interrupted.

It's not your fault if you miss clues like these. That's part of having ASD. As you get older and keep working on communication skills, you'll read these clues more easily. You'll learn ways to watch for signals that tell you, *without words*, what another person might think or feel.

Your own facial expressions communicate to others, too. It's been said that some people with ASD have a blank look. (This is another way of saying "not much facial expression.") Maybe this describes you. If so, then it's probably difficult for other kids to imagine what you might be thinking or feeling. They may even get the impression that you're not thinking about much at all. *You* know your mind is filled with interesting thoughts, dreams, and feelings—but other people may not.

Here's something you may not realize: Many "typical" kids spend a lot of time looking in mirrors to check themselves out, especially when they're preteens or teens. They stare at their reflection, making all sorts of expressions—mad, glad, sad. It's almost like they're posing for a camera. Many younger children do this, too. They discover how they look as they make different faces or imitate other people. "Typical" kids of all ages also study photos of themselves, trying to figure out if they're attractive. Chances are, you haven't done a lot of this yourself. It's possible that faces simply don't hold as much interest for you.

As humans, we look at faces as we communicate. We do this to try to understand another person's thoughts and feelings. We listen to the person's words, but we also concentrate on the eyes and expressions to see if the person seems truthful or to make sure we really understand. This ability to read faces is like a built-in navigation system (like GPS) that "typical" people are born with. If you don't have the same system, you get lost more often when it comes to communication.

This means you need to create your own navigation system if you want to get better at communication. Start by working with an adult to become more familiar with different facial expressions and the emotions they express:

- Look at faces in magazines and try to identify people's feelings.
- Together, take photos of family members making "emotion faces." Then label them with the matching feelings: shy, happy, anxious, furious, sneaky, giggly, mad. Place these photos in an album you can look at again and again.
- With a parent, go online to look for posters, books, apps, and other tools designed to help kids with ASD recognize facial expressions.

At home, practice making pleasant expressions you can use when you're speaking with people. Smile in different ways—with your teeth showing or your lips closed. Try to look relaxed and approachable, but not "blank." We're not suggesting that you go around with a fake smile! Just become more aware of your facial expressions and what they might say to people. This is where a video camera comes in handy. A parent can record what you look like when you're talking to friends and family. When it's your turn to listen, do you look interested? When it's your turn to talk, do you change your facial expressions to match what you're saying?

School is a good place to practice paying more attention to faces. There, you're surrounded by kids of all ages who look different and whose expressions are always changing throughout the day. Pretend you're a spy, gathering information about what people might be thinking or feeling. Notice when different classmates seem annoyed, pleased, or confused. At the lunch table, look around as you eat, watching how the other kids interact. Can you tell, just from facial expressions, who likes their lunch and who doesn't? Or who's having a good day and who's not? What more can you learn from what you see?

Let your friends help you get better at reading their thoughts. Every so often, you might say, "You look excited. Did something good happen?" Or "You seem sad. What's up?" If you notice an expression on your friend's face and wonder what it means, speak up. You could say, "What are you thinking right now?" This is a step toward *good communication.*

Plus, you get to learn from real-life situations, which is even better than practicing skills at home.

Personal Space

People like to have some personal space around them during conversations or when standing in line. There are rules, often unspoken, about what is considered a polite distance. Have you ever been in a situation where another kid at school says, "You're too close to me" or "Back up"? Maybe you didn't realize you had crossed a boundary— because it's an invisible boundary! You can't *see* it, so you have to *sense* it. But having ASD can make it difficult to sense those boundaries.

Imagine that each person is contained within a clear bubble. The unspoken rule is that other people shouldn't get inside that space— unless they're family or very close friends. If it's hard for you to picture an imaginary bubble, try this: Put your arm straight out in front of you. Where your fingertips are right at this moment is an *arm's length* away. That's a good distance to put between yourself and your classmates. Now you're setting personal boundaries that help you and the people you talk to feel more comfortable.

If you tend to get very close to people when you speak to them, they may back up. Watch for that clue (the backing away). It tells you you've accidentally gotten inside their "bubble." Other kids at school might be direct enough to say, "Can you move back?" But if they're not, it will help if your teacher knows you're working on personal-space issues. Ask your teacher to give you a secret signal that tells you

Take a Look!

Personal space can be a big issue when playing with other kids. Sometimes, play gets rough (like when you're racing, wrestling, or having pretend battles). During those times, the personal-space boundary doesn't seem to apply. But it actually does! There are **rules about not getting too rough.** There are also **rules about knowing when to stop.**

ASD can make the rules harder to understand. For example, you may tag or hit people too hard but not realize it. What feels like a light touch to you could feel like a smack to someone else. How confusing! Talking to an expert on sensory issues can help you better understand how this works.

Sometimes, during rough and active play you might miss some of the signals your friends are sending. For instance, you and your buddies might shout so loudly during a wrestling match that you don't hear someone yell, "Stop! That hurts!" Or, you might tickle a friend to make him laugh and not real-ize that you're tickling too hard.

It's important to have fun—but also to know when the fun has stopped. A parent can help you become more aware of whether you're being too rough with friends and siblings. You could make up a signal for all of you to use, like forming your hands into the shape of a letter T to say "time out." Whenever someone uses that signal, it's a clue to stop, take a few deep breaths, and step back. Instead of physical play, move on to something quieter, such as art or a board game.

if you're overstepping a boundary. Your teacher could tap you on the shoulder and whisper a word like "bubble." Or your teacher could draw a circle shape in the air to let you know you need to back up.

With family members, standing or sitting close isn't usually as much of an issue. Unless, of course, it's an issue for *you*. Maybe you sometimes feel uncomfortable if your siblings or parents get too close to you. They may not even realize that you need a little distance at times. Let everyone at home know what you've learned about a need for more personal space. You can use hand signals at home, too: You might draw a circle in the air or use a gesture your family makes up. You might also decide on a family phrase you all agree on, such as "Please give me some space."

With close friends—kids you frequently spend time with at your home or theirs—the personal-space issue gets a little trickier. Often, friends don't require as much distance during conversation or play. In fact, you might sit close to each other while you play video games, do art, or talk. It all comes down to what you and your friends prefer.

If you need more personal space, you could say it in a friendly way: "I'm backing up a little because I need some space. No offense, okay?" Or, "I'm having one of those days where I need some personal space. Do you mind if I sit over here for a while?" (Then move to a chair or a different area of the floor.) If you tend to be the one who gets a little too close, let your friends know you're working on it. Show them the circle signal, which they can use to quietly say, "Back up a little, please."

Learning to Listen

Do people have trouble getting your attention? Do they usually call your name several times before you notice? Do they say stuff like "Pay attention, please!" or "Did you hear anything I just said?" Many people on the spectrum find it challenging to tune in and listen. Or, they may be listening quite well but aren't showing it in a way that other people understand.

Listening is an essential part of good communication. You have to listen carefully to:

- follow instructions
- learn what you're being taught in school
- do what your parents ask you to do
- get along with siblings at home
- make friends and have lasting relationships

Adults are often pretty good at being patient with someone who has ASD. For example, your parents are probably used to calling your name a few times before you respond. Your teacher might know you have a condition that affects your ability to communicate, so he or she makes accommodations for you at school. The adults on your team (see Chapter 7) realize you need more time to listen to the directions you're given at appointments and will take extra time to explain things carefully.

But guess what—*kids* often aren't as patient. If other kids get the feeling you aren't listening, they might simply walk away. If they don't know how to get your attention, they'll probably give up after one or two tries. Other kids may not realize you have ASD. If they don't understand you and your special needs, they might not make much of an effort—and they'll miss out on getting to know you. They shouldn't miss out on this chance, because you're worth getting to know!

You don't *have* to tell other kids, "I have some trouble with communication, so I hope you can be patient with me." But you *can* if you want to. Sometimes, giving other kids information about ASD can help.

You could say, "Sometimes I forget to look at people when they're talking" or "If it ever seems like I'm not listening, just tap me on the shoulder or say my name a little louder. That will get my attention." Then, instead of thinking you don't listen or you don't want to be friends, other kids might realize, "There's a difference here, and now I know what to do." That opens a door to friendship.

Eyes Listen, Too

Listening with your *eyes* is often as important as listening with your ears. Focus your eyes on other people when they're speaking—even if eye contact is difficult for you.

How to Be an Active Listener

The rule is you should face the person you're listening to. Turn your body toward the speaker, focus your eyes on the person's face, and nod your head every so often. Nodding shows that you're taking in the information.

Remember all you read about eye contact and facial expressions? Now is the time to use what you've learned. When other people are talking, try to look as if you're actively listening:

- Keep your eyes focused on the person's eyes or forehead.
- Smile when appropriate, and try to look interested.
- Make sure not to interrupt.
- Nod your head (or say "Yeah" and "Uh-huh" a few times) to show you understand.

> I have to work hard to pay attention to what is happening, because I have an auditory [listening] problem. I don't always catch what people say, or I can't follow, or I'm thinking of something else.
>
> —14-year-old boy with autism

Learning to listen is a skill that *all* kids have to learn, not just kids with ASD. So you're definitely not alone when it comes to needing practice in this area!

Your family can help you and your siblings learn better listening skills by using a timer and a prop. The prop can be a hat, a stick or wand, a ball, or another object that can be passed back and forth. Sit together in a room and take turns talking, so you can all practice listening. The person who's talking should wear the hat or hold the stick, wand, or ball. No one can interrupt while the speaker is talking. When the timer goes off, it's the next person's turn to talk—the visual prop is passed to him or her. The prop is the tool that reminds everyone to stay quiet and be good listeners.

Next, figure out how well people listened. Go around the room, taking turns saying something about what each person spoke of and what was said. (Keep passing the prop, if you'd like.) Here's where it gets interesting. What did you notice? Was everyone paying close attention? Were you all able to remember what people said—or did some of you get confused along the way?

This is helpful information to know. If you have trouble remembering things you hear, then you might need more visual aids at school so you have a better chance of success. Your speech therapist might be able to suggest certain activities and skill-builders to help you improve in this area, too.

Putting the Skills Together

After you've focused on using body language and active listening, you can work on putting the skills together. Combining the skills takes practice. You may need prompts and reminders from an adult—that's okay. You'll feel more comfortable once you've had time to run through the skills over and over. The more you can use them in daily life, the better. Get out the video camera and spend time recording conversations that take place at home. (Ask permission from the people who are talking.)

First, pay attention to the speakers. If you're handy with the camera, you can focus on each speaker's face when he or she talks. Then pan out again to get a view of all the speakers. What do their facial expressions tell you? Can you identify people's emotions by the expressions on their faces? While talking, where do the speakers' eyes look? What are their hands doing? What do the different gestures mean?

At times, focus on the listeners instead of the speakers. Later on, watch the video with your family. Conversations aren't always easy to follow in the moment. But when you have one recorded, you can push *pause* whenever you'd like. You can rewind to go back and listen more closely or to watch how someone's facial expression has changed.

You might see all sorts of interesting clues that tell you what people are feeling and thinking.

- Do their voices get louder or softer, depending on their emotions?
- Does the conversation speed up and slow down at certain · points? Is there a sort of natural rhythm to the conversation?
- Do the speakers interrupt each other? If so, what happens?
- What do different people's hands, body postures, eyes, and facial expressions tell you?
- Do you see some active listening going on? Do the listeners focus, nod, and seem interested?
- What do you notice about eye contact?
- Do the speakers seem to be making a connection? Why or why not?

The suggestions in this section—like all the ones in this chapter—aren't meant to be used only once. Do them again and again. It's almost like being an athlete in training: You have to keep doing the exercises (in your case, *communication* exercises) to make progress.

Your family and helpers can add their own original spin to any of the activities:

- A homemade prop can make listening more fun. How about a funny crown you decorate together?
- Create your own phrases about personal space. Maybe if someone is standing too close, you'll say, "Don't be a space invader!"
- Invite relatives and close family friends over for gatherings where you record conversations to listen to later. You might be amazed at the stories that come out. Some of these recorded conversations might even become family treasures.

Chapter 11

Good Communication: Making Conversation

Conversations are complex forms of communication, even if the talk sounds something like this:

Person 1: "Dude."
Person 2: *"Duuuude."*
Person 1: "Can you believe that happened?"
Person 2: "Totally."
Person 1: "I know. He's out of control."
Person 2: "You said it."
Person 1: "Catch you later."
Person 2: "Cool."

If you overheard that, you might think, "What in the world are they talking about?!?" Sometimes two people say only a few words but still have an intense conversation. And messages come through what *isn't* being said. All sorts of nonverbal (without words) communication occurs. So much is expressed through gestures, tone of voice, and facial expressions. You can read more about that in Chapter 10.

But the *words* matter, too.

One of the hardest things for kids with ASD is making conversation. Even kids with Asperger's who started talking early in life and have large vocabularies may find conversation challenging. In conversations, people interrupt and talk over each other. They change the subject unexpectedly. They have "inside jokes" only they understand, and use all sorts of slang words and nicknames. That's a lot to follow.

This chapter offers tips to help you become a better conversationalist. It's likely that you're already working with a speech therapist at school or a special center—and that's great. Speech therapists are trained to help people learn communication skills. But it's also important to work on your skills at home as often as you can. Why? Because conversations happen at home every day, and it's a convenient place to practice.

Conversation: It's Complicated

Conversations have a back-and-forth rhythm, almost like a ball being tossed from one person to another.

Person 1: "Hey, how's it going?"
Person 2: "Okay. That test was so hard!"
Person 1: "Yeah. What did you put for number three?"
Person 2: "I think it was 100. What did you put?"
Person 1: "I don't remember, but I think I got it wrong.
What's for lunch today, anyway?
I'm so hungry!"
Person 2: "Some slimy casserole. I brought cold lunch."
Person 1: "You were smart."
Person 2: "Not smart enough to ace the test!"

When two people talk, they go back and forth, taking turns making statements and asking questions. That back-and-forth isn't as easy for you because of your difficulties with communication. When you add more people into the conversation, it can seem as if words are flying back and forth so fast you can hardly keep

Take a Look!

This chapter focuses on the *verbal* aspects of communication—using words. You'll learn about starting a conversation, asking questions, giving responses, staying on topic, and understanding tone of voice. In Chapter 10, you can read about the *nonverbal* (without words) part of communication. The 3 Tools for Learning Good Communication in Chapter 10 (page 78) will help you work on all the conversation skills in Chapter 11.

track. It's a challenge to follow the words and to know who's saying what. Then there's the body language, the facial expressions, the eyes flitting back and forth . . . confusing!

Like many kids with ASD, you may feel more comfortable with *monologue*, which means only one person is speaking (you). Maybe you can talk at length about topics that really interest you. You might even be a budding performer who can recite passages from books or movies, or tell funny stories and jokes you've memorized. These are great skills that can help you in life. But the goal of this chapter is to help you with *dialogue*, where two speakers do the talking.

Developing that back-and-forth conversational rhythm between you and another person is really important. It's the basis for friendships, classroom participation, and (someday) a job. Conversation is a form of *connection*. You reach out to someone by asking a question. That person reaches back by giving you an answer, and then asking *you* a question, too. Back and forth, and back and forth. With every question and answer, you learn more about the other person, and that person learns more about you.

Tips for Starting a Conversation

So, how do you *start* a conversation? Sometimes, it's hard to know what to say. Maybe you're a little shy, and you hang back and don't say much. Or maybe you walk up to people and blurt stuff out, instead of letting a conversation begin in a smoother, more natural way. There are some basic "rules" for starting a conversation in a way that makes other people feel comfortable. Learning these rules will help.

Say hello. Greeting people when you first see them is a nice way to show you care and to help them feel welcome. Remember to say hi to the kids you sit by on the bus, and greet your classmates when you first get to school. Say hi again when you sit at the lunch table. Greet your family members, too. It makes them feel good when you notice them. Saying good-bye when someone leaves is polite and caring, too.

Learn people's names. Sometimes, kids with ASD have trouble remembering other people's names. If this is the case for you, spend some time looking through old yearbooks or class photos so you can match names to faces. Another idea is to ask a parent to take pictures of the kids in your class. Your parent can collect the photos and names in a book you keep with you. If you have a smartphone or an iPad, the pictures and names can go there, too.

Pay compliments. Compliments are positive comments you make to another person. For example, you might compliment someone on his appearance or on how well he played a game. A compliment can be as simple as "Nice haircut" or "Great job!" If someone compliments *you*, you can smile and say "Thanks."

Find a way to connect. There are lots of ways to start a conversation with someone. You could begin with a greeting: "Hi," "What's up?" or "How's it going?" Then you could add a compliment like "Cool shoes." Here's a greeting and compliment:

"Hi, Maria. I saw your artwork hanging on the bulletin board. It was so good!"

Another option is to make a comment. A comment is a simple statement about something you notice or have on your mind. Try comments like "That looks like a fun game" or "It sure is raining hard out there." Just make sure the comment actually fits the situation! Here are a couple:

"Hi. I heard we're having outdoor gym today and we get to play softball."

or

"Hey, Ethan, I saw that movie you were talking about yesterday. It was really cool."

Be sure to listen to the person's response! And then say something more to keep the conversation going.

Make a list of topics. If you can memorize a list of topics that kids commonly talk about, you'll be able to start a conversation more easily. Most kids talk about:

- school
- sports
- movies or television shows
- popular music
- pets
- food
- vacations
- favorite things

At home, practice what you've learned so far. Start with greetings. Say hi to family members when they come home and when they enter the room you're in. Next, work on compliments. Tell your dad what you liked about the meal he cooked, for example. Or let your sister know you like her new jeans. Your family will probably love hearing such nice things from you.

Try making more comments at home, too: "Mom, I had a great day at school." Or "The weather looks pretty bad out there. I'd better bring a jacket." Maybe you don't usually say things like this because you believe that other people already know. But they don't necessarily know! Remember, just because you are thinking it doesn't mean other people are thinking it, too. Your thoughts are separate from everyone else's.

By the way, try to keep your comments positive. Say something nice whenever you can because people will respond in a friendlier way. Avoid saying things like "You have bad breath" or "You did terrible on that test." These comments may be true, but they could hurt someone's feelings.

The Next Level: Questions

Many kids with ASD have trouble with questions. Do you forget to ask people questions? Maybe it doesn't even occur to you to ask them. You might be used to finding answers in books or doing research on the computer. You probably love finding out facts or learning trivia! And you probably *don't* love learning about other people's opinions or emotions.

But questions connect you to other people in a powerful way. Most people like being asked questions about themselves. It makes them feel noticed and appreciated. This is a *great* skill to learn (in fact, it's an essential one). Asking questions of people you meet, and people you already know, is a way to reach out. You'll seem friendly, curious, and interested. And you'll be opening a door so that other people will ask *you* something, too. That's how the back-and-forth begins.

Asking someone a question is one of the best ways to start a conversation. Here's an easy question: "How are you?" The person will probably answer "Fine. How are you?" If you're not used to asking this question when you see people for the first time each day, now is the time to practice. Start within your own family. When you wake up in the morning, try:

"Hi, how's it going, Mom?"

or

"Good morning, how'd you sleep last night, Grandpa?"

When you come home from school, ask:

"Hi, how was your day?"

Whenever someone else comes home, try a version of the same question:

"Hello! How's it going? What's new?"

Once these questions become a habit, you can practice other conversation starters:

"What are you thinking about?"

"Is that a good book?"

"What do you like about that game?"

"What did you do last night?"

"Are you going anywhere special today?"

Questions, questions, questions . . . keep asking them!

 I have trouble communicating, especially around a lot of people. Like it's hard for me to say, 'What's up?'

—14-year-old boy with autism

Responses

Once you're better at asking questions, you can focus on how you respond to questions others ask of you. Some kids who have ASD tend to keep their responses pretty short:

> **Parent:** "Did you have a good day at school?"
> **You:** "Yeah."

That conversation was stopped right in its tracks! Here's how to get a dialogue going:

> **Parent:** "Did you have a good day at school?"
> **You:** "Yeah. We learned about volcanoes. It was pretty cool. I want to learn more about them on the computer. How was your day?"
> **Parent:** "My day was great—thanks for asking! Maybe you and I can look up some stuff on Pompeii later. Did you learn about Pompeii?"

See the difference? When you respond with more than a simple yes or no, a conversation can happen.

At home, practice adding a comment each time you answer with a yes or no:

"No, thanks, I don't want seconds—I'm full.
Was that a new spaghetti recipe?"

or

"Yeah, I had art today and we did self-portraits.
Did you do anything fun today?"

To get better at asking questions, listening to what the other person says, and giving responses, try this:

Practice using the phone. (You might be groaning right now. Lots of kids with ASD don't like using the telephone!)

Talking on the phone will give you a chance to concentrate on the conversation. You can close your eyes to block out distractions, and the other person doesn't have to know. (*Bonus:* You don't have to remember eye contact when you're on the phone.) If your phone has a volume control, you can turn it up to make sure you hear everything that's said.

For this exercise, practice with a family member. Talk to him or her for a certain amount of time—maybe five minutes. Focus on asking some questions and answering the ones the other person asks you. Try to keep the conversation going so it doesn't "die" too fast. When the timer goes off, you might be ready to end the conversation—or let it continue if you're enjoying it. When you're ready to say good-bye, you can end with one of these statements:

"Well, it's been great talking to you!"
"I have to go now, but let's talk again soon."
"I'll talk to you later, okay?"
"Call me again sometime. Bye!"

Talking on the phone is a skill everybody needs to learn. Once you have the basics down, it gets easier—and so does conversation in general. You just might discover that asking questions isn't as hard as you thought. And your curiosity about other people will grow.

Talking on Topic

There's probably a subject or topic you love *so* much that you want to talk about it almost all the time: animals, football, stickers, video games, your collection, or whatever it may be. Sometimes, you might even interrupt conversations so you can talk about your favorite topic. Other times, you might forget to listen to people's questions or ideas because you're thinking of a way to bring up your best subject. This is known as talking off topic.

Notice how the conversation went from soccer to Pluto? In fact, this isn't actually a *conversation* in the true sense, because the people involved were talking about separate things. No real connection was made.

Your goal is to talk ON TOPIC. Why do you have to talk about other stuff if it really doesn't interest you? Because it's part of good communication. Think of communication as a two-way street: The traffic goes in two directions, not one. You need to pay attention to the other "drivers," because you share the "road" with them. They listen to you—and *you* listen to *them*.

At home, your family can give you little reminders, like "Talk on topic, please." That's your signal to pay closer attention to the conversation and participate in it—without going back to your familiar subject.

Another idea is to keep a timer in a handy spot at home. Then you can talk about your favorite thing for a limited time. A parent could say, "I know you want to talk about *Star Wars,* so let's set the timer for five minutes and I'll listen. But after that, you need to agree to change topics." After you've had a chance to talk about what interests you, you have to give the other person an opportunity to do the same. It's a good way to practice the back-and-forth aspect of conversation.

Remember that list of common kid topics on page 98? You might want to write down some questions to ask other kids to get a conversation started or to keep it going. If you have a list in your mind, you'll be ready to talk about things other than your favorite topic. Examples:

"Do you play a sport?"

"Seen any good movies lately?"

"Are you going on a vacation this summer?"

"What's your favorite activity?"

"Who's your favorite teacher?"

"What kind of music do you like?"

Listen to the person's response. Then say something ON TOPIC to keep the conversation going.

Does talking on topic mean you shouldn't *ever* talk about your favorite subject? Definitely not. You probably have lots of knowledge about whatever it is you love. You can share what you've learned with others. Just be sure that the people you're speaking with seem interested.

How will you know? They'll probably show the signs of active listening: They'll look at you, nod their head, and ask appropriate questions.

If someone is trying to get you to stop talking about a topic, he or she might say one of these things:

"Cool. Can we change the subject?"

or

"Yeah. Want to go play a game or something?"

or

"Let's talk about something else."

Those are clues for you. You can then tell the person something like this:

"Sorry, I just realized I'm doing all the talking. What do you want to talk about?"

or

"Oops, I may be boring you. Want to talk about something else?"

or

"There I go again! I can get carried away when I talk about this topic. Let's change the subject."

Tone of Voice

In conversation, it's not only *what* you say that matters but also *how you say it*. People listen for clues that come through your tone of voice:

- Do you speak louder when you're excited? Do you talk softly if you don't want others to overhear?
- Do your words speed up when you get to the "good part" of the story?
- Do you pause when you want to make a point?
- Do you slow down your speech to emphasize certain words?
- Do you sometimes change your voice to imitate someone else's speech?
- Do you phrase questions as *questions* by raising the pitch of your voice at the end of the sentence?

All of these clues are considered standard speech patterns. No matter what language is spoken, many of these patterns serve as hints about the *meaning* behind the words.

When you have ASD, your speech might not fit the usual patterns. Back in 1944, Hans Asperger* worked with a group of children who would now be identified as having ASD. He noticed that many of these children spoke in a monotone, meaning their tone of voice stayed at the same level, almost as if they were giving a lecture. Perhaps this describes the way you talk, too.

You can't help it if your way of speaking differs from many people's. But if you're interested in making some changes in how you communicate, it *is* possible to do.

It's best if you work with a speech therapist who's trained to help kids with a variety of communication issues. A therapist can work with you on the pace and rate of your speech, pronunciation, tone of voice, or problems with the constant repeating of words or phrases. Challenges like these require the help of a specialist who can work up a plan for you and give your parents ideas on how to help you at home.

* Asperger's syndrome is named after Hans Asperger, a pediatrician who did lots of research about autism.

Still, there's a lot you can do on your own to practice communication skills. Following are ideas you can use at home and at school.

Putting the Skills Together

Record yourself. There's a reason you keep seeing this suggestion: Recording is a really helpful tool in learning new communication skills. Have your dad, your mom, or another family member record you talking to someone. Use a video camera or a tape recorder. Later on, you can watch the video or listen to the tape together to find out what your conversation strengths and weaknesses may be. For example, are you good at sharing your knowledge about certain topics or listening to other people share theirs? Awesome, keep it up! But do you need help remembering the back-and-forth aspect of conversation? Maybe you interrupt or forget to ask questions. Well, now you have something to work on . . . so get started! Bring the recorded conversations to your speech therapist so he or she can help you practice, too.

Talk during meals. The dinner table is a great place to practice conversation, because the whole family is gathered. Use this time to improve your conversation skills, your listening, and your ability to ask questions.

Here's an activity to try: Let each person talk for two minutes, using a timer if you'd like. After each person has spoken, the other people at the table get to ask questions about what was said. (You can pass around a prop if you have one. See page 92 for prop ideas.) Many families use mealtime to talk about their day. They discuss what happened at school or work, what they had fun doing, whether the day was "good" or "bad." Other families use decks of conversation-starter cards, which offer prompts for interesting things to discuss. You can find cards like these at gift stores—or your family can create homemade ones. That way, the conversation goes beyond "How was your day?" into brand-new territory.

Practice talking during activities. This is more challenging than you might think. Your brain likes to focus on one thing at a time, or to concentrate deeply on something that interests you, like a game or puzzle. When you're playing, you probably don't like to stop and talk—and if you *do* talk, it's only about the game. What if, in the middle of the game, your friend asks you a question about school, or your sister starts cracking jokes? You probably find that pretty annoying! It's like you suddenly have to "switch gears," and that isn't easy for you.

Switching gears and doing more than one thing at a time are skills. You can build these skills through practice. One way to practice is to throw a ball back and forth to a family member while you talk about your favorite topic. Your brain and body suddenly have to do two different things at the same time. An activity like this helps you improve your coordination and rhythm. (Remember, conversations have rhythm!) Another way to practice is to work on talking during games—but *not about the game*. As you play, tell the other players about a test you took, a movie you saw, or what you want to eat for lunch. This helps your brain focus on two different things at once, which is a great skill-builder.

The Last Word . . .

People in your life and on your team of helpers will keep pushing you to talk—even if it's really hard for you. They'll prompt you to say hello and good-bye. They'll ask you questions and expect answers. They'll tell you to speak more quietly or in less of a monotone. They'll even try to get you to talk about your feelings, or to stop talking about the same things over and over. At times, you might feel frustrated with all these demands.

Because these people care about you and your future, they're asking you to go beyond what's comfortable or easy. They know that *communication* is the key to so many things: Making friends. Having strong relationships with family. Succeeding in school. Pursuing what interests you. Feeling comfortable in the wider world. If you work hard to improve your communication skills, they'll get stronger and you'll grow more confident. Keep trying!

> ASDs can be very challenging at times, but they also can make you see things in a new way. Take life one step at a time, and no matter how bad things get, never give up.
>
> —17-year-old girl with ASD

Chapter 12

Your Social Skills Survival Kit

On TV, there are reality shows where people are put into highly unusual situations to test their Survival Skills. For example, they'll be dropped into the wilderness with very few supplies. There, they must pass every test of their courage and skill until they're the last "survivor." (No one actually dies, though.)

In another show, contestants pair up in a race to an unknown finish line. The racers are placed in foreign countries and cultures. They may not know the language and still must find their way. Mysterious clues direct each step in the confusing journey. Teamwork helps—but it would all be so much easier with a map and compass or GPS.

Do you ever feel like one of these reality-show contestants, dropped into the middle of a puzzling environment where you're not sure what to do, what to say, or how to get along? So many new skills to learn. So many hard-to-follow clues. So much language to figure out. You know what would be useful? A special Social Skills Survival Kit to help you through this often-confusing, fast-paced world.

It's not an actual kit you can hold in your hands—more like one you imagine in your *mind*. It includes four important tools that give you information, skills, and support for surviving social situations and feeling confident. These are the tools that will help you find your way through the social world and survive tough situations. Use your imagination to picture your kit and each tool in it. Ask a parent or another trusted adult to be your partner—someone who can give advice, offer solutions, and stand by you when you're feeling lost.

Survival Tool #1:
Imaginary GPS Device

One of the challenges of ASD is how it affects your level of awareness. What does *that* mean? It means you don't have a built-in ability to know where you're going, how to get there, and what you might face along the way.

For example, you might need help remembering what day or time it is, what's on your daily schedule, and what tasks you're expected to complete. The adults in your life probably keep you focused. They might provide a visual schedule or prompt you about what comes next. Many kids with ASD rely on routines to help them feel prepared and safe. Sometimes, any kind of change in the routine is upsetting and confusing.

Often, life isn't as predictable as we'd like it to be. Schedules change. New people arrive on the scene. Rules we've come to count on don't always apply to every situation. That's when we end up feeling lost and worried. Maybe you feel this way a lot of the time.

One thing that helps is developing a greater sense of awareness about what's happening around you. Not what you *expect* to happen or what you *want* to happen—but what's *actually going on*. This means opening your eyes and your mind a little wider than usual.

Think of it as turning on your GPS, or Global Positioning System. Beep! Locating . . .

Look where you are at various times of the day, and then think about what the situation requires. Different settings mean different types of behavior. Your *awareness* tells you what you might need to do. Here are some examples:

Nick is getting in trouble at school for things he didn't realize were a problem. During class, his teacher often says, "Nick, this isn't the time for jokes." But the kids are laughing! Nick likes the attention, and he feels like he's making friends. Isn't this what his parents and therapists want—for him to make friends and have more fun?

Jessie likes having her buddy Ben over on the weekends. They're neighbors, and they have a lot in common. They like to build with Legos, collect rocks, and make elaborate sand castles in the sandbox. Sometimes, Jessie gets so involved in building her structures that she forgets to talk to Ben. Other times, she gets bored playing the same old things. Then she wanders away, looking for a new activity. Ben is left all alone. Soon Jessie's mom yells, "Jessie! Aren't you forgetting something important? You have a guest."

Hakim has occupational therapy on Thursdays at 6 PM. His therapist is Karen. Karen follows a certain routine: First she does therapeutic brushing on Hakim. Next come several skill-building activities. After that Hakim gets time on the swings. This is what Hakim is used to and what he expects. But when Hakim and his mom arrive one Thursday, they learn that Karen hurt her ankle and can't do the session. Another occupational therapist smiles at Hakim and says, "I'll be your 'Karen' today." Hakim hates this. Another lady can't be Karen! Standing in the waiting room, Hakim starts to cry hard. "No!" he says. "This isn't how it works." He runs out the door and makes it as far as the parking lot. There are lots of parked cars and moving cars, but Hakim doesn't care. All he wants to do is get away.

In these examples, Nick, Jessie, and Hakim weren't thinking about the setting—about where they are, why they are there, and who else is there. They could have been more *aware* of what's really going on. Can you think of some ways these kids could use their (imaginary) GPS to handle these situations more successfully?

For **Nick,** the setting is his classroom. That's a place where he could show better "student behavior." Instead of making jokes, he could pay attention to the teacher and listen harder. Because he likes to joke, and he seems to get a good response from other kids, he can save his humor for lunchtime. That's a better place for his comedy show!

Ben is **Jessie's** guest. When she has Ben over, she needs to remember to treat him like one. During playdates, she'll have to talk with Ben to make him feel welcome. If Jessie gets tired of an activity, she might say, "Hey, Ben, want to do something else instead? How about a board game?" Then she can listen to what Ben wants to do. Together, they can decide on an activity they both like.

Running out of the waiting room was dangerous for **Hakim.** He could have gotten hurt in the parking lot. It's understandable that Hakim was upset by the change of plans. Taking deep breaths might have helped. While Hakim was calming down, the other therapist might have been able to explain that she knew Karen's routine and could follow it. Hakim could have asked questions about what might happen. He might have said, "I'm nervous. What can I do to feel better?"

The imaginary GPS could help each of these kids be aware of what other people around them expect. That's an important social skill! With help from an adult, practice using your personal GPS. It's a helpful tool to fine-tune your awareness. Keep paying attention to where you are and who you're with at different times each day. This is what tells you how to act and react appropriately.

Survival Tool #2:
Handbook of Customs

Did you know that before a trip to a foreign country, most travelers look at a handbook to get helpful information about the people and places they'll see? Travelers need to know about all sorts of stuff:

- traditions, customs, and manners of people in the area
- the local rules and laws
- handy phrases from the language

You may not be a traveler. But sometimes you might feel like you're in a foreign country—where people speak quickly and behave in ways you're still trying to figure out.

It feels like kids are either mean to me or they treat me like I'm invisible.

—**11-year-old boy with ASD**

Another way some people with ASD describe their experience of the world is "being from another planet." Perhaps you feel like an outsider in a world of insiders, at least some of the time. If so, you need a handy reference guide, one that can serve as a little handbook of social customs. Well, now you have one, right here, as part of your Social Skills Survival Kit. If you can memorize these customs and guidelines, you'll have an easier time in the social world.

Basic greetings. When you enter a room, or when someone else enters, say "Hello" or "Hi," or give a little wave. Do this at home, at school, and in places where you see people you know. Be sure to say good-bye when you or someone else is leaving, too. You don't have to greet anyone when you're going into a store or walking around in your neighborhood, unless you see someone you recognize.

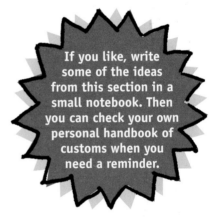

If you like, write some of the ideas from this section in a small notebook. Then you can check your own personal handbook of customs when you need a reminder.

Formal greetings. When you're meeting someone for the first time, there are a few rules to follow. Stand up if you're sitting down. Smile politely. Look the person in the eye, at least for a moment. If eye contact is hard for you, here's a trick to help you remember. Think to yourself, "I wonder what color eyes the person has." Take a quick look and find out. (For more on eye contact, see page 82.) Then say, "Hi. My name is _____(your name). Nice to meet you."

Introductions. Sometimes you'll be in a situation where you have to introduce someone. For example, maybe you have a friend over, and then another friend comes over. If the two friends don't know each other, you can introduce them like this:

"Jaden, I'd like to introduce you to my friend, Lee. Lee, meet Jaden."

or

"Jaden, this is Lee. Lee, this is Jaden."

Awareness of your "audience." You don't have to be onstage to have an audience. The people around you at home, at school, and in your community are like an audience. They listen to your words and watch your actions. Because of your ASD, you may not always be aware that you're surrounded by others—people who think their own thoughts and feel their own feelings. You may often believe that your thoughts match everyone else's, but they *don't*. Each person is unique in his or her own thinking.

"Typical" kids have a built-in awareness of this. Even at a very young age, they figure out that they need to change their words and behavior to suit their audience. For example, one moment a young child might be acting silly with friends. But what happens as soon as a parent or teacher enters the room? The child will probably notice and stop the silliness. The moment the adult leaves, the child might go right back to being silly again.

Here's another example: A group of boys might be standing around talking about how girls "are girly" and "like stuff that's pink and sparkly." Even if some of the boys don't agree, they might nod their heads and go along with the talk, just to feel like they're part of the group. Then, the moment a girl comes by, all the boys might suddenly go quiet or change the subject so she doesn't hear what's being said. They realize the girl could be hurt or annoyed by their comments, so they quiet down. That's an awareness of their audience—even if it's a girl just walking by, who isn't part of the conversation at all.

People with ASD often need to work harder to gain the same level of awareness that many people already have. It takes practice to develop the skill. But you can do it! With an adult's help, you can work on adjusting how you talk depending on who you're talking to and where the conversation takes place. For instance:

If you spend time with young children . . .
you'll learn patience and how to speak more slowly and clearly.

When you're with people your own age . . .
it's appropriate to use more slang or to talk openly about your likes and dislikes.

If you're with a teacher . . .
you'll need to speak more politely, as a sign of respect.

How you talk in a library (in a whisper) . . .
is different from
how you might speak at a noisy sporting event (shouting to be heard).

So much depends on the listener or listeners around you. You'll need to learn ways to adjust your words and volume. You'll be developing "audience awareness," a skill you can use all your life.

Polite remarks. As a person with ASD, you're probably very honest. That's a great quality to have. Telling the truth is important, and so is saying what you think. If you're doing these things already, way to go! But in some cases, people with ASD are a bit too blunt. (*Blunt* means you say something abruptly, without thinking to tone down your words.) Here's an example of being blunt: "Your hair looks awful. Why did you get it cut that way?" You might be telling the truth, but your words could hurt someone's feelings. It's better to make *polite* remarks. For example, you could instead say, in a friendly way, "I see you cut your hair. Do you like it the new way?" Or you could skip mentioning the hair at all, and just say something else: "I like your green jacket" or "Did you think the homework was hard?"

You won't always know when you're being too blunt. This is why it's helpful to ask an adult to help you work on this issue. (Find a parent or ask someone on your team of helpers. You can read more about this team in Chapter 7.) The grown-up helping you can point out times when you're a little too blunt. She or he can then help you rephrase the words in a more polite way.

As time goes on, you'll probably start noticing other people's reactions to your words. You'll be able to better read their body language and facial expressions (see pages 80–89). These things can tell you a lot about the effect your words have.

Private thoughts. This relates to the idea of being too blunt (see previous page). Because of your ASD, you might speak your thoughts aloud at times when it would be better to keep them to yourself. *Lots* of kids have this problem, even if they don't have ASD! The words just come out, before they can be stopped. Then—*oops!*—there's trouble. Feelings get hurt, or someone ends up angry.

Keeping your thoughts to yourself is a skill that speech therapists and autism experts can help you with. Your dad or mom can help, too. It takes practice. You'll need to work on knowing whether what you want to say is appropriate. Plus, you'll need help noticing if what you've said has caused hurt or angry feelings. All this takes time. As you grow older, you'll gain a better sense of what's appropriate and what isn't. Keep asking for help.

Saying you're sorry. Sometimes, you'll make a mistake or hurt someone's feelings. What can you do? Apologize! Two small words—"I'm sorry"—can make a big difference.

It takes courage to admit when you're wrong, especially after an argument. You may still be angry and upset, and those strong emotions may get in the way of saying you're sorry. Practice can help. With a parent or another adult, you can role-play different ways to apologize. Like this: "It's my fault, and I'm sorry." Or: "I'd like to apologize for what I did. Can you forgive me?"

Asking for help. What do you usually do when you're feeling lost and confused? Do you speak up? For example, if you're in math class and you're having trouble understanding something, do you raise your hand and let the teacher know? It's important to do that! In fact, it's a *skill*.

Admitting you need help isn't a sign of weakness. It doesn't mean you're not smart. Anyone can get lost or have difficulty understanding. But no one will know it's happening to you unless *you* say something. Raise your hand and say, "I'm confused about what you just said. Can you repeat it more slowly, please? Thanks."

You can use this skill in all sorts of situations, even conversations. In Chapter 11, you'll find many tips on communication skills. Even if you follow them all and practice often, there will still be times when you don't understand what someone's saying. When that happens, you can say, "Sorry to interrupt, but I'm having trouble understanding you. Can you please slow down or say it again?" You might feel a little awkward, but it's worth being honest about your confusion. Otherwise, you'll probably misunderstand the person and that can lead to frustration.

Survival Tool #3:
Skills for Being Assertive

Even if you're by nature a peaceful person, and you don't like fights and arguments, they happen. Conflicts occur when people don't treat each other fairly. In conflict situations like these, an important conflict-solving skill is Speaking up. When you speak up for yourself in a strong but polite way, you are being assertive.

Sometimes a conflict can take you by surprise. For example, you could be playing a video game, and then one of your siblings marches into the room and says, "*My* turn to use the TV!" You didn't start the disagreement, but suddenly you're right in the middle of it. Other times, conflicts keep happening. Maybe your friend always wants to choose the game the two of you will play. Maybe your sister thinks she should always get to use the computer first because she's older. Or, perhaps one of your classmates looks at your schoolwork and copies it.

In each of these situations, you're not doing anything wrong, but you probably feel annoyed, frustrated, and cheated. Feelings like that are challenging. They make your day harder and can add to your level of stress. What should you do? You may be able to help yourself if you use assertiveness skills and speak up for yourself.

> Chapter 8 (pages 63–65) talks about handling conflicts that come up at home using STOP THINK GO. You can also use that skill when you have conflicts with classmates or friends.

Here are some examples of speaking up assertively:

"Let's take turns choosing. That's more fair."

or

"I need to use the computer from 4:00 till 5:00 today to work on my project."

or

"Please don't copy my work. It's against the rules."

Sometimes, it's hard to speak your mind like this—but you can do it! Use a kind but firm tone. Practice at home with a parent. See if you can make your voice sound confident but not harsh. Usually, speaking your mind is more effective if you can make eye contact with the person, too. (Read more about eye contact on pages 82–83.) If eye contact is hard for you, then work on using your voice until you're more confident about assertiveness skills. Later on, practice looking the person in the eye when you speak your mind.

Speaking up usually works, but not always. What happens if you say what you want, and the other person doesn't agree? In this case, you might have to stick up for yourself even more. Here's an example of how to do it:

You: "Please don't copy my work. It's against the rules."
Other person: "I wasn't!"
You: "I saw you look at my paper. I've seen you do this before. I won't let you keep copying me."

(Notice the word "I" here. When you use "I," your words sound calm and straightforward. If you say something like *"You* looked at my paper" or *"You* are a big cheater," the other person is likely to feel accused and get angry.)

Other person: "Oh, yeah? What are you going to do to stop me?"
You: "If I see you copying me again, I'll report you to the teacher."

(Stay calm. Let the other person know you'll get adult help, if needed.)

Other person: "You're a jerk."
You: "Please leave me alone."

(If someone calls you a mean name, this doesn't mean it's true! Don't let yourself get caught in a name-calling contest. Instead of calling the person a name back, say that you want to be left alone.)

Other person: "Whatever!"

Even if the person stops doing what angered you in the first place, you'll probably feel upset after a disagreement. Take some deep breaths. If you're at school, you might need to take a break somewhere safe, like the resource room, media center, or front office. Talk to your teacher about what you might do to calm down and feel better. You can also look at Chapter 18 for other ideas to help you calm yourself.

Sometimes, people start shouting if they disagree. When this happens, the conflict gets worse instead of better. It's important to always try to speak up for yourself in a strong but *polite* way. This is a verbal skill all kids need to learn, not just those with ASD. Practice using a firm, strong voice, but don't yell.

Other times, people who are in arguments use their hands instead of their words. That's when the hitting, pushing, and punching start. Physical violence is never a good solution. If a disagreement with someone starts to get out of control, use your *feet* and walk away. Get help from an adult you trust.

Survival Tool #4:
Bully Radar

Sheila dreaded going to school each day. Another girl was making Sheila a target. The girl would whisper mean words like, "You smell," "Here comes Sheila the Stupid," and "Why don't you just go home so no one has to look at you?" Sheila was surprised at how those quiet words rang loud in her mind, over and over, long after they'd been spoken.

Andre had a similar problem. A boy named Tate just wouldn't leave him alone. Tate and his friends would come up to Andre when no teachers were around, and they'd call him "Psycho" and "Andre the Giant." Even though Andre was tall for his age, the other kids weren't scared of him. They knew it didn't take much to make him cry. Sometimes, they flicked his cheek with their fingers or tried to trip him in the hall.

Theo, a fifth grader, wanted to be liked and admired. After joining the soccer team, he thought he had a group of instant friends. Some of the other guys on the team liked to make jokes and pull pranks. The guys were funny and they made Theo laugh. But sometimes, things went too far. They'd snap the waistband of his shorts and bounce the soccer ball off his forehead. Sometimes, Theo's teammates would tell him to go sniff a girl's hair or stand up in the lunchroom and do a huge burp. When he did these things, other kids laughed. For a while, Theo thought all of this was part of friendship and fitting in. But one day, his coach took him aside and asked Theo if he knew the difference between kids' laughing *with* him and laughing *at* him. Theo thought about the coach's words all day and realized he didn't like being the victim of jokes and pranks. He decided that he'd be more careful about letting his teammates take advantage of him.

In each of these situations, someone is being bullied. Bullying is when a person or group of people hurt, scare, or embarrass another person on purpose over and over again. The person being bullied has trouble defending himself or herself. You probably already know that bullies tend to push, shove, hit, punch, and insult others. But not all bullying is easy to identify. This is why you need bully radar. It helps you tune in to a kind of bullying that's a bit harder to understand.

Diego's Story

New schools are hard—so many unfamiliar faces, classes, and teachers. Twelve-year-old Diego knows all about having to start over in a new place. Right now, he's in a small private middle school. He had started sixth grade at the public middle school, like all his friends and classmates from fifth grade. But that school was so big! Diego was overwhelmed by its size and by having to change classrooms for each subject. Partway through the year, his parents helped him switch schools. They found a place that was smaller, quieter, and easier to get around in.

But now that he's here, Diego is having a hard time. At his other school, the kids knew about his autism. Not everyone was nice to him, but he had friends. Now those friends seem so far away. Diego wanders the hallways of his new school, watching other kids talking and laughing. He feels lonely.

The kids at Diego's new school aren't used to having a student with autism in their classes. They don't seem to understand that when Diego gets upset he may talk too loud or flap his hands. The kids give him strange looks.

Diego realizes there are many good things about the new school. It's quieter and he knows what to expect. The classes are small, and the teachers treat Diego well. But, even so, Diego's organizational skills seem to be getting worse. Just yesterday afternoon, his favorite pen went missing. This morning, his science folder wasn't in his locker where he'd left it. And now his lunch is gone! All the kids are on their way to the cafeteria, but Diego is at his locker feeling confused.

He decides to go to the front office to call his mom. He tells her he forgot his lunch at home. "No, you didn't, Diego," says his mom. "I saw you walk out the door with it. Did you leave your lunch on the bus?"

"Maybe," Diego answers. "But I'm pretty sure I put it in my locker. The locker doesn't have a lock, Mom."

Someone must have taken Diego's lunch. He doesn't want to believe that. But what about the other items that seem to have disappeared?

The trouble doesn't stop there. Friday at the end of the school day, Diego goes to his locker to get all his stuff. To his surprise, the locker is empty. There's nothing there but some dust. Where are his books? His supplies? His gym shoes? Diego can't help it—he starts to cry.

The other students hurry to their buses, and Diego is left behind. He returns to his classroom and tries to find his missing stuff. No luck. He goes through the hallways, still looking. His belongings are nowhere to be found. What should he do? Call his mom? Then he realizes he's missed the bus! The halls are empty. Diego sits down in front of his locker and puts his head on his knees.

That's where his mom and the principal find him later. Diego's mom hugs him. "I was so worried when you didn't get off the bus with the other kids! What happened?"

Diego tells her about the mystery of the disappearing stuff. "It's not my fault, Mom. I didn't lose my stuff. Someone took it."

"Of course it's not your fault, Diego," his mom replies.

Diego's mom and the principal find a custodian who can help Diego search for his belongings. "While you're doing that," says the principal, "your mom and I can go have a talk in my office. We're going to solve this bullying problem. You need to feel safe at school, Diego."

Diego is relieved. He's even more relieved when they find his backpack stuffed in the corner of the auditorium, with all of his belongings still inside it.

The following Monday, there's an announcement about an assembly that will take place in the auditorium. All students are required to attend. The principal, some teachers, and the guidance counselor all talk about how the school needs to be a bully-free zone. That means students aren't allowed to fight, call people names, send rude emails or text messages to other students, or steal another student's belongings. All students, they say, should feel safe and cared for at school. The principal says that if any students see or hear of a bullying incident, they should report it immediately.

Diego feels better after that. He knows that if he's ever picked on again, he can go right to a teacher or the principal for help.

Later that day, after lunch, there's another surprise in Diego's locker. It's a handwritten note that says, "I'm sorry, Diego."

Asking for Help Isn't Tattling

Because of your ASD, you might find yourself in situations where other kids tease you, call you names, or pick on you in some way. Lots of kids who have ASD say that "typical" kids often don't treat them well. Have you been called names like "dummy," "loser," "freak," or something else? These names are meant to hurt your feelings and make you doubt yourself. Unfortunately, people sometimes make fun of what they don't understand. If you haven't been teased this way yet, it will probably happen sometime. It's part of life. A hard part!

Every kid is called names or bullied at one time or another. Sad but true! Why do people use hurtful names? Maybe they think being mean makes them more powerful. (It doesn't.) Keep in mind that their words aren't true. You're a great person who deserves respect—and that's what really matters.

If someone is bothering you, you can stick up for yourself by holding your head high (to show pride) and speaking with a firm voice. Being assertive like this shows you're willing to face the person, even if you feel scared inside. You can say things like "Back off," "Stop bothering me," or "I don't like what you're saying. Leave me alone." Another option is to ignore the person. Say nothing, turn your body away, or walk away.

Sometimes this is enough. Sometimes it's not. If you're being teased or treated poorly, get an adult's help. At school, you can tell your teacher, another teacher who's nearby, a recess monitor, the social worker or guidance counselor, the principal, the psychologist, your speech or OT teacher, or any other adult you recognize in the school building or on school grounds. It's helpful to let your parents or other grown-ups at home know what's going on, too.

What if kids call you a "tattletale" or some other rude name because you've reported them? Try not to let it bother you too much. You haven't "tattled"—you've told an adult about a situation you need help with. The most important thing is for you to feel safe and supported.

Have you ever been bullied at school or in your neighborhood? Is there someone who targets you by saying mean things, pushing you around, taking your belongings, or making you do things that get other kids to laugh? Being bullied is scary and stressful. You might feel nervous, unhappy, lonely, or even helpless.

But you're *not* helpless. You *can* take a stand against someone who's bullying you. Here are 10 strategies that might work in your situation:

1. **Ignore the person who's bullying you.** Don't make eye contact, and pretend not to hear the bully's words. Keep doing whatever it is you're doing: schoolwork, playing, talking to a friend.

2. **Try not to show emotion,** if possible. Bullies like to get a reaction. They want to see another person cry or get upset or angry. Even if you feel afraid and hurt, try to keep a calm expression on your face. You can talk about how you feel later, or you can write down the feelings to express them.

3. **Tell the person to leave you alone.** Do this in a straightforward way. Depending on the situation, you could say: "I don't like what you're saying," "That isn't true," "Leave me alone," or "Stop bothering me." Use a strong, firm voice. It's okay if other people overhear you. These people may be able to help if they realize you're being bullied.

4. **Walk away, quickly—or run.** Go to a place where there are more people so the bully is less likely to keep bothering you. Find an adult and tell him or her exactly what happened. You can say, "I'm being bullied, and I need some help, please."

5. **Know that a true friend won't bully you.** If someone you consider a friend is doing the bullying, that's a particularly difficult situation. But a *true* friend wouldn't want to embarrass you or hurt your feelings. If a friend is making you do things you're not comfortable with, *stop.* Say "No," "I don't want to do this," or "I refuse to do what you're asking." Just because you've done it once or twice before doesn't mean you must keep doing it. You have the right to stop, and to make your own decisions.

6. **Let your family know about the problem *right away.*** Tell your parents so they can help protect you. Their job is to report any bullying to the school. That way teachers and the principal

become aware of what's going on. If you have older siblings at your school, you might want to tell them what's happening, too. Then they can look out for you in the hallways, on the bus, and in other busy, crowded places.

7. **Get help from a trusted grown-up.** If your family isn't a strong source of support for you, find an adult you trust who can help you deal with the bully problem. It's not your fault if you're being bullied. You deserve to feel safe at school, at home, and in your community.

8. **Surround yourself with people at school.** Walk through the hallways with friends, stick with your buddies at recess, and avoid being alone in the school bathrooms. (You might be able to get permission to use the bathroom in the nurse's office for a while, for example.) Bullies like to catch their targets when they're alone.

9. **Be aware of cyberbullying.** This takes place through Internet or cell phone communication. People who bully online might make fun of someone in a chat room or post cruel messages on a person's MySpace or Facebook page. They might send threatening emails or put up unflattering pictures of someone online. They might call another person's cell phone over and over, or send rude text messages. Only use the Internet or a cell phone with a parent's permission. And be sure you know the rules about cyberspace safety. If you're bullied online or on the phone, tell an adult. Keep all the records for proof!

10. **Don't bring expensive or special belongings to school,** especially if another kid is taking your stuff. Label all your notebooks, jackets, and the soles of your shoes with your name, using permanent marker.

You know what else will protect you from bullying? And you know what can help you during those times when you're feeling lost and left out? FRIENDS. Friends are there for you in good times and bad. They help you out, make you laugh, and teach you how to get along with others. In Chapter 13, you'll learn about the importance of friendships. Keep using your Social Skills Survival Kit, and keep reading!

Chapter 13

Making and Keeping Friends

Making friends is a lifelong skill—for anyone, whether the person has ASD or not. It's a skill you can start working on now, and one you'll continue to develop as you learn and grow. *Everyone* can improve their friendship skills—even adults. Talk to some grown-ups and you'll see! You'll probably hear that their friends still teach them about some of the most important things in life:

- sharing interests and activities
- spending time together
- connecting with others on a deeper level

Friends, in other words, are protection against loneliness. Do you get lonely sometimes? Maybe you're a person who enjoys spending time alone and has lots of cool hobbies. You still need other people. Humans are social creatures—even if they have problems with social skills! We all need to feel a connection with others. We need that feeling of being liked and accepted for who we are.

J.D. Kraus is a young man with Asperger's. In his book *The Aspie Teen's Survival Guide*, J.D. describes his experience of coming home after school on Fridays. There he would wait for his parents to get home from work: "I would . . . go to my room, close the door, and lie on my bed. I would stare at the ceiling and feel the isolation and loneliness build inside of me. There was no one to call, no one to hang out with. No one. Nothing." That changed when he found a friend in ninth grade. His new friend, another boy with ASD, helped J.D. experience the benefits of friendship. Together, they were no longer isolated and lonely.

What Is Friendship?

That may seem like an easy question . . . but it's more complicated than you think. Kids who have autism spectrum disorders don't always understand the difference between a *friend* and an *acquaintance*.

So, what *is* the difference, anyway?

An acquaintance is someone you see on a regular basis but may not know well. You might know the person's name and recognize his or her face. You might say hi to the person or make "small talk" by saying stuff like "How are you?" or "What's new?" Acquaintances may include: classmates, kids in higher and lower grades at school, neighbors, and teammates (if you're on a team). Kids who go to your place of worship, community center, or park are also acquaintances. So are adults you recognize—your parents' friends or people they work with, a librarian or coach, and neighbors.

An acquaintance is someone you might see almost every day or a few times a week. That person might be nice to you. That person might speak with you briefly. He or she may even hang out with you for short periods of time. But it's usually not *friendship*. Friendship is bigger—and better.

A friend is someone you spend time with, doing things you both enjoy. There's a spark, a connection that's meaningful and worth building on. The two of you might go to each other's homes. You might share a meal, see a movie, or play games. You might spend time talking and laughing face to face. You have something in common—like a hobby, an activity, or a collection. You like being together. Together, you have FUN.

The most important piece is *togetherness*. A friend wants to spend time with you. He or she will call you on the phone or invite you over. You'll spend time together in places other than school.

> I have a best friend. He has been kind to me and understands me. We've been friends since kindergarten. He doesn't have autism, but he doesn't care that I do.
>
> **—14-year-old boy with autism**

Some kids who have ASD believe that classmates are the same as friends. But there's a difference. Even if you've known certain kids since kindergarten, you share a classroom, and you say hi each day, it's not necessarily *friendship*. But it could become a friendship! First, you've got to show people that you want to become friends. You might:

- Invite someone over after school.
- Send emails back and forth (if you have a computer and you're both allowed to use email).
- Join the same club or try out for a team together.
- Make a plan to see the person during the weekend—for example, at a park or movie theater.
- Ask your dad or mom for help making social plans with a kid you want to be friends with.

It helps to choose someone who's *likely* to be a friend. Think of someone who's usually nice to you, doesn't tease you, and seems to care about you in some way. Look for a person who shares your interests or talks to you at school. Someone who invites you to play at recess. Someone who asks you questions or seems open to being friends.

You might say, "I noticed you signed up for chess. I did, too. Would you like to come to my house sometime for a game?" If the person says yes, then be ready to get his or her phone number and set up a time to come over. Your mom or dad can help with that, too.

> It takes a while for me to make new friends. You can't just run around and say to people, 'Hey, do you want to be my best friend?' They would think you're weird. If they talk to you a lot or wave to you or say hi, that means they might want to be your friend.
>
> **—14-year-old boy with autism**

Why Is Making Friends Hard to Do?

Many kids struggle to find friends. They might not have strong social skills. They may be shy or get picked on. They may just feel more comfortable spending time alone. There are lots of different reasons why it can be difficult to make friends. But it's *so* important to try. Why? Because having friends leads to better health. People who have friends say they're happier and less stressed because they have people they can count on (other than family).

> Is there something I'd like to tell people who don't seem to understand me? Yes: I don't bite.
>
> **—11-year-old boy with Asperger's**

When you have ASD, "typical" kids may sense you're different in some way but may not know why. To them, you might seem a bit "odd" or somewhat of a loner. They may not realize you want to make friends. Or, they may have the (wrong) idea that you prefer to be left alone. If you've had any behavioral problems at school in the past, other kids might be a bit scared of you. Or they may not realize that, in some ways, you've grown. Many kids in your class or neighborhood may already have close friendships, and perhaps you've been left behind. Any of these situations may be true for you—but it's not too late! You can still make friends, and you can still learn to *be* a good friend. It's never too late for that.

Sometimes, no matter how hard you try, certain kids won't want to be your friend. It's not your fault. Find other kids and focus on them instead. Don't give up on making friends!

Being a Good Friend

Friendship means sharing more than interests and activities. It means sharing parts of *yourself*. You'll need to talk about your thoughts and feelings, even if it's hard to do, because that's key to friendship. Sometimes, you might share your knowledge or advice. Other times, you'll tell some of your secrets (like your most embarrassing moment or your dreams for the future). That's what friends are for.

Communication and conversation are big parts of friendship. You'll need those skills to be a good friend. If that seems scary, don't worry. All kids your age are learning those skills, not just kids with ASD, and not just you. You don't have to have perfect communication (no one does!) or be the world's greatest conversationalist. Do the best you can, knowing that your skills will improve over time.

Be open with your friends—let them know what you're working on. Here are some things you might say:

"I have a problem with interrupting, but I'm working on it. I hope you can be patient with me! If I interrupt while you're talking, you can let me know."

"Every once in a while, I say something that I wish I hadn't said. You can let me know if I ever hurt your feelings. Don't be afraid to tell me, because I might not figure it out on my own."

"Sometimes I talk too loud. Can you tell me if I do that?"

Liam's Story

Liam is in the fifth grade and has ASD. He knows the names of all the kids in his classroom and in other classes, too. He loves to raise his hand to answer questions in class, because he's smart and he likes learning. He always sits next to someone during lunch at school. In gym class he's almost always picked for one of the teams for dodge ball. Liam thinks he has lots of friends and feels good in school.

But outside of school Liam doesn't have much of a social life. He hardly ever gets invited to someone's house to play, and he's never been asked to a sleepover. Liam doesn't understand why it's so hard for him to have friends to do stuff with after school. Sometimes he hears kids talking about a playdate or a birthday party, and Liam feels left out and sad because he wasn't invited.

Liam knows he has ASD, but he's not always sure just what it means. He gets good grades, and other kids are friendly to him—but Liam feels as if something is missing in his life. He decides to talk to his mom about the friendship problem.

Liam tells his mom that he's lonely and doesn't know if he's doing something wrong. His mom says that it's not his fault if friendship isn't easy for him. She tells him that friendship is challenging for many kids who are on the spectrum. But, she says, they can learn the social skills that will help them succeed. Liam feels better, especially when he and his mom come up with a Friendship Plan.

As part of the plan, Liam's mom calls Carl's mom. Carl and Liam have been at the same school since kindergarten, and they ride the same bus. Back in kindergarten, Liam went to Carl's birthday party and they had a few playdates. But that ended in first grade, when Carl found other friends in school and on his soccer team.

Liam's mom gets some helpful information from the phone call. Later on, she tells Liam that Carl admitted some of the other kids at school are a little afraid of Liam. Liam can hardly believe his ears! What could they be afraid of? His mom explains that the other students think of Liam as "the smartest boy in their grade." They like sitting with Liam at lunch.

But Carl said that sometimes Liam talks really loud. Then people think he's angry or upset. Also, some of the guys think Liam sits too close. They don't know how to ask him to move, so they try to avoid him instead.

Liam is confused by all he hears. He never realized he spoke too loud or sat too close to people. But he also knows he can change that. He likes it that the other kids think of him as smart, but he wants them to realize he's *more* than smart—he's friendly and fun, too! He asks his mom what to do.

"Well," his mom says, "what would you think about telling the kids in your class about your ASD? Maybe that would help them understand you better."

Liam considers this. His classmates might tease him or think he's weird. On the other hand, being on the spectrum is a part of who he is. He decides that, with his mom's help, he can talk about ASD so other kids might better understand him. His mom tells him she will ask his teacher, Mr. Gilbert, to help Liam talk to the class.

Mr. Gilbert starts the presentation by saying, "All people are different. Everyone has strengths. Everyone has challenges. Today, Liam is going to tell you something about himself that you may not have known."

Suddenly, it's Liam's turn to talk. He's nervous, but he glances at his mom, who is smiling and looks proud. Liam takes a deep breath and imagines he's a teacher at the front of the classroom, explaining a lesson. He says: "I have something called ASD, or autism spectrum disorder. It means I have some problems with social skills." He goes on to describe his symptoms, such as talking too loud or not realizing when he's standing or sitting too close. He finishes by saying, "I don't mind if you ask me questions about ASD. And I really hope that some of you will be my friends."

Right away, kids raise their hands to ask questions. "How did you get ASD?" "What does it feel like?" "Is that why you're so smart?" Liam answers the questions as best he can, and sometimes his mom and Mr. Gilbert help with the answers, too.

Then, to Liam's surprise, the kids clap. He sits down in his seat, feeling relieved—and happy. He knows he's something else besides smart: He's brave.

Like Liam, some kids who have ASD share that information with their classmates. This is a way to help others better understand how they act and communicate. It's up to you—and your family—to decide if that step is right for you. Some kids and families prefer to keep the diagnosis private, telling only relatives and very close friends. Talk to your parents or caregivers about the issue before deciding.

If you've made a friend, that's terrific! Now you'll probably need ideas for staying friends. A friendship is lots of fun, but it's also *work*. Staying connected takes effort. Here are some tips to try:

Be flexible. Do what your friend likes to do, even if it's not your favorite activity. Being flexible is important because otherwise your friend might feel as if you're making all the rules or decisions. Take turns choosing activities, and be a good sport by not complaining. For more on being a good sport, see pages 61–62.

Reach out. Even if you're not used to making phone calls or texting friends, you sometimes need to make the first move. Invite your friend to your home, plan a fun outing like going to the arcade, or have a sleepover.

Go places together. This helps create a stronger bond. Together, you'll have experiences out in the world, instead of only at home. Your outing doesn't have to be expensive. You could go to a free concert or museum, or try hiking or playing in a park. If you can spend a little money, head to a skating rink, an indoor play park, or a water park. See movies, go to sporting events, or volunteer together. If outings tend to be difficult for you, remember that your friend can support you and help make the experience more fun.

Show appreciation. Let your friend know you care. Do simple things: Make a birthday card or send a funny email. Give compliments. Help a friend with homework. Send your buddy a postcard if you're on vacation. Give your friend little gifts like a fun pencil or eraser or something you made yourself. You don't have to give presents often, but it's a thoughtful gesture when you do.

Be loyal and caring. If your friend gets a bad grade, say something kind, such as, "You seem upset. Is there anything I can do to help?" Show you care in other ways, too. For example, stick up for your friends if they're being teased. Give friends a call at home when they're sick and can't go to school. Save a seat for a friend at the lunch table or on the bus, if you're allowed to. Leave a funny note at your friend's locker.

Take a Look!

Many of the skills you've read about in this book will help you make friends:

- Have you been working on getting along better with family members? (See Chapter 8.) *That* can help you get along better with kids your own age.

- Have you tried any of the ideas in Chapter 9—joining a club, starting a social skills group, or finding other kids who have similar hobbies? If so, the kids you're getting to know might become your friends.

- Are you practicing the listening skills from Chapter 10? Being a good listener is a key to friendship.

- The conversation tips from Chapter 11 can help you become more confident about talking with friends one-on-one and in groups.

- Finally, the Social Skill Survival Kit in Chapter 12 can help you build confidence in many social situations.

Kiko's Story

Kiko is 10 and very independent. Everyone always tells her dad how mature Kiko is for her age. They say she's "almost as responsible as an adult." Sometimes, people tell Kiko's dad: "She must be so popular."

Kiko is proud about the compliments. But she's also sort of sad, because the truth is she doesn't have many friends. In fact, she's not popular at all. Deep down, she knows popularity doesn't really matter—but she sure would like to have a couple of friends. Kiko's ASD makes it hard for her to be social in a way other people understand.

At school, the speech therapist helps Kiko practice her social skills. Kiko is learning appropriate ways to start conversations. She practices asking social questions. Kiko also works on listening, so she can be part of conversations at the lunch table and during recess. Kiko also practices in the cafeteria while eating lunch with the other girls. Things are going better. The other girls seem to notice her, and they don't drift away when she talks.

Today in the lunch line, Kiko decides to ask Megan a social question: "What do you like to eat?"

Megan says, "I like cookies. But my mom won't let me use any of the money from my lunch account to buy them. Can you believe that?"

This gives Kiko an idea. She puts a cookie on her lunch tray—not for herself but for Megan. Kiko knows this is *showing interest in what other people like,* something she's learned about in therapy. Then she goes to Megan's table and sits near her. "I got this for you, Megan," Kiko says, smiling.

"Thanks!" says Megan. Kiko can tell by the expression on her face that Megan is pleased.

The next day at lunch, Kiko buys two cookies with the money in her lunch account. She gives one to Megan and another to a girl named Janelle. After that, Megan and Janelle are extra nice to Kiko. They save her a seat at lunch and seem excited when she brings them more cookies. At home, Kiko tells her dad all about her two new friends.

For a month, Kiko keeps buying cookies for Megan and Janelle. They seem to like sitting with Kiko at lunch. For the first time in a long time, Kiko feels included.

But one day after school, Kiko's dad is waiting to talk to her. He says he got a notice from the school that all the money in her lunch account is gone. He's surprised, because he had paid enough for several months of lunches. That's when Kiko tells him that her new friends love to eat the cookies she buys them every day. "I have to buy the cookies, Dad," she explains. "Megan and Janelle expect it."

Kiko's dad tells her that real friends don't expect you to buy things for them. He says it's okay to buy treats or give little gifts once in a while, but it's not a rule or an expectation. And you don't do it all the time. "There's more to friendship than that," he says. "It's about having fun together, playing together, and helping each other out."

Now Kiko feels confused. Has she done something wrong? Is it possible that Megan and Janelle only like the cookies and don't really like Kiko herself? Will they still sit with her if she doesn't give them a treat each day? It's a lot to consider.

"Dad, what should I do?" Kiko asks.

He puts his arm around her shoulders. "I have an idea," he says. "What if you invite Megan and Janelle over this Friday after school. You can spend time together here, getting to know each other better."

Kiko agrees to the idea. Then she has a thought. "I know what we can do while they're here!" she says.

"What?" her dad asks.

"We'll bake cookies," Kiko replies, grinning. "I'll send Janelle and Megan home with a bunch of cookies, and they can bring them as snacks all week."

Friendships can be *forever*. Ask some of the adults in your life if they have friends they've known since childhood or their teen years. Chances are, they'll say yes. Maybe they've been close friends for 20 or 30 years—or longer! Keep working on your friendship skills so these relationships can grow as you grow. And so they can last and last.

Chapter 14

School Success

Many kids with ASD agree on this: School is harder for them than it is for most kids. There may be a struggle to learn or to fit in (or both). School is challenging because of all the "extras" that go along with it:

- crowded classrooms and hallways
- bells ringing, messages over loudspeakers, shouting at recess
- moving from subject to subject and place to place
- an expectation of neat work, even handwriting
- lunch and recess, where you're on your own to figure out what to do
- the need to listen continuously, even if listening is difficult
- feelings of confusion or not knowing what might come next
- assignments to keep track of and bring to and from school

No wonder school can be tough! Even if you love certain subjects and get good grades, some aspects of school may be hard to handle. At times, you might think it would be a lot easier if you could sit alone in a quiet room with books and a computer. Then you could learn in your own way and at your own pace. There'd be no extra demands. But unless you're homeschooled, that won't happen very often. In a school setting, being part of a *community* is at the heart of the learning process.

This has its ups and downs. On the downside, when you're in a building full of people, your sensory system (see Chapter 3) is under added stress. You might be bothered by bright lights, sudden noises, crowds, and having to stand in line. And when you're surrounded by kids all day, your social skills are tested again and again. You have to listen, talk, and interact, which raises your anxiety level. By the time you get home, you might feel exhausted. Or, you might be all wound up from stressful experiences in your school day.

But there *is* an upside. Besides learning, one of the positives of being in school is that you have daily opportunities to grow in areas that are difficult for you. Every day is a test of your communication skills and a chance to explore the social world. Every day is an opportunity to discover more about yourself, your needs, and how to get them met.

Take another look at pages 73–77, which focus on ways to get involved in special activities that help you learn and have fun. Many of these opportunities start at school: clubs, band, orchestra, school plays, sports, volunteering, and more. Activities like these can help extend your learning and increase your brain power—just a few more advantages of school.

Your IEP

IEP stands for Individualized Education Program. It's the written plan outlining the educational program and services that will meet your needs as a student. You need a special plan because you have a disability (ASD). Your ASD affects your ability to learn in school. A law passed in 1975, now called the Individuals with Disabilities Education Act (IDEA), helps make sure that *all* children, including those with a disability, have a right to a quality public education.

You may not think of yourself as disabled. Instead you might consider yourself "quirky" or "different" or "unique." You may be all those things! But it's still important to have an IEP. This plan helps the teachers and other adults at school understand you better.

As a student, you don't have to put together the IEP yourself. That's a job for your parents or caregivers and your school. There are steps that must be taken before an IEP is created, such as having a doctor or another expert let the school know about your diagnosis. Show this chapter to the adults at home so they can learn about IEPs or let you know if you have one in place.

You can be part of your IEP meetings, if you wish. Those meetings take place at school. They include your teacher, a special education teacher, and other experts who can support you.

An IEP includes many ways the people at school will help you, depending on your needs and what your parents, caregivers, and teachers request. Parents might request that their child:

- be able to sit near the teacher, and never have to change seats, even if the classroom is rearranged
- be allowed to take "sensory breaks" throughout the day, as needed, in a resource room or another place at school
- get extra time on tests
- receive special help in speech, social skills, or occupational therapy (OT) skills such as handwriting (if needed and approved)
- have a classroom aide to help with academics
- may call a parent during the school day, if needed, as a way to calm down or stay focused
- be allowed to use a special bathroom at school
- have extra classroom tools (such as a mini trampoline, an exercise ball to gently bounce on, a weighted vest or blanket, headphones, or communication tools)
- have a reward system in place, to encourage positive classroom behavior
- get extended deadlines on longer homework assignments
- have an additional set of textbooks at home, in case the child forgets them at school and needs to study or do homework

Each student's IEP is different. Yours might include some of the previous ideas, or other things. You can help with your IEP by letting the adults who teach and take care of you know more about your school experience:

- What's hard for you? What's easy for you?
- What do you like and dislike about school?
- Where might you need extra assistance?
- Is there anything that could help your days go more smoothly?

Keyan's Story

Keyan is in fourth grade, and because of his autism, he has sensory issues. Sometimes at school, he gets over-whelmed by all the noise, lights, and people. His IEP plan tells his teacher specific ways to help Keyan calm down and focus so he can learn better.

Keyan's teacher made a special space in the back of the classroom where Keyan can take breaks. Other students can use the space when they need time away, too. This makes Keyan feel good. Something that helps him can help others as well!

Today in science, the students are doing an experiment with pop-ping balloons. Keyan gets startled and bothered by loud noises. His teacher knows that Keyan may not want to participate. She tells him all about the experiment ahead of time. Then she asks if he'd like to wear his special sound-blocking headphones but still watch. Keyan decides he'd rather read about the experiment instead. Then, when the experi-ment takes place, he'll head to his quiet space at the back of the room.

When the time comes, Keyan goes to the back of the room. There, a bookshelf makes a divider. Behind the shelf, Keyan finds the giant beanbag chair he loves. He has a printout of the experiment to read. And there's a CD player with headphones. Keyan turns it on and listens to calm music that blocks out the rest of the classroom noise.

Before the school year and before your IEP is written, talk with your parents or members of your team of helpers (for more about this team, see Chapter 7) to come up with ideas for what might help you in the classroom and throughout the day. Your family and team members know you best—they can help make your IEP into a document that makes a difference in your school day.

Your family has opportunities to make changes to the IEP when something isn't working. A parent or caregiver can let the school know if it's time to meet about the IEP again. You and your family have a right to stand up for your needs. You don't have to wait!

Tools to Help You Get Organized

You might be one of those kids who has a clean locker, an organized backpack, and a nice, neat desk. Maybe you like rules and a sense of things being orderly—which helps you focus and feel safe. It's great that you're already focused on being organized. That will help you a lot in middle school and high school, where you have more classes, teachers, and schoolwork to keep track of.

Many kids on the autism spectrum don't have strong organizational skills, however. This is because of how their brains are wired. It's not a matter of intelligence—it's a matter of being weaker in the area of *executive function.* What does that mean? The executive function area of the brain helps a person plan and organize. It's like having a "personal assistant" inside your head, telling you how to stay on top of your day. Don't worry if your brain's "assistant" isn't so great at the job. Lots of tools can help you better focus, plan, and organize. They're right at your fingertips when you need them.

Handy-Dandy Planners

Using a daily planner can be the key to knowing what comes next. When you know what comes next, you feel more comfortable and confident. You'll be more likely to have what you need when you need it.

Kids with ASD do better when they have a daily schedule they can count on. Are you already using a visual schedule, a planner, or a calendar? If you're not, ask an adult at home to help you plan your days from morning until evening. Then you'll have a routine you can count on.

Page 142 has a sample daily schedule for at-home use. Some families use a special planner or a dry-erase board. The schedule needs to be in a place where you can easily see it throughout the day. Check off each item as you finish—it feels great to accomplish your tasks!

For school, try a planner with one day per page so you'll have more room for all of your activities (see bottom of page 142). Write down all of your homework assignments and which materials to bring home. It's stressful when you forget to take home the books or folders you need. Or, when you do your homework but forget to bring it back to school.

Wednesday

Morning:			
	☐	7:00	Alarm goes off, get dressed, get backpack and lunch ready
	☐	7:20	Breakfast
	☐	7:40	Wash face and brush teeth
	☐	7:45	Playtime until bus comes
	☐	8:00	Bus!
After School:	☐	3:30	Arrive home! Eat snack! Relax!
	☐	4:30	Piano lesson
	☐	5:00	Piano lesson ends—FREE TIME!
	☐	5:30	Do two chores from chore chart—then more FREE TIME!
Evening:	☐	6:00	Dinner (try one new food tonight)
	☐	7:00	Start homework (Dad will help)
	☐	8:00	Fun time with Mom
	☐	8:30	Start getting ready for bed
	☐	9:00	Bedtime, lights out!

Day of Week: Monday   **Date:** March 3

Assignment	Due
Reading Textbook pp. 140–150 — Bring book home!	tomorrow
Math Worksheet, pre-test handout — Bring math folder home!	tomorrow
English/Language Check out poetry book from library — Find library card!	by next Tuesday
Spelling Test Friday (study unit words) — List is at home	
Science No homework tonight—yay!	
Social Studies Work on report for 30 mins. tonight — Materials are at home	Friday

Teacher Message	Parent Message
Kira needs more graphing paper. —Mrs. M.	

"Neater Meter"

You may be disorganized and not even know it. Maybe you overlook the mess, or just become used to it. But having a sloppy desk, locker, or backpack slows you down. It's hard to find what you need, and the work you hand in to your teachers might be messier than it should be. Time to turn on your "Neater Meter"! Look at the areas around you.

You can start with your desk at school. What's inside it?

Take a peek in your locker. Is it a disaster, with old papers, rotten food, or out-of-season clothing in it (like a mitten from last winter)?

Now look inside your backpack. Take everything out of it and see what you've got. Are there several broken pencils at the bottom of it? How about bent, torn papers? Old snacks or used tissues?

Ask a parent or another trusted adult to help you clean out these different areas and get them in better shape. It's best to work with

someone instead of trying to do this on your own. Cleaning up can be a long, difficult task. You may not know where to begin or how to keep going. Having a helper is motivating. That person can sort through your belongings. She or he can also purchase any organizing supplies you may need, such as new folders or a pencil pouch.

Once you've tidied up, it's a matter of keeping your "Neater Meter" turned on and tuned in. How?

- **Locker.** Use the hooks and shelves provided to hang up your jacket and store extra shoes or boots. The top shelf can hold your books and notebooks. Never leave food in your locker, because it can rot.

- **Lunchbox.** Remember to bring your lunchbox home with you each day. Make sure you have your thermos, containers, or utensils. At home, give the lunchbox to your dad or mom to wash and repack (unless you do those tasks yourself).

- **Desk.** At the end of each week, examine the inside of your desk. Are there papers you can take home? Do you need to sharpen your pencils or bring in new markers? Is the cap on your glue? Are your folders and notebooks stacked neatly? Is there food or candy that should be removed?

- **Subject folders.** Use color-coded folders for each subject. Write the name of each subject clearly on the front. Then place the folders in your backpack in subject order. (If you start the day with math, your math folder goes in first. If science is next, put the science folder behind the math one, and so on.)

- **Zippered pouch.** This can hold pencils, pens, erasers, a small ruler, highlighters, a glue stick, a calculator, tissues, and other items you need each day. With these things in one place, they won't get lost in your backpack or get smashed by your books.

- **Backpack.** Go through your backpack each night at home. Put your papers in the correct folders and toss any trash. After you do your homework, place your assignments and textbooks in the backpack so you won't forget them. Be sure to check your daily planner one last time to see if you've finished all your work.

- **Gym bag.** If you have a gym bag or sports bag, be sure to regularly clean that out, too. Remove the dirty clothes for washing. Give your shoes a chance to air out. Wash the water bottles. Place everything back in the bag before your next practice.

Being neat and tidy can become a good habit. You'll probably discover that having a clean desk, backpack, and locker makes it easier for you to find your belongings and homework and keep track of them. All of this can add up to higher grades and increased confidence. Keep trying—it's worth it! Ask for help anytime you start to feel as if the needle on your "Neater Meter" is pointing to the sloppy side.

Homework Habits

Homework is a "have to." It's not fun, but you have to get it done! To make sure your homework time is efficient, set up a routine you can count on:

- Work at a desk or table in a quiet place—a *homework station*. Use a bright lamp so you can see well.
- Gather all the materials you'll need so you don't have to stop your work to go find markers, a pencil sharpener, glue, etc.
- Eat a healthy snack like a piece of fruit so you won't get hungry. Keep a water bottle nearby to sip from.
- Do the hardest work first to get it done while you're still energized. (Later in the evening, you'll probably be more tired.)
- Focus on using neat handwriting and the correct pencil grip—it's frustrating sometimes, but you can do it!
- Set a timer for breaks. Maybe you need to get up and stretch every 15 minutes.

- Ask a parent or another grown-up to check over your work once you've finished. Make any needed corrections. Then put your homework back in the correct folders. Put all your folders and books in the backpack, zip it up, and you're done!

"Unstructured" Times at School

Most of the school day is *structured,* meaning there's a schedule of tasks and activities to complete. For example, you have math class, where your teacher stands at the front of the room and goes over the lesson. Students are expected to listen and learn the material. This is true for most classes throughout the school day, even gym. In gym class, you may play a game or do a workout. But there are still rules, and an adult who watches to be sure kids are doing what they're supposed to do.

What about the unstructured times like when you're walking through the hallways? Or recess and lunch? Many kids with ASD say the *unstructured* parts of the day are the most difficult for them. It may seem as if lunch should be easy. All you have to do is eat, right? And it may seem as if recess is pure fun—all that shouting and running around. But for kids with ASD, these times are loud, crowded, and confusing. There aren't clear rules they can count on. Things change all the time: where kids sit, what they talk about, who they hang out with, and what games they play.

If lunch, hallway time, and recess are difficult for you, you can let the adults at school and at home know this. Maybe you've felt stressed during these parts of the day, but didn't know why. Or maybe you never realized things could change for the better. But they *can*—there are lots of ideas to try.

Hallways

- Ask to have your IEP state that you're allowed to leave the room five minutes before the other students are excused to go to the next class or activity. This gives you extra time to get where you need to go while the halls are quieter.

- What if you don't want to walk alone or have trouble finding your way around the building? Ask to have an aide, a teacher, or another student accompany you each time.

- Keep a set of ear plugs in your pocket or desk. Put them in before hallway time to block out some of the noise.

- To further block out sounds and commotion, recite some kind of memorized list in your mind: the multiplication tables, the U.S. states in alphabetical order, or whatever you'd like.

Recess

- Try to join a game like tag, four square, hide and seek, or chase. This is an easy way to be social and have a structure—a game with rules!

- Swing to calm yourself down. Or, have fun on the slide. The rhythm of waiting for your turn, climbing up, and sliding down can feel familiar and soothing.

- Avoid being alone. It's stressful to wander around the play-ground, not knowing what to do or who to hang out with. Is there at least one friend you can count on? Make plans with that person ahead of time. Say something like, "Want to play with me at recess?" Stick together!

- Ask for a recess buddy. If making friends is difficult for you and you need some help with social skills, a recess buddy is a great option. This student gets the special responsibility of helping you at recess. You can play together, join in a game, or practice conversation. Your mom or dad can help arrange for this.

- Bring something special to play with at recess: trading cards, a toy, or a ball, for example. (Get permission first.) This way, you can invite other kids to share the item with you. Instant fun!

- Some days, you might need to skip recess. It's true that recess is a great opportunity for exercise. Still, there may be days you need time alone between classes to settle down and de-stress. Find out if there's a place in school where you can go on days when recess is too hard for you.

Jordan's Story

Recess is fun, but boy can it get crazy, thinks Jordan, a third grader. All the screaming and running around gets on his nerves. He has tried wearing ear plugs, but they fall out when he hangs from the monkey bars or zooms down the slide. Jordan's autism makes it harder for him to join other kids in their games. He likes calmer activities. It's frustrating that the other kids seem to know just what to do. Some of them run right to the jungle gym. Others quickly start a game of Freeze Tag. A few hang around the edges of the playground to talk. By the time Jordan gets up the courage to join in, it's time to go to lunch.

Today Jordan's class is having indoor recess because it's raining. All the students will go to the Multipurpose Room. Jordan thinks it will be noisy, and he isn't looking forward to it. Then he remembers his marble collection in his backpack. He'd brought it in for Sharing Time to show his class.

Jordan loves his marbles. Some of them were given to him by his grandfather, from the days when he was a boy. They're all the colors of the rainbow. He loves how they sound when they roll and click together.

Jordan decides to ask his teacher if he can bring the marbles to indoor recess to play with. She says it's fine. *Cool,* Jordan thinks. *Now I have something to do!* He goes to a quiet corner to play to make sure the marbles won't roll away and get lost.

Jordan is having so much fun shooting marbles that he doesn't notice the crowd of boys gathered around him. One of them asks, "Hey, Jordan, can we play too?"

Jordan can't believe it. Usually, *he's* the one who has to ask others to play. Jordan shows the boys his collection and teaches them different marble games. "Maybe you can start your own marble collections," he tells them. Jordan hopes that some of them will. Then they could trade marbles and learn more marble games together.

When it's time for lunch, the boys help Jordan clean up the marbles. "Thanks for playing, Jordan," they say.

"Any time!" he says. And he means it.

Lunchtime

- If waiting in the cafeteria line is difficult for you, bring your lunch every day or a few times per week.
- If noise is a problem, sit at a table where students are quieter.
- Think of a subject to talk about. Then use lunchtime to practice your conversation skills. (Read Chapter 11 for more on this.)
- If talking is difficult, start with simply listening. Make some eye contact, nod your head when appropriate, or laugh along with others. (See Chapter 10 for more on listening.)
- Invite a parent to join you at lunch once in a while. It's a good chance to spend time together.

Making the Most of School

At school, you have so many people you can go to for further assistance. If you're in special education, your teacher is trained to help you in subjects you struggle with *and* to come up with ideas for improved behavior and social skills. You may spend part of the day in a resource room where you get extra help and a break from larger classrooms. You may also work with an occupational therapist or a speech therapist at school. The school counselor or social worker is trained to help you, too.

Any time you're facing tough challenges at school, talk to your mom or dad, your teachers, your principal, or your aide (if you have one). They will probably have good ideas for making the most of school. You may need a tutor in certain subjects, or to take special tests designed to help experts figure out your unique learning style. It's important to explore options so you can find what helps you succeed.

But YOU play a big role in your own success, too! How? Try hard in all your subjects. Do your homework, and make sure your work is neat and correct. Whenever something isn't working well for you at school, speak up. Changes can be made to your IEP. It's an important tool for helping you get the most out of your school experience.

School teaches you not only about academics but also about getting along in a community of your peers. Your school can be a place to discover your talents, make friends, and learn. All that learning makes you smarter, stronger, and more prepared for the future. Think of school as a *positive* in your life—even if your days are sometimes difficult because of the social demands you face. You're a special kid with a lot of potential and so much ahead of you in life. Always believe in yourself!

Part 3 Body and Brain Basics

Chapter 15

How to Handle Hard-to-Handle Feelings

People who have ASD often describe themselves as very logical. That's a great asset! Using logic can help you make sense of situations and figure out what might happen next. You're most likely a fact-lover, too—someone with a great memory for information and trivia. But when it comes to understanding and expressing emotions, that's probably a challenge for you.

Everyone has strong feelings at times. But when you have ASD, you tend to have a lot of intense emotions that come on suddenly. Your feelings may be hard for you to handle, especially if you also have sensory issues like those described in Chapter 3.

What does this mean for you? Well, it might seem like you have more bad days than good ones. Or there may be times during the day when you feel like you just can't handle the stress. That can add to the tension you're already experiencing. Stress often leads to an increase in those hard-to-handle feelings. And so it goes, around and around, as if you're caught in a circle:

To top it off, you probably find it hard to communicate what's bothering you. For example, if someone bugs you at school, you might not know what to say right at the moment to make the person stop. Or maybe you dislike riding the bus because of all the movement and sounds. Your reaction might be to get frustrated and "shut down." At home, you might feel angry about the amount of homework or chores you have, which can lead to a feeling of . . . ACKKK! When you feel like that, you might want to yell or be by yourself. It's sometimes difficult to say, "Help me, I'm stressed." But asking for help is the key to getting a handle on those hard-to-handle feelings.

What's the Problem?

Something a lot of people with ASD have in common is that emotions can be like a puzzle to them. This is true for their own feelings and other people's, too. For example, studies have shown that people on the autism spectrum don't look at the human face in the same way that a "typical" person does. They look not at the *eyes* but at the mouth or nose.

Eyes give us a lot of information. They've been described as windows into what a person is thinking and feeling. If you're not looking in the window, you might miss important clues about another person's emotions. Sometimes, what someone *says* doesn't match what the person really *feels.* But you wouldn't necessarily know that unless you were looking the person in the eye and "reading" the emotions.

You can find out more about "reading" other people's thoughts and feelings in Chapters 10 and 11. Before you take on the challenge of trying to understand other people's emotions, a great goal is learning to recognize and understand your *own.*

How to Identify Your Emotions

How do you start to identify your feelings? There are signs that give you clues to what you are feeling.

Signs That You're Feeling Good

Good is a general term. It's a word most people use in everyday language to express that they're "okay" or not feeling "bad." So, *good* can mean you feel any of these ways:

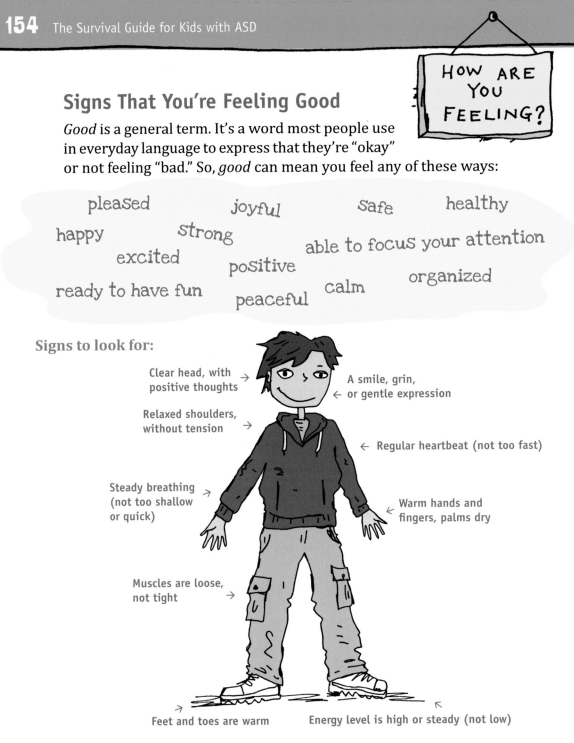

HOW ARE YOU FEELING?

pleased   joyful   safe   healthy

happy   strong   able to focus your attention

excited   positive

ready to have fun   peaceful   calm   organized

Signs to look for:

Clear head, with positive thoughts →

A smile, grin, ← or gentle expression

Relaxed shoulders, without tension →

← Regular heartbeat (not too fast)

Steady breathing (not too shallow or quick) →

← Warm hands and fingers, palms dry

Muscles are loose, not tight →

→ Feet and toes are warm   ↖ Energy level is high or steady (not low)

When you feel this way, you're *balanced*. You're ready to learn. You're able to listen and follow through. You feel friendlier and more relaxed. Being balanced feels . . . good.

Signs That You're Feeling "Bad"

Bad is another one of those all-purpose terms—in this case one that people use to describe negative feelings. Feeling "bad" doesn't mean you're a "bad person." And it doesn't mean it's *bad* to feel "bad." Confusing, right?

When you're feeling *bad*, you might feel some of these ways:

worried   unhappy   down   angry

sad   Scared   stressed out   alone   frustrated

sick   disorganized   upset

panicky   anxious   freaked out   confused

overloaded

Signs to look for:

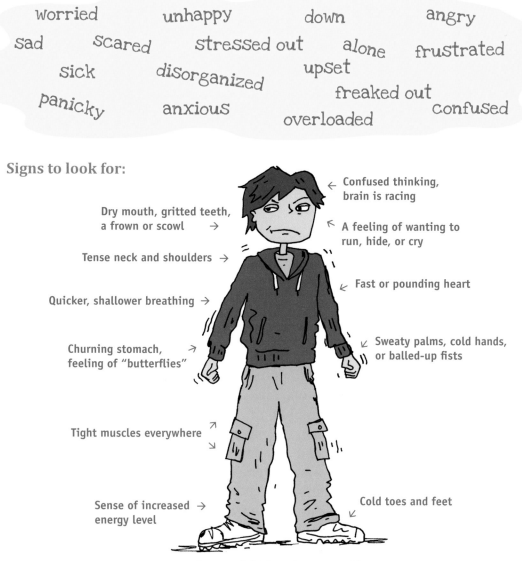

← Confused thinking, brain is racing

Dry mouth, gritted teeth, a frown or scowl →

↖ A feeling of wanting to run, hide, or cry

Tense neck and shoulders →

← Fast or pounding heart

Quicker, shallower breathing →

↙ Sweaty palms, cold hands, or balled-up fists

Churning stomach, feeling of "butterflies" ↗

Tight muscles everywhere ↗↘

Sense of increased → energy level

Cold toes and feet ↙

Or you might have *low* energy if you feel sad, down, and lonely.

These physical and emotional symptoms are signs that you're feeling *out of balance.* Your body fills with adrenaline—energy-boosting chemicals that make you feel like running, hiding, or even hitting. In a flash, you might feel out of control. This can lead to a meltdown.

Sometimes, young people with ASD have meltdowns because the strength of their emotions is confusing and upsetting. Do you often (or sometimes) get so angry or stressed out that you:

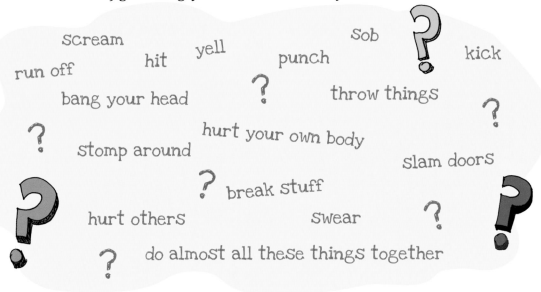

scream
run off
hit
yell
punch
Sob
kick
bang your head
throw things
stomp around
hurt your own body
slam doors
break stuff
hurt others
swear
do almost all these things together

Meltdowns are really tough—on *everyone!* When you *feel* out of control and *get* out of control, it's scary. You might briefly feel a sense of power when you're melting down. But you're probably left with negative feelings afterward—like sadness, regret, and confusion. You might worry that a punishment will follow. That never feels good.

When you're in the middle of a meltdown, one of the last things on your mind is what *other* people are feeling. But the truth is, they're probably getting frustrated with you or angry, upset, and hurt.

If you're at school, a big, angry outburst or meltdown puts negative attention on you. Other students might say something not-so-nice to you later. You might feel embarrassed afterward. In some cases, other kids might even try to get you mad again, just to see if you have another outburst.

At home, your family probably has a hard time handling your meltdowns, too. Your parents and siblings get upset when you're upset. Often, they're the ones who have to clean up if you've damaged stuff in anger. Nobody feels better after a meltdown. Not even you.

Guess what? You can learn to stop a meltdown before it starts. It takes some work and some practice—but it's worth it. There are *lots* of healthy ways to handle feelings.

How do you begin? You can start by doing your own "emotions self-check." At different points during an average day, take a moment to ask yourself how you feel. Notice your breathing, your heartbeat, your body temperature. Are you calm? Focused? Alert? Good!

Look around. *Who* are you with when you feel positive and content? *What* activity helps you feel this way? *Where* do you feel good? (At home, at school, in an after-school club?) *When* do you feel good? (Certain times of day or night?) *Why* do you feel good? Is it something you're doing—and can do *more* of?

Or, are you getting a bit stressed and worried? Does your body feel unbalanced? Is there something on your mind?

Again, ask yourself the *who, what, where, when,* and *why* of it. Pay attention to the situations that lead to stress or other difficulties.

If you're feeling bad at any given time, it's okay. Take a deep breath and get ready to use some tools from your toolbox.

Your Tools for Handling Emotions

Four tools can help you as you work to understand and handle your feelings. They aren't tools like a hammer and nails. Instead, they're an imaginary set of tools you can picture in your mind. Each tool can be used to take care of yourself when you're getting upset or experiencing intense emotions you need to get a handle on.

Tool #1: Oxygen

As soon as you start to feel "bad" or off-balance, close your eyes and your mouth and take a deeeeep breath through your nose. Shallow breaths go only as far as your chest. Deep breaths go down to your belly. Your stomach should rise as you inhale. Now exhale through your mouth. Do it again, and again. Getting oxygen to your brain helps you think more clearly. (See Chapter 18 for more breathing exercises.)

Tool #2: Antenna

You don't have an antenna growing out of your head, giving you information about yourself and your environment. (But it sure could come in handy.) Often, having ASD means you aren't "in tune" with yourself and what's going on around you. This can lead to that off-balance feeling mentioned earlier.

Sometimes, it's the simplest things that can help when something doesn't feel right. Tune

Take a Look!
This chapter has tools to help you figure out HOW you feel, WHY you feel that way, and how to help yourself cope with intense feelings. It would be nice if you could read the chapter and then—*presto!*—be an expert on emotions for the rest of your life. But it doesn't work like that. Learning to understand your feelings takes time and practice. In fact, many people work on this *all their lives,* whether they have ASD or not. As human beings, we're emotional creatures, even if we're capable of logic. We have a lot of feelings that leave us confused and uncertain where to turn.

Learning to understand your feelings and express them is a skill to work on now—and forever! The more you do it, the easier it gets.

in by asking yourself some basic questions: *Am I thirsty? Hungry? Overtired? Do I need to use the bathroom?*

Make sure to keep yourself hydrated by drinking water throughout the day. Eat a healthy snack between meals. Get the rest you need. When you feel the urge to go to the bathroom, try to notice it right away—don't wait until the very last minute. Remembering to take care of your body helps you feel more balanced—physically *and* emotionally.

Tool #3: Walkie-Talkie

One of the best things you can do when you're off-balance, stressed out, or upset is to *communicate* these feelings. Walk over and talk to someone! Go to a parent, a teacher, or another adult you trust. Sometimes, the words don't come easily, so memorize a few phrases you can say:

- "I'm upset. Can you help me?"
- "I'm having feelings I don't know how to handle."
- "I need to talk to you about something."

Cry if you need to. Get the feelings out by talking about them. Listen to the adult, too. This person might be able to help you solve the problem. He or she might also find a place for you to calm down.

Remember to try *talking it out* instead of *acting out.* (Acting out is doing something with your body instead of your words—things like hitting, kicking, punching, destroying property, or hurting yourself.) Let your feelings be known so other people can help you.

> Now that I am older, I can better express myself when things are vexing me. There are still times when I am bottled up like a clam, but talking to someone about my troubles has been good medicine for relieving my stress.
>
> —J.D. Kraus, from his book *The Aspie Teen's Survival Guide: Candid Advice for Teens, Tweens, and Parents from a Young Man with Asperger's Syndrome*

Note for Adults

ASD makes it very difficult for children and teens to manage their feelings when they're angry, upset, or melting down. Challenging as this is for you, the calmer *you* are, the easier you make it for your child to gradually calm down. Stay quiet and patient; guide your child to breathe deeply. Calming down after any kind of upset can take a while, for your child and you. See Chapter 18 for tips on creating a Calm-Down Space at home.

Tool #4: Rubber Band

Picture a rubber band. What's it like? *Rubbery, stretchy, flexible.* You can twist it and bend it in many directions, but a rubber band still goes back to its original shape without breaking.

What does this have to do with you? Like a rubber band, you can become more flexible.

Part of having ASD is *liking things a certain way.* Maybe you fear change. Maybe you feel safer when you know what to expect each day. For example, perhaps you eat only certain foods. Or maybe you have a hard time at school when the unexpected happens, like you get a substitute teacher one day. You may be afraid to try new things because something new feels scary or threatening to you—even if the new thing is something fun, like a movie or a different restaurant.

All of these are signs of *rigid thinking*—of being less flexible than you could be. When something happens that you don't like or didn't expect, you might suddenly feel "bad." (The physical symptoms mentioned on page 157 are signs to look for.) You get frustrated and angry more quickly, because you're locked into a certain way of thinking. That's known as *rigidity.*

But you can learn to be flexible. You probably know that you can make your body more flexible by bending and stretching your muscles. You can also become more flexible in your thinking. Using your "rubber band" tool (thinking of yourself as willing to bend), you can make little changes in your thinking. Over time, these small changes can make a BIG difference in how you feel.

At times when something isn't going the way you want, bend your mind a tiny bit. Take a deep breath first. Try not to react or act out. Instead, tell yourself:

- "It's okay. I can find a way to solve this problem."
- "I can try, even though I'm scared."
- "People will help me. I can go to [think of an adult you trust]."

You're being a rubber band, remember? You can bend in new ways without snapping or breaking. Ask for help when you need it.

Flexing (being flexible) is something that you'll need to practice at home and in therapy. It's part of managing the symptoms of ASD. The more you practice, the more flexible you'll be. And that means you'll feel good more often.

Look back at "Signs That You're Feeling Good" on page 154. That's what you're aiming for—feelings of calm and confidence, even when you're bending and stretching. You can do it!

Whenever you're faced with those hard-to-handle feelings, picture your Emotions Toolbox. Use the tools to help you start to feel better:

| **Breathe!** | **Tune in to what you're feeling and why.** | **Talk to someone— get help.** | **Flex!** |

With time and practice, some of those "bad" feelings may happen less often, and you'll have more good feelings more of the time.

Jackson's Story

Jackson is in the fourth grade and has autism. He spends most of the school day with his regular fourth-grade class. He has an aide, or helper, with him part of the day.

One thing Jackson struggles with is leaving the classroom to go to other places in the school. Jackson hates the hallways—they're *so* loud, and the noise hurts his ears. He hears footsteps, voices, doors opening and closing, bells dinging. For Jackson, the hallways have too much movement and confusion. He gets nervous and upset.

It's Wednesday, which means Jackson has gym. He doesn't like going to gym because he has to walk through a bunch of hallways to the other side of the school. He knows that when he gets there, the gym itself will be loud and full of too much action. Kids will be screaming. Balls will fly through the air. He never knows what might come at him. But whatever it is, it won't be good.

Usually, getting to gym makes him feel so anxious that he slaps himself on the head and tries to run away. But today Jackson and his aide are trying something new to make gym a little easier. They're going to leave for gym class five minutes earlier than the other kids. This means the hall will be clearer, and Jackson will have extra time to try to relax.

As he and his aide walk down the hall, Jackson stays quiet and tries to think about what his doctor taught him about relaxing: take big, deep breaths very slowly and focus his thoughts on a calm place. He does that now. He breathes in and out. "Stay calm," he tells himself.

When he gets to the gym, Jackson sits in the corner, breathing deeply, waiting for the other kids to arrive. His aide smiles at him.

The quiet hallway helped, Jackson thinks to himself. *Maybe the deep breathing will, too.*

Chapter 16

"Stims"

I never sat still; I bobbed and weaved and bounced. . . .
Most of the time, I stayed alone, in my own little world,
apart from my peers.

—John Elder Robison, from his memoir about Asperger's, *Look Me in the Eye*

People who write about their autism or Asperger's often tell of a deep need for rhythmic motion and repetition. These repeated motions are what experts refer to as "self-stimulatory behaviors," or "stims." When people use stims, it's called "stimming." Maybe you do some of these:

- rocking back and forth
- flapping your arms or flicking your hands
- banging your head or tapping your fingers on a surface
- twirling or spinning around and around
- humming
- rubbing a piece of cloth or another object
- staring at patterns or observing objects that spin
- lining up objects in a particular order
- dangling string or other objects in front of your eyes, or looking at things from the corners of your eyes
- picking at parts of your body (nose, fingernails, pimples, scabs)
- pacing or walking on your toes
- licking or mouthing objects
- asking the same question over and over, or repeating favorite words
- whatever else you may do repetitively that's unique to you

Chastain's Story

Chastain is a third grader who has autism. He likes string a lot, and he carries it everywhere—something he's done his whole life. His mom has pictures of him at two years old holding string in his hands.

When he was younger, Chastain liked to wave the string in front of his eyes. But once he started school, the other kids couldn't understand why Chastain always had his string. Sometimes, they'd tease him when he'd take out his special string and give it a wave. He learned to keep his string in his pocket. Throughout the school day, he'd put his hand in his pocket to make sure the string was there. Touching the string felt good.

This morning when Chastain gets to school, he reaches into his pocket. He can't find his string. He knows he had it earlier. Now he's worried. He looks in his backpack. No string. He looks in his desk. No string. Chastain starts to cry. He *has* to have his special string!

He goes into the hallway to calm down, but he's crying so loud his teacher sends him to the office. The health aide calls Chastain's mom, because he can't stop crying. His mom arrives to take him home. When Chastain gets in the car he's still upset. That's when he sees it—his string! It's right there on the floor of the car, where it must have fallen out that morning.

Chastain picks up his string, gives it a happy wave, and asks his mom if he can go back into the school. He knows he can stay calm. The day will go better now that he has what he needs.

Stims are often done automatically, without your noticing. But sometimes, you might stim on purpose to calm yourself down or deal with worries or boredom. Stims may be your way of feeling "safe" because stimming is familiar and soothing.

Everyone has habits of some sort—some of yours may just happen to be stims. People with ASD stim the way "typical" people twirl their hair, bite their fingernails, or tap their feet. But if everybody has habits, how come stims get a special name? And why are stims often seen as something you need to stop doing or "control"?

Those are tough questions! The answers differ, depending on who you talk to. Parents, doctors, behavior therapists, teachers, and other experts all have points of view. So do people with ASD. Here are some of the different ideas:

- Teachers may notice that a student's stims are a distraction in the classroom. In their view, too much stimming might interfere with everyone's learning.

- Many behavior experts say that stims set a child apart. The behaviors look "odd." They may lead to teasing from other children. According to these experts, if the goal is to increase positive social behaviors, then stimming needs to be done less often. (Or at least not in social situations.)

- Sometimes stims become a medical issue. Kids might pick their nose until it bleeds. Or they may scratch their skin until sores develop. Kids who bang their head are at risk of injury.

- In some families, parents and other family members might say that stimming is "annoying," "pointless," or even "harmful." That can seem really unfair! But perhaps it's the family's way of protecting their loved one. They want him or her to fit in and feel comfortable.

- In other families, the parents are more accepting of stims. They may see stimming as a symptom, a quirk, or something that simply comes and goes.

- Occupational therapists (OTs) look at how stims connect to the senses. They ask, "What does the stim do for the person's sensory system?" or "What sensory input is the person craving or creating?" (You can read more about the senses in Chapter 3.)

- Lots of people with ASD say that stimming is really soothing and relaxing. Some say that stims help them focus or think better. They wonder, *Why can't autistic behaviors become an accepted part of the world we all share?*

As you can see, there are many different opinions. Even the people on your team of helpers (see Chapter 7) might disagree about this topic. It's easy to get confused about stims or to get confused about who's really the "expert."

Well, maybe you can become your *own* expert here. Think about whether your stimming might be:

- a way to wake up your brain and body
- a way to soothe yourself and relax
- how you get rid of pent-up energy and emotions
- a symptom you'd like to learn to handle
- part of who you are—something you're not ready or willing to change
- a result of your unique sensory needs

Maybe your different stims create different feelings at different times of day. How can you find out? By noticing when you do them. Keep a notebook with you so you can write down the stims you catch yourself doing. Or ask an adult to point them out. This way, you'll learn more about yourself. You'll start to tune in to your emotions and your unique ways of handling them. You'll also get a better understanding of what your stims do for you.

Depending on how you feel about this, a parent, family member, or therapist could make a video of you when you're stimming. Then you can look at the video later and decide what you think. Is the stim something you want to change? Do you want to do it less often? Would you like to do it only in private, so you're not stimming at school or when you're with friends? You can figure out your answers to these questions by thinking them over and talking to adults you trust.

Maybe stims aren't a big concern for you at this time. As you get older, some of your stims might go away on their own. Or, your feelings about them may change.

To work on these behaviors, here are some ideas to try:

Keep them private. Stim in your room or just at home.

Have a secret signal. Ask a family member to give you a secret signal if you stim in public or with friends without being aware of it. (A signal works better than saying "Stop doing that!") The person could tap you on the shoulder, touch your hand, or whisper in your ear.

Try a different behavior. Find a different way to get the same feeling that stimming gives you. For example, if you like to tap, maybe you'd enjoy drumming. If you hum, try singing along to recorded music or using a karaoke machine or game. If you pace, you could try jogging or walking on a treadmill. If you like doing things with your hands, play with puppets, do crochet, or tap some piano keys. Experiment with different types of art.

Do high-energy activities. Get the sensory input you need by doing activities that offer lots of stimulation: Bounce on a trampoline. Swing at the park. Rock back and forth in a rocking chair. Get a spinning chair you can use at home (sit in it or just watch it go around). Do somersaults, roll in the grass, or wrestle. Figure out what your body and brain *needs*—then do it.

Work on relaxation techniques. Learning these will give you different ways to calm yourself. Chapter 18 discusses many ways to relax.

> I like to set up my action figures to match what happens in my video games. I imagine the game in my head over and over. While I'm doing that, I put my face very close to my action figures and move them with my hands so they do what's in my head. It's almost like I watch the action figures while I watch the game in my mind. I like the way this repeats. I call it 'staging.' It's fun for me when I'm alone, and I feel good when I do it.
>
> **—10-year-old boy with autism**

Chapter 17

Toilet Time

Our bodies are amazing: they can run, leap, think, sleep, talk, smile, and laugh. They're built to be efficient, well-run machines. One thing many machines need in order to work well is a source of fuel. For example, the fuel for cars is gasoline, while the fuel for humans is *food* (see Chapter 21 for more about that). All those fruits, vegetables, and other foods you eat each day turn into energy, which helps you work and play.

As a car uses fuel, it produces waste in the form of exhaust from the tail pipe. Bodies produce waste, too. Body waste includes *urine* (liquid waste, which is made by your kidneys), and *feces* (solid waste made in your intestines). Maybe you use other words to describe these waste products, like *pee* and *poop* or *BM* (for bowel movement). In this chapter, we're mostly going to say pee and poop, to keep it simple.

Going to the bathroom is a basic human function, but that doesn't mean it's easy and problem-free. Many kids with ASD have difficulty with *toileting* (as experts refer to it). This chapter talks about some of these toilet troubles and what you can do if you need help. If you don't have problems in this area, you may want to skip to another chapter.

Bathroom Basics

Bathrooms can be scary or uncomfortable places if you have ASD. Some kids don't like the cold surfaces of toilets, sinks, and bathroom floors. Other kids hate the loud, echoing noises—especially the sounds of flushing. Maybe you're worried about germs, or using the toilet paper correctly, or having someone walk in on you. All of these issues lead to feeling anxious, which makes bathroom time more stressful.

Plus, not all bathrooms are exactly like the one you have at home. At home, you know the sound of the flush, how to lock the door, and how the toilet paper comes off the roll. You know how to turn on the faucet afterward to wash your hands. You can find the soap and a towel. But at school, it's a whole different bathroom. The flushing noise is louder. The toilet paper dispenser may be harder to use. And there's a lot less privacy. If you're in the boys' bathroom, there are urinals, which you don't have at home. Because things are different from home, you might not want to use the bathrooms at school unless you really need to go.

Some kids with ASD have a hard time with public bathrooms at restaurants, theaters, and other places. Some places have huge bathrooms with rows and rows of stalls. They can be intimidating! You might discover you can't work the lock on the door . . . or the toilet seat is dirty . . . or you can't even locate the flusher to figure out how it works. Then there are all the smells—you know how bad it can get. And what about those portable toilets at parks and playgrounds? Public bathrooms at crowded places can be a real challenge.

Bathroom problems can be hard to talk about, too. We've known kids with ASD who have toileting challenges that go on for a long time. Why? Because the kids kept their problem a secret or didn't realize they could ask an adult for help.

Alisha was very bothered by the loud noises in her school bathroom. The sound of the toilet flushing hurt her ears and echoed everywhere. If she had to poop, she'd get worried because she knew she'd need to be in the bathroom longer. That meant hearing the sounds even more. Instead of going, she'd hold it until she got home, even if she had horrible stomach pain as a result. This made it more difficult to poop later on, because by the time she was ready, it hurt to go.

Samir didn't always realize when he needed to pee. He would get so busy or interested in an activity that he didn't seem to notice when his body was telling him something. That meant he would "leak." At times the leaking went through his pants and the other kids noticed. Sometimes the kids said he smelled like pee. Samir didn't want to be known as the guy who smelled. But he didn't know what to do.

Sophie's problems with coordination made it hard for her to wipe after pooping. Sometimes she used big wads of toilet paper and would accidentally clog the toilet. That scared her. Sometimes she used too little toilet paper and didn't do a good enough job of getting herself clean. She thought it was gross when she got poop on her fingers or underwear by mistake. She didn't want to talk about it, but she needed help.

If you have *any* kind of bathroom problem, don't try to hide it or ignore it. This will only make the problem worse. Something that Alisha, Samir, and Sophie all had in common was that they finally told an adult about their challenges. This meant help was on the way!

Alisha's mom knew about the problems with going to the bathroom at school. Together, they came up with a plan. They talked to the principal and got permission for Alisha to bring her MP3 player to school to use only in the privacy of the bathroom stall. When Alisha had to go to the bathroom, she brought the MP3 player with her and put on the headphones to block out the noise. This helped her relax and made it possible for her to go. What a relief!

Samir and his dad talked about the "leak" problem. They realized it might help if Samir went to the bathroom on a schedule. Then he would be less likely to wait too long to pee. At home, he would use the toilet every hour, even if he didn't feel like he needed to. At school, he followed a routine: He went to the bathroom before his first class started, right before lunch, and after his afternoon gym class. He also brought an extra pair of underwear and pants to keep in his locker in case of an accident. Then he could change his clothes if needed.

Sophie decided to talk to her mom. Her mom understood and made a special point of showing her daughter how much toilet paper was enough, and how much was too much. She told Sophie it was okay to flush after using a couple handfuls of toilet paper, even if she wasn't completely done wiping. After the first flush, she could use more toilet paper as needed, and then flush once again. (They called this a "two-flusher.") Her mom also bought moist wipes to keep by the toilet so Sophie could get herself cleaner. Now Sophie felt more confident.

Bathroom challenges affect a lot of kids with ASD, so you're not alone. If you talk to your mom or dad, your doctor, or your teacher, a plan can be worked out. Some kids have a special bathroom plan at school. For example, the student might only use the bathroom when it's less busy, or an aide might come along to help. Often, there's a different, more private bathroom to use, like in the health office.

If public restrooms are a problem for you, you might look for family restrooms that are set apart from the men's room and women's room. Family bathrooms often have more space so that parents can be in the stall with their kids. These bathrooms might be more private or quiet.

Pee Problems

Many kids—not only those with ASD—have different types of problems when it comes to peeing. Some kids have trouble getting to the bathroom on time. Some forget to go, and then wet their pants. Another common problem is bedwetting, which can happen to kids of any age.

Take a Look!

Some kids with ASD forget that bathroom time is private time. Be sure to shut the door so other people won't see what you're doing in there. Remember to flush, too. (No one really wants to see what you've left behind!)

The first step in dealing with either challenge is going to the doctor to find out if there might be a physical problem. Special tests can be done to find out. If everything is in working order, then the problems might be a result of something else.

Forgetting to Go

The best way to fix this problem is to set up a bathroom schedule for yourself, with help from a parent or doctor. (A schedule also helps if you have poop accidents because you've waited too long to get to a bathroom.)

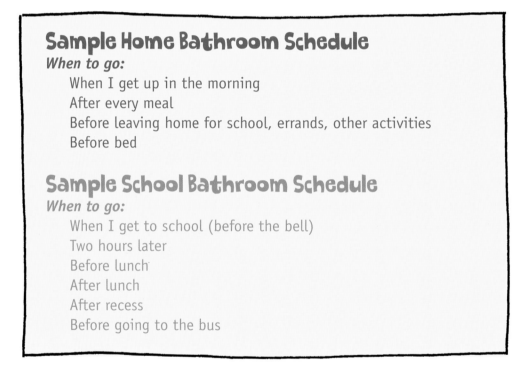

Sample Home Bathroom Schedule
When to go:

- When I get up in the morning
- After every meal
- Before leaving home for school, errands, other activities
- Before bed

Sample School Bathroom Schedule
When to go:

- When I get to school (before the bell)
- Two hours later
- Before lunch
- After lunch
- After recess
- Before going to the bus

For some kids and teens with ASD, the problems with peeing are a result of missing the signals their bodies are sending. Your body "tells" you when you have to pee. You'll notice your bladder feels full, for example, or you'll have a sensation of pressure in that area. Anytime your bladder feels full, listen to that message. STOP what you're doing, even if it's fun or you think you're too busy and can wait. Peeing *as soon as* you feel that urge teaches you to listen closely to your body.

Bedwetting

If you're wetting the bed at night, that's a challenge, too. Bedwetting is more common than you may think. And it can be frustrating. You need to know that you don't wet the bed because you're "lazy," "dumb," or "a baby." Wetting the bed often happens because the connections between someone's brain and body aren't fully working yet. The connections usually work better during the day, when the person is awake. But if the person is sleeping, the signals from the brain to the body "sleep," too! Maybe the person is a heavy sleeper, and sleeps too soundly or deeply to wake up to go to the bathroom. Or maybe the "I need to pee" signal happens, but not quickly enough for the person to wake and get to the toilet in time.

If you sometimes wet the bed or wet it every night, there's help for you. Here's what helps many kids and teens who wet the bed:

Fluid restriction. This means you cut way back on the amount of liquids you drink from late afternoon into the evening. Drinking less at

this time of day means you'll produce less urine at night. Your bladder won't be as full when you go to bed, so you'll be less likely to wet the bed (or less pee will come out if you do). Try not to drink anything at all two hours before bedtime. It's especially good to avoid caffeine (drinks like soda, coffee, or tea), because it makes you have to go more.

Schedules. Set up an evening bathroom schedule so you "go" frequently before bedtime. For example, you might make a point of peeing every hour from the late afternoon until bedtime. If your parents stay up later than you do, you could have them wake you right before they go to sleep. That way, you can get up and pee one last time before you fall into a deep sleep.

Bedwetting alarms. These devices wake you up when you start to pee in your bed. (They're designed to make a noise or a vibration the moment they sense liquid.) The alarm wakes you, which allows you to stop peeing and get to a toilet before wetting the bed completely. After frequent use, the alarm trains your brain to pay closer attention to the signal from your bladder. Alarms usually attach to your pajamas and have a wire that goes to your underpants—if any part of the wire gets wet, the alarm alerts you.

　　Alarms are safe and can be helpful for some people. Ask your doctor for a recommendation. One thing to know ahead of time is that bedwetting alarms can be *very* loud. Some kids with ASD get so scared or upset from the noise that it's hard to go back to sleep afterward. However, many alarms have a vibration setting that can be used instead.

Medications. There are medications that can help stop bedwetting. They require a prescription from a doctor. Some of these medications are taken every night. Others are taken only on nights when they're needed (like if the person has a sleepover or is going camping).

Pee pads. Your dad or mom can buy special pads that absorb urine. One kind goes inside your underwear. Another is made of waterproof material and goes on the bed over the sheets. You can also consider adult diapers or the extra-large size of kids' "pull-ups."

Bedwetting can be embarrassing and frustrating. Here's the good news: Help is available. Your doctor can give you advice, or you and a parent can find books or websites about bedwetting. There's more good news: The problem will lessen as you get older and the connections in your brain get stronger.

Note for Adults

Bedwetting isn't a sign that your child "isn't trying." Kids who wet the bed need help, not anger or disappointment. Even when you're exhausted, try not to yell or make your child feel guilty if you're changing sheets in the middle of the night or every morning. This only makes the situation more frustrating for everyone in the family. Instead, buy several absorbent protective pads for the bed. Use easy-to-wash blankets instead of goose-down comforters or bedding that must be dry-cleaned. It's simpler that way.

Poop Problems

Having bowel movements is just one of those things we all have to do—it's part of life. But for some people, it's a part that's hard to deal with.

Many kids with ASD have difficulty with pooping because it's a sensory activity. There are noises and smells involved, plus internal feelings that are hard for some kids to handle. This can lead to resistance: In other words, you try to avoid pooping or put it off until you absolutely can't wait any longer. This isn't good for your body, though. Your body *has* to get rid of waste to stay healthy.

Here are some ideas that may work for you. But first, talk to a parent about the trouble you're having in the bathroom.

- **Try to keep a schedule.** Poop first thing in the morning or right after breakfast, if you can. (That way you're still at home and can more easily relax.) Eating a meal often signals to your body that it's time to get rid of the waste.

- **Keep yourself hydrated.** This makes it easier to poop. Drink lots of water during the day.

- **Exercise regularly.** Movement helps the poop make its way through your system. The more you move, the more your poop moves!

- **Take your time.** A bowel movement is more likely to occur if you're relaxed. Take a book or a portable music or video player with you into the bathroom and sit for a while.

- **Fix the sensory problems.** If the toilet seat feels too hard or cold, ask your parents to get one made of softer material that stays warmer. Put a portable heater in the bathroom if you get cold sitting with your pants down. If you don't like the smells, then you can use sprays or deodorizers while you "go."

- **Change your diet.** Sometimes, kids with ASD get *constipated* (meaning, it's hard to poop) because their diets are so limited. Maybe they're mostly eating hot dogs, French fries, cheese, and milk—which tend to be constipating. Chapter 21 talks about the importance of eating healthy foods. If you're constipated, your poop might get so big that it's painful to get it out, or you might start having stomach cramps. To avoid this, eat fresh fruits and veggies and drink more water.

If you try these suggestions and still have problems, it's important to talk to a doctor. The doctor will check to make sure everything is working properly. If needed, there are medications you can take to help keep your poop soft and make it easier to have a BM.

The Final Flush

In general, kids with ASD just need more practice when it comes to going to the bathroom. It may sound strange, but toileting is a *skill*—just like other self-care skills such as bathing or brushing your teeth. Give yourself time. Ask your family to be patient with you. Don't be afraid to get help.

Chapter 18

Learning to Relax

"Relax!" "Chill out!" "Take it easy!" Do people ever say that to you? (Like when you seem nervous, upset, or frustrated?) Sure, it would be great if you could instantly relax the moment someone suggests you do so—but *that* probably doesn't happen. Often, hearing you need to relax can make you feel even more stressed out.

Having ASD may mean you're more anxious than the average person. Why? Maybe it's sensory issues (see Chapter 3). Maybe it's because you have trouble in social situations, and that makes you feel nervous. Or, maybe you have more stress hormones floating around in your brain and body. Whatever the reason, the stress is there, and it doesn't go away just because someone *tells* you to relax.

> One thing I don't like about my ASD is I'm more nervous than other people.
>
> —12-year-old boy with autism

This chapter is about *how* to relax. Did you know that relaxation is a skill you can learn? Once you know how to do it, you can use this skill to stay calmer in situations that cause you stress. Here you'll read three ideas to help you develop this skill. Some of the ideas work best at home, and some can be used at school or anywhere.

A Calm-Down Space

At times when you're stressed, scared, angry, or frustrated, it helps to have a place where you can calm down. Think about a place at home where you can go to feel peaceful. Ask a parent to help you design a special place—a Calm-Down Space—just for you. It doesn't have to be fancy to work well.

Your Calm-Down Space can be:

- your bed
- a beanbag or cozy chair
- a cleared space inside your closet
- a blanket-covered table you can fit under
- another comfy spot at home

> I 'crash' on my beanbag in my room. I flop onto it a bunch of times. *Crash-crash.* It helps me feel calmer.
>
> —11-year-old girl with ASD

It's really important to get some help finding this place and making it yours. That way, when you go to your Calm-Down Space, your family will know where you are. You'll be safe there.

How to make your Calm-Down Space comfortable:

- Have a few blankets and pillows handy.
- Keep a music player and headphones there so you can listen to relaxing music, like instrumental jazz or classical.
- Use noise-blocking headphones or ear plugs.
- Turn the lights low or off. (If you can't change the lighting, use sunglasses if you'd like.)
- Have something to hold close, like a stuffed animal, a small pillow, or a body pillow.
- Keep a water bottle handy.
- Have a journal and pencil for writing or drawing.

A Calm-Down Space can be so relaxing you may want to spend all day there. But it's important to allow time for family and friends, too!

What you can do when you need to calm down:

- cry
- yell into a pillow
- flop into the beanbag
- snuggle under the blankets
- write about or draw your feelings

- take a nap
- think, dream, remember, wish, or pray
- try Belly Breathing (described below)

Belly Breathing

It's hard to believe, but something as simple as *breathing* can help you feel less stressed and more in charge of your emotions. Belly Breathing is a special way of controlling how you breathe, so you feel calmer and more relaxed.

You can use this type of breathing when you're upset, worried, or stressed. It's a tool to help you calm down and get a handle on your emotions before they spin out of control.

Belly Breathing does three great things:

1. It calms your nerves.

2. It relaxes your muscles.

3. It helps release *endorphins*, or chemicals that reduce pain, increase energy, and help you feel positive and happy.

Take a Look!

Sometimes, kids with ASD leave their home seeking a quiet place to help them settle down when they're upset. That's really scary for the family, because they know their loved one could get lost or hurt. Other times, kids might hide somewhere inside the home, yard, or car to get a little peace and quiet—and then not realize that the family is looking everywhere for them. **Make sure your Calm-Down Space is a place everyone at home knows about.** Use it when you need to. Let your family know that you like to be alone there, and when you're ready to come out and talk, you will.

Here's how to Belly Breathe:

- Use your imagination to pretend you have a balloon in your belly.
- Put one hand on top of your belly.
- Breathe in *slowly* through your nose. As you do this, count to three, pausing in between each number (1, *pause*, 2, *pause*, 3). Feel the imaginary balloon filling with air.
- Breathe out *slowly* through your mouth. Count to five, pausing between each number. Imagine that the balloon is getting flat. Imagine your bad feelings leaving your body as you breathe out.
- Repeat the Belly Breathing several times. Notice your muscles relaxing as you do. *Ahhhhh . . .*

Belly Breathing is even more relaxing and fun if you have a little something extra to help you—especially when you're learning to do it. For example, you can use a colorful pinwheel that turns as you breathe on it. (You can find pinwheels at a dollar store or drugstore.) Or, you can get a small container of bubble stuff and blow through the wand as you breathe out. Watch the bubbles peacefully drift through the air.

A Relaxation Exercise

Sometimes, you might want to do a longer relaxation exercise that helps clear your mind and calm your body. Use the following one any time you want to relax from head to toe.

Ask a parent or another trusted adult to read each of the steps as you do them. After you've done the sequence many times, you'll probably have it memorized and can do it on your own.

1. Find a quiet place (if possible, do this outside because the fresh air feels great).
2. Lie down on the grass (or floor, if you're indoors) and get comfortable.
3. Close your eyes, but don't fall asleep.

4. Breathe deeply, focusing on your breath going in and out. Count to five as you breathe in, and count backward from five as you breathe out. Take your time. Pause between each number so the counting doesn't go too fast.

5. When you feel calmer, continue breathing deeply. This time say the word *relax* as you breathe in and out.

6. In time with your breathing, begin to relax your muscles from head to toe. Start with your forehead. Tense those muscles as you inhale. Then relax them as you exhale.

7. Continue tensing and relaxing your muscles, moving downward from your head to your neck and shoulders, to your arms, stomach, legs, and feet.

8. When you've reached your toes, tense and relax them. Then take a rest. Keep breathing deeply.

9. Slowly open your eyes. You are now relaxed.

10. Enjoy this feeling!

Don't wait until you're stressed to learn the techniques in this chapter. Practice them at home when you have time and when an adult can help guide you. Then, once you know how to do Belly Breathing and deep breathing, you can use these tools whenever you're angry, scared, nervous, or upset. If you have an OT (occupational therapist) he or she can show you other ways to calm down and relax. You may also want to learn yoga, a form of exercise that involves stretching and paying special attention to the breath.

Chapter 19

Is There Medicine for ASD?

Doctors and other experts believe that autism is a medical condition. Many medical conditions have cures or treatments. But how about ASDs?

Today there is no proven cure for autism. But there *are* treatments that can make a positive difference in your life.

Maybe you're already doing therapy treatments to help improve how you communicate and get along with others. Your therapies might take place at home, school, or a special therapy center that helps people who have disabilities. Many families work hard to find treatments to help relieve the symptoms of ASD and make life better. You're probably working hard yourself, trying to gain new skills.

In the search for ways to help, your family might see a doctor who suggests a medication that focuses on (targets) certain symptoms. Only a medical professional, usually a doctor, can prescribe (order the use of) medication. Most likely, the doctor will ask a lot of questions about you: Do you sleep well at night? Is it easy or difficult for you to pay attention in school? Do you have a lot of stress or worries? How do you handle them? Do you have trouble managing anger? The doctor's job is to get information about your physical and mental health. This helps him or her better understand you and how medication ("meds" for short) might help.

If you need a medication, or if your family agrees that it's time to try one, you might be confused and worried at first. You might wonder what the medication looks like and how it will make you feel. Your doctor can answer these questions, so be sure to ask (or have a parent or caregiver ask with you).

Usually, meds come in a pill or capsule you swallow or crush, or a liquid you drink. But some even come in the form of a bandage you wear. Some people take a medication once a day, while others take it several times a day. In some cases, more than one type of medication may be prescribed.

Getting Medication: Three Important Steps

Step 1: Deciding which symptom to target

Remember back in Chapter 1, where you learned the symptoms of autism? You read that differences in your brain make it more difficult for you to communicate, be social, and have a wide variety of interests. ASD also affects your senses: sight, smell, hearing, touch, taste, and more. Does this mean you can take a medication to make you "talk better" or find more friends? Nope, it doesn't work that way. The symptoms that medications target are much more specific.

This is why a doctor has to ask a lot of questions before helping your family decide if medication may be an option for you. Most medications prescribed for ASDs will focus on treating particular kinds of ASD symptoms. These are the four categories of symptoms:

1. **Attention and focus.** Some kids on the spectrum have trouble sitting still, getting organized, or paying attention. They might do things too quickly without thinking first.

2. **Worries and repetitive thoughts.** This category includes having trouble being alone, or feeling nervous or anxious when making changes or being in new places. Kids with these kinds of symptoms might do the same thing over and over or ask things again and again.

3. **Being too aggressive.** Lots of arguing, yelling, and hitting are *aggressive* behaviors. Kids with problems in this area might also cry uncontrollably or hit or scratch themselves when they're scared or upset.

4. **Sleep issues.** Some young people with autism spectrum disorders have trouble getting to sleep at night. Or they may wake up in the night or too early in the morning.

Each type of symptom calls for a different kind of medicine. You, your parents, your teachers, and all your other helpers play a role in thinking about symptoms to target. You can start by making a list of things you struggle with on a daily basis. A parent can note what gives you trouble at home. Your teachers can offer

Take a Look!
This chapter talks about medication and the role it may play in ASDs. The chapter isn't suggesting you *should* or *should not* use medication. That decision is up to your family, with input from your doctor and other helpers.

suggestions for what might help you do better in school. Once your doctor has all this information, he or she can see if the symptoms you most need help with match the list on page 184.

Step 2: Discussing meds and possible side effects

The second step is to talk with your doctor about which medications might help your symptoms. You'll also learn what, if any, *side effects* you might experience. Side effects are the unexpected or unintended results of taking a medication. For example, you may take a medication to help you sleep, but then discover it also gives you headaches. Some side effects are mild, but others aren't. Some are temporary, while others last as long as you take the medication. You and your family can talk with the doctor about any questions or concerns you have.

Your doctor will choose from different medications that may target the same symptom. He or she will look at the possible side effects of each one, the dose to take, and the cost. With some medications, it's first necessary to have medical tests to examine your blood or your heart. You may need to go back for further testing while on the medication.

For some people with ASD, other health conditions might be important, too. If you're already on medication for any reason, your family needs to report this to any other doctor you see. Then the doctor can make sure *not* to prescribe medications that might not work well with one you're already on.

Step 3: Tracking whether the symptoms improve for you

Follow-up is an important part of taking a new medication. Your doctor—and you and your family—will want to be sure the medication is making a positive difference in your life. It helps if your parent or caregiver keeps a daily log of any changes you experience. Bring the log each time you see the doctor. Show the doctor records of:

- when you started the meds
- what time of day you take them
- any times you've missed taking them
- what improvements you've noticed

- any side effects you may have
- if the side effects are mild or severe, and how long they last

If you have side effects, your doctor may try these different ways of getting rid of them:

- changing the medication
- adjusting the dose
- changing the time of day you take the medication
- asking you to take the medication with food

Your doctor will require you to come back for another appointment. There, you and your family can discuss whether it's a good idea to stay on the medication, try another, or stop medication altogether.

Keep Communicating

Finding a medication can be a long process—a long process that not every family chooses to go through. Your family gets to decide what's best for you.

If you do take medications, *communication* is a very important part of the process. Let your family know how your meds make you feel physically. Are there any side effects, for example? Then your family can tell your doctor what's working and what isn't.

Most of all, be sure to follow the medication instructions your doctor gives you. Go to your appointments, too. Together, you, your family, and your doctor can track your progress and figure out what's most helpful to you.

Vicki's Story

Vicki is 8 and has Asperger's. She has *lots* of friends, energy, and interests. Sometimes she feels like her head is going to explode with ideas.

When she's supposed to be doing math, Vicki might be thinking of her favorite hobby: trading wristbands. She has over 200 wristbands. She likes to organize them every night and put some in her backpack for school the next day. She sometimes gets in trouble at school because she can't get her mind off her wristbands.

Vicki's teacher says Vicki talks too much in class, interrupts, and has trouble staying on task. Vicki, her dad, and her teacher meet with the school psychologist to talk about this. Together, they decide it would be a good idea to ask a doctor about medication.

After a few meetings, the doctor prescribes a medication for Vicki that helps with focus and attention. Vicki learns that she might have side effects, like trouble sleeping or changes in her appetite. The doctor also explains that Vicki should tell her dad if she notices any "funny feelings," like not being hungry or getting nervous and upset.

Vicki starts the medication. On the very first day she notices a difference. She can pay attention more easily. She doesn't talk as much. She can wait her turn, and she patiently raises her hand in class instead of interrupting. Her teacher calls Vicki's dad to share the good news.

Vicki likes feeling happy and focused in school. But the hours after school are terrible for her! The medication gradually leaves her system during the day, and then Vicki feels crabby. At home at night, she yells at her sister, cries, and doesn't even want to play with her wristbands.

Her dad calls the doctor about these side effects. Over the next few weeks, Vicki's doctor keeps changing the medication. The dose goes up. It goes down. Sometimes Vicki has to take one pill; other times, two. She starts to feel like a yo-yo—up and down, up and down.

After weeks of adjusting the dose, Vicki's family decides meds aren't the answer. It's more important that Vicki feels good *all* day long, even if it means she has difficulty paying attention in school.

Now Vicki feels like herself again. She knows she has to work harder to focus, but she's trying. And she's decided, with her dad's support, that when she's older she might want to try medication again.

Jamal's Story

Jamal collects, organizes, sorts, counts—and sometimes he can't stop. He likes things to be the same . . . every day.

Today, his mom says they need to go buy him a new pair of shoes. Jamal hates the idea. He runs and hides in his closet. He thinks, "I don't need new shoes! New shoes are always too tight or too loose!"

Outside the closet door, Jamal's mom tries to reassure him. She says new shoes will be great. She even promises to get him a Lego set if he cooperates.

Hmmm, Jamal thinks, *I love Legos. Maybe I should go.* But he can't stand new shoes and doesn't want to have to try them on. Jamal stays in the closet, and finally his mom gives up.

It's not just shoes that are a problem. Jamal's mom has a hard time getting him to do lots of things, even coming to the table at dinner-time. He doesn't like to stop what he's already doing, especially if it's something fun like building with his construction kit.

Jamal and his mom know he has autism. But Jamal's mom feels it's important for him to try new things and not get "stuck" so often. She tells him they're going to the doctor to get some help.

Jamal's doctor knows him well. He understands that Jamal prefers "sameness" and has a hard time moving from one activity to the next. Jamal practices being flexible, but it's getting harder for him to do. The doctor suggests a medication that might help Jamal be less rigid in his thinking and learn to accept change. Jamal thinks, *Whoever heard of a medicine that helps with shoes and coming to dinner on time?* But he says he's willing to try it, because he knows he needs help.

He takes this new medication every day, just like his doctor said to do. Jamal and his mom watch for side effects, like trouble sleeping or feeling restless. So far, so good.

One night a few weeks later, Jamal is organizing his Lego collection, thinking about all the awesome things he can build. "Jamal, dinner!" his mom calls.

Jamal runs downstairs, hungry. Then he notices the strange look on his mom's face. For a moment, he's confused. Then his mom smiles. "Jamal, you came right to the table without any fuss!" Jamal smiles back at her, proud of himself.

After dinner, Mom says, "Maybe tomorrow we can buy new shoes?"

"I'll think about it," Jamal answers. And he wonders to himself, *Maybe the medication is helping?*

Chapter 20

Move Your Body

So far, you've learned a lot about autism spectrum disorders and how they can affect your brain and body. You're probably starting to better understand your own ASD and how you can manage it, with support from your team of helpers. You've also discovered that you have a few things to handle on a daily basis: your symptoms and sensory issues, for example. Guess what can help you better manage both?

Exercise!

Regular physical activity will help you build a stronger, healthier you. You'll get fitter and feel better—and that's just for starters. Studies show that kids who exercise have stronger muscles, bones, hearts,

lungs, and vital organs. Plus, they get better sleep and better grades. Besides keeping your body in good shape, exercise can help you burn off extra energy or cope with stress. If you start now, healthy exercise habits (and their benefits) can last a lifetime.

Get Active!

The National Association for Sport and Physical Education (NASPE) says that school-age children should get 60 minutes or more of physical activity per day. If you want, you can break up the minutes. For example, you could do four sessions of activity for 15 minutes, or do two sessions lasting 30 minutes. Activities include anything that gets your heart beating faster, or that stretches and strengthens your muscles.

play outside

go for a run, jog, or hike

go to the park or playground

shoot hoops or toss a ball against a wall

take a long walk with your family

learn to do yoga or simple stretches

swim at a community center

play tag or other neighborhood games

run races with your friends

bounce on a trampoline

ride a bike or scooter

make up crazy dances

Use a Wii or Xbox to exercise your whole body—not just your fingers!

What about trying out for a sport or joining a team? Many young people with ASD tend not to be great at team sports. Maybe you happen to be a proud athlete and member of a sports team—if you are, way to go! But if you aren't, that's okay. Team sports may not be your thing. Team sports can be difficult because there's a social aspect to team play. You need to read your teammates' body language. You have to be able to predict what they might do next on the field or court, or what they need *you* to do. Team sports are often loud, too. Team sports also call for coordination. Many people with ASD have difficulty moving their bodies in a coordinated way.

Imagine all the steps a baseball pitcher takes to wind up for a pitch: He puts his arms over his head, starts his pitching motion, and turns his body while one arm goes back and around. His opposite foot then strides toward the plate, and he throws the ball forward. Then he quickly gets back into position, ready to field the ball if it's hit. Pitchers do all these steps so smoothly that fans who are watching hardly notice all that's really involved.

If you were doing the pitching, you might have to stop and think about each movement: What your legs must do. Where your right arm should be. Where your left arm needs to go. Where to focus your eyes. How to hold the ball, how to let go, and where to aim. And so on. If your brain has trouble planning the order of the movements, then your body doesn't act on them as quickly or smoothly.

If coordination is a problem for you, you might think of yourself as "clumsy." But it's really an issue of needing extra help, time, and practice. You have to train your brain and body more than the average person—but it *can* be done. Ask a parent, older sibling, or buddy to help you practice swinging a baseball bat, tossing a football, or working on lay-ups at the basketball court. These are great ways to build your strength and get the physical exercise you need.

If you want to play team sports, you can practice the coordination skills your sport needs. It might also be helpful to work on "reading" other people's body language and making eye contact. You can learn more about these communication skills on pages 80–89.

Many kids with ASD prefer solo sports like swimming, tennis, archery, rock climbing, golf, karate, track and field, dance, gymnastics, or tai chi. These sports involve seeing and interacting with other kids, too. But your performance is "just yours" and you can work at your own pace. Baseball and softball are often good "compromise" activities. This is because even though they're considered team sports, the focus is mainly on the individual performance of each player.

> To me, [basketball is] the perfect sport for someone who's autistic, because there are all these drills you can do by yourself. You can shoot hoops in your backyard all day long. You can practice your dribble. Whatever you want to work on, you can just work on it and work on it.
>
> —Jason McElwain, from his book *The Game of My Life: A True Story of Challenge, Triumph, and Growing Up Autistic*

To get involved in athletics, see what your school has to offer. Ask your dad or mom to help you find community sports opportunities. Maybe there's a sports program just for kids with special needs. You can also look for a local center for people with disabilities, where you can use a special pool, track, or other equipment. Some communities offer horseback riding therapy for children with ASD or other disabilities.

Looking for more options? Join the YMCA or YWCA. Go to your community's recreation center several times a week. Take lessons (tap dance, martial arts, whatever!). Run around during recess. Participate in gym class at school. Spend lots of time outdoors. Ask neighbors or classmates to join you on bike rides. Or invite them to go on a walk with you and your dog or play a game of catch. When you're busy doing a physical activity together, conversation is usually less important. This makes things easier if talking and listening are difficult for you.

If motor skills and physical coordination are an issue for you, you may find it helpful to try physical therapy (PT) or occupational therapy (OT). Read more about them on page 49. Both types of therapy are great for improving balance and strengthening the core muscles of your body.

Want to make exercise a part of your daily routine? Try these ideas:

- Make it a rule for yourself. This is especially helpful if you find that life is easier when there are guidelines to follow.
- Put it on your daily schedule, your calendar, or your to-do list each day.
- Give yourself a fun reward afterward, like extra time on your favorite hobby.
- Think of physical activity as something that helps you feel good.

Bonus: Exercise can be a social activity. You'll meet new people if you join a team or take lessons. You can find other kids to hang out with at the community center. If you go to a playground, you're sure to find other kids there, too. It's fun to exercise with others. Try it!

Take a Look!

No matter where you are on the autism spectrum, it's important for you to get some exercise. Don't make excuses like "I hate sports" or "I'm no good." Physical activity releases feel-good chemicals called *endorphins* in your brain and body. Exercise also lessens stress, which is especially important for kids with ASD.

Gretchen's Story

Gretchen is 10 and has Asperger's syndrome. Her older brother Ian is a good downhill skier. Gretchen doesn't ski, but she thinks it looks *so* fun. Her family lives in a state where it snows a lot, and winter sports are a big deal. She's tried skiing before, but it was complicated. First, she had to put on a helmet. It felt heavy and kind of tight. Then there were ski goggles to wear—also tight. Gretchen found it hard to keep the skis pointing straight and to hang onto the poles. The squeaky sound of the snow under the skis made her nervous, too. But the scariest thing was the chair lift. Gretchen just couldn't get on it. The chair was so high, and it kept moving. She watched as the chairs swung around and picked people up, carrying them to the top of the hill. They dangled so high in the air! It looked way too dangerous.

So Gretchen decided not to ski, at least for a while. Instead, when her dad and brother ski, she likes to look out the window of the building where people warm up. One day as she does this, she takes a closer look at the chair lift. It's made of tall poles, heavy chains, and turning wheels. Gretchen likes to count, so she starts counting the wheels and the poles. Soon her dad comes to check on her. Gretchen says, "The pulleys and poles work together to get the skiers up the hill." Her dad smiles, and then he says, "If you ride on the lift with me, we can see if you're right." But Gretchen isn't ready for that.

At home later that night, her mom notices that Gretchen seems to have something on her mind. "What's up, Gretchen?"

"I want to ride the chair lift, but I'm scared," Gretchen tells her. "I want to ski, but it's too hard."

Ian and Dad join the conversation. Everyone's excited that Gretchen wants to ski, because they know it's something the whole family could do together. Their dream is to take a trip to the mountains and stay at a ski lodge. There they would spend long days skiing and having fun as a family. Gretchen likes that idea a lot.

Together, the whole family makes a plan: Gretchen can get used to skiing very slowly. She'll start by wearing her brother's helmet and goggles around the house. Then she can take her time getting used to skis. Finally, she can practice riding the ski lift with her dad.

And that's exactly what happens. For a little while each day, Gretchen sits indoors with the helmet and goggles on. She knows she looks funny, but it's all for the ski trip! After a few weeks, she learns to get the skis off and on and walk around with them in the snowy back-yard. This takes some coordination, but Gretchen doesn't give up.

Now, she's feeling ready, but she's still scared. She and her dad are at the ski hill. Gretchen has on a helmet, goggles, skis, and a ski jacket like Ian's. The chair lift looms before them. Gretchen's dad talks to the man running the lift. He agrees to slow it down so Gretchen can get on more easily. She holds her dad's hand tight. Here comes the chair . . .

In a flash, she and her dad are on the chair lift. Gretchen closes her eyes and hangs on tight. She's doing it! She's riding through the air like all the other skiers. It's not long before her dad says, "Gretchen, we're at the top—let's get off."

It all happens really fast. Her skis hit the ground, she slides down a little hill, and then she falls on her butt, laughing. She's *at the top*—she can practically see the whole world! Gretchen is *so* proud of herself. She can't wait to tell Mom and Ian about her ride up the hill.

Now all she has to do is go *down* the hill. She thinks she's ready!

Check Your "Engine"

Imagine for a moment that your body is a car. The engine is what keeps it running. It's time to check that engine of yours. Does it often run too fast or too slow? For example, are there times when you're expected to be calm and quiet (like in the library), but you're zooming around like it's NASCAR? Or, are there times when everyone around you seems to be talking loudly and having tons of fun, and all you want to do is park yourself in a quiet corner?

Sometimes, it probably feels as if your engine speed doesn't match the "driving conditions" around you. At times, your engine may be out of control, out of rhythm, or out of gas. Want to know what can help?

There are things you can do to rev up your engine or bring it down to a nice purr. The chart on page 198 explains more about "checking your engine" and giving it what it needs. This chart includes ideas that many OTs and PTs use during their sessions with kids. You and your parents can pull out the chart whenever you need an engine check. Make photocopies, if you'd like.

How to "Speed Up" or "Slow Down"

The day goes more smoothly when your engine speed fits what the situation demands of you. For example, you might be at a "60" just before gym class at school—perfect timing! When you head back to class afterward, you might be at a "40" and ready to learn. Late in the day, sitting on the school bus, you might be at a "20," which helps you stay calm on the ride home—*ahhhh.*

What if you're still at "20" when you get home from school, and your mom expects you to start your homework? Roadside emergency service needed! Better get the chart and show your mom how you feel.

Or, what if you're at "80" when you get to school the next morning? This makes it hard to settle down and focus. You need ideas for putting on the brakes.

There are lots of ways to slow down your engine or rev it up, depending on what speed you need. Here are some tips to help you get in the right gear.

Move around (a lot). Maybe you need to bounce, run, jog, spin, tumble, or climb. Jump on a trampoline or an old couch (ask permission first), play tug-of-war with a friend, or go to a park. If you have to stay indoors, climb up and down stairs. Even chores can help you get physical: rake leaves or sweep the floor.

Move around (a little). If you're in class and have the urge to move, stand up if you can. Take a bathroom break so you can walk down the hall, or maybe get a drink of water. Just ask your teacher first. Maybe your IEP (see page 138) allows you to take breaks during school in a quiet place. Use those breaks to move your body so you feel better.

Some classrooms have ball chairs you can sit and gently bounce on. Others have sensory areas you can use during breaks (if you have permission). If moving around isn't possible, you could go out in the hall to briefly stretch your neck, shoulders, arms, and legs.

Check Your Engine

Your Engine Speed		How do you feel at this speed?
80: Too fast, out of control (you might crash!)		You might feel disorganized, angry, or scared. You may want to run or fight, or to tune out and shut down. Your behavior might get too wild. Or you might feel like you can't deal with anyone or anything for a while. This is a good time for a break.
60: High energy		You might feel excited, energetic, and ready for a challenge. This is a good time to do some physical activity.
40: Running smooth, humming and purring		You might feel confident, happy, and tuned in. This is a good time for some mental activity, like learning.
20: Running slow but still chugging along		You may not feel you're at your best, but you're getting somewhere—slowly. This is a good time for quiet activities, where people won't expect a lot out of you. If you still have homework or chores to do, you could try a little exercise so your engine speeds up again. (Aim for "40"—"80" is too fast.)
0: Running too slow— you need a little push		You might feel bored or sad. It may be hard to do what a teacher, parent, or therapist tells you to. This is a good time to ask for some help and support.

Do "resistance work." You can work your muscles through *resistance.* How? Push your arms against a wall. Or pull something (like a rolling backpack). Carry some heavy books. Jump up and down, or roll around in the grass or on the floor.

When you don't have much room to move around, try palm presses: Interlock your fingers and press your palms together, with your elbows up and out at shoulder level.

Resistance activities like these help your body feel more organized and get your engine numbers up or down.

Find your rhythm. Many people with autism or Asperger's find that rhythmic body movements calm them and help block out noise and activity. Maybe you rock back and forth or flap your hands and arms for this purpose. Sometimes, you might pace when you're anxious or bored. If pacing, rocking, or flapping are things your school or family are comfortable with, they can help you steady your engine.

Some teachers and families will want you to find other ways to get that soothing feeling. Here are some examples of different things that may relax and calm you: swinging, bouncing on a workout ball, rocking in a rocking chair, dancing, or swinging back and forth on a hammock. Some families get mini trampolines for year-round use. Others get an indoor swing that can be safely hung from the ceiling.

Keep your hands busy. If you feel bored or fidgety, it helps to do something with your hands. For example, doodle, draw, or play with clay or a stress ball. If you need something that won't draw much attention, carry a straw, twist tie, or paper clip in your pocket. You can bend and twist it in your pocket or pull it out and bend it in your hands.

Keep your mouth busy. Sometimes, you might feel like you need to eat a crunchy food, suck on ice cubes or hard candies, or chew something chewy. Doing something with your mouth can help your brain focus. At home, chew sugarless bubblegum. At school, see if you can chew gum during times when you need to wake up or keep your mouth busy. Keep a water bottle at your desk so you always have something to drink. You can talk more about this with your OT at school or at a therapy center. OTs usually have lots of great ideas for helping kids with sensory issues that have to do with the mouth.

Check your ears. Sometimes, you might feel too revved up by the amount of noise around you. Loud noises might startle you. And they might leave you feeling jumpy long after the sound has passed. At other times, even everyday background noises (like the TV, other people's voices, or a ticking clock) might bother you a lot.

It's helpful to keep a pair of ear muffs or ear plugs handy. If you're in the car or on the bus, use headphones to listen to soothing music. Or, choose a CD of rhythmic sounds such as ocean waves or falling rain.

Go someplace quiet. Chapter 18 talks about creating a Calm-Down Space at home—a place where you can go for some peace and quiet when you feel wound up. Keep soothing items there, like blankets and pillows, so you have what you need to feel cozy.

Relax. Even though school and therapy help you succeed in life, they can be tiring, and sometimes it's just hard to keep going. At times like these, a break is essential. After a long, *active* day, you can:

Take a warm bath or hot shower.

Get a hug from someone you love.

Take a nap.

Hold someone's hand.

Curl up with a good book.

Turn off the overhead lights, or put on an eye mask for a while.

Ask a family member to rub your feet or lightly tickle your back.

Snuggle up with your cat, or pet your dog.

Watch your fish swim around and around in their tank.

Chapter 21

Feed Your Body

If you read Chapter 20, you've already learned how to take care of your "engine." Now it's time to check your fuel supply. Your engine's fuel isn't gasoline—it's *food*. The human body needs food to survive. Normal body functions like digestion and breathing rely on energy from food. Food contains essential *nutrients* that get absorbed by your bloodstream. There they are changed into blood sugar and delivered to your cells.

What are nutrients? They're the parts of food that provide your body with the fuel it needs to run. They include vitamins, minerals, proteins, complex carbohydrates, and *good* fats and oils. (Bad fats and oils are the ones found in snack foods and sweets.)

A good diet keeps you healthy and strong—but it also helps you better manage the symptoms of your ASD. Why? Because ASD affects your brain. Think of your brain as a hungry part of your body. It craves nutrients! It needs them to function in the best way it can.

Getting Enough Nutrients

Different nutrients do different jobs in your brain:

Vitamins. They're found in fruits, veggies, juices and milk, tofu, and enriched breakfast cereals, and in the form of supplements.

What they do:

- Keep your brain cells alive and healthy.
- Keep your brain cells "awake" so you're alert and thinking clearly.
- Boost your mood.

Minerals. They're found in fruits, veggies, juices and milk, nuts, meat, fish, and enriched grains, and in the form of supplements.

What they do:

- Help your brain send messages back and forth.
- Act as "bursts of energy" that help different parts of your brain communicate.

Proteins. They're found in eggs, meat, fish, nuts and seeds, veggies, tofu, soy, whole-grain foods, nut butters, milk, and other dairy products such as yogurt and cheese.

What they do:

- Build muscles.
- Become protein "messengers" inside your brain and body.

Good **fats and oils.** They're found in raw fruits and veggies, eggs, nuts and seeds, fish (especially salmon), olive oil, and grapeseed oil. Some good fats—like fish oil—are available as supplements.

What they do:

- Keep the walls of your brain cells healthy and flexible.
- Keep your nerves healthy.
- Boost your mood.

Take a Look!

Bad fats and oils—the ones found in French fries, potato chips, corn chips, deep-fried foods, donuts, brownies, cookies, and many kinds of candy—aren't good for your body or your brain. Try to limit these kinds of foods. They clog your engine!

Complex carbohydrates. Your body also needs the nutrients found in complex carbohydrates, like breads, whole-wheat pasta (noodles), brown rice, and cereal.

Dealing with Food Sensitivities

Some parents of kids with ASD have reported that their children have sensitivities (reactions) to *gluten*. Gluten is found in products containing wheat, oats, barley, and other grains. Sensitivity to gluten can create problems with digestion and behavior. For this reason, these families may decide to go gluten-free. They carefully choose foods and drinks that don't contain any gluten at all, even trace amounts.

You still need to eat complex carbohydrates, even if you're on a gluten-free diet. Many grocery stores and special bakeries offer gluten-free breads, pizza crusts, bagels, muffins, and waffles. You can also find tasty pasta made from brown rice, corn, or potatoes.

Some families with children who have ASD also choose to go dairy-free. They have found that their kids do better if milk from cows is removed from their diet. So, products from dairy cows—like milk, butter, cheese, yogurt, and ice cream—are no longer allowed. All sorts of replacement products are available, though. For example, you can find milk made from soy, brown rice, or almonds. Dairy-free margarine is a good substitute for butter. Cheese and yogurt can be made from goat's milk or soy. If your regular grocery store doesn't carry these items, you can go to natural foods stores or order special foods online. It's essential to take calcium supplements if you go dairy-free because calcium helps build your bones.

Just because you have ASD doesn't mean you automatically have food sensitivities. And it doesn't mean you will do better if you're gluten- or dairy-free. But if you have ongoing problems with your digestion and seem to react to certain foods, your family can explore special diets as an option. Just be sure your doctor plays a role. You may want to see an allergy specialist or a dietician, too.

Avoiding Dyes, Chemicals, and Sweeteners

Even if you don't go gluten- or dairy-free, it's important to watch your diet for foods and drinks that affect how you feel. Many kids with special needs react badly to foods with dyes that turn the food bright colors. The same is often true with foods containing chemicals called *preservatives* that help keep them fresh on the shelf or in the fridge. You should also avoid foods and drinks that use artificial sweeteners like the ones found in soda, sports drinks, and candy. Try to stay away from sugary treats and caffeine (found in coffee and cola drinks), because you'll probably feel jumpy and out of sorts.

What can you have instead? When you're in the mood for something sweet, try foods sweetened with honey, brown sugar, molasses, or stevia. Instead of soda, drink some fruit juice (not the kind sweetened with corn syrup). You can still bake cookies and other treats, even if they aren't made with gluten or dairy.

Choosing Healthy Foods Every Day

Changing your diet will mean making different choices at the school cafeteria. You might bring a lunch from home each day. If you're at a relative's home or visiting a friend, you'll probably need to take along your own snacks, too. Then you'll be sure to

Take a Look!

Your doctor may tell you it's a good idea to take a multivitamin every day—one made especially for kids or teens (depending on your age). This will help ensure you get the nutrients you need. Vitamins come in all shapes, sizes, and flavors. You can find them in the form of a pill you chew (hard or soft), a pill you swallow, a liquid, or a powder you mix into foods or drinks. Try different ones to see what you like (but avoid ones with added dyes and chemicals).You can also ask about adding omega-3 fatty acids in the form of a "fish oil" pill, if you'd like. Experts believe that essential fatty acids help in brain development and overall health.

have something you can eat. If people ask why you eat the way you do, you can say, "I have sensitivities to certain foods." These days many kids have food allergies and sensitivities, so it's often no big deal to eat differently.

Choosing healthy foods is something your whole family can work on together. You can learn about the importance of:

- eating lots of fruits and veggies each day
- choosing healthy proteins and whole grains (found in whole-grain breads and cereals)
- avoiding too many packaged and "processed" foods (they have added chemicals)
- drinking lots of water to stay hydrated
- buying as many organic or fresh foods as possible
- consuming fewer foods that are high in fats, sugars, and sodium (salt)

In the end, you may find that a diet rich in fruits, vegetables, good proteins, and fresh ingredients helps you feel better overall. Your engine will run more smoothly and efficiently, and you'll be healthier!

What If You're a Choosy Eater?

Many kids who have ASD are *very* choosy about food . . . so choosy that they're often called "picky eaters."

Bella knows when her family's having pot roast for dinner. *Yuck*—the smell! The meat will be hard to chew, and there will be all those different vegetables swimming in the juices. She hates the smell *and* the taste. But she knows the rules. She has to take at least one bite of each food. Her parents stick to this rule because they're sure that someday Bella will learn to like new tastes and textures. So she does it—one bite of each. Then she's off to the fridge, where she finds her favorite food of all, mashed potatoes. She puts them in the microwave, and *beep,* they're ready! She sits at the table again, pleased she gets to make some choices about what she eats, even if it means following the rule about "one bite."

Danny loves all things salty. His favorite foods are French fries and potato chips. He would eat salty foods all day long, if only he was allowed. To him, one of the best parts of sharing a big bowl of popcorn with his family is licking all the salt off his fingers afterward. His parents have to watch to make sure Danny doesn't sneak salty foods when they're not looking.

Tameka has been having a hard time at lunch. The school cafeteria is always noisy and busy, and Tameka hates most of the foods that are served. She doesn't like crunchy foods or foods that smell too strong. This limits her choices. But now things are better: The school has agreed to let Tameka eat lunch in the special education room with her teacher. Tameka brings her lunch. She has whole-wheat macaroni and cheese along with peas that her grandma cooks just right for her. Her teacher heats up her lunch in the microwave. Now she can look forward to eating her favorite food in peace and quiet.

Breakfast is such a bother for **Levi.** He's supposed to be at the bus stop at 7:30, but he's hardly ever ready on time. The trouble is that it's really hard to get ready in the morning *and* eat breakfast, too. Levi can't finish his cereal, and it's hard to try to sneak a piece of fruit on the bus. Levi's mom is worried he won't have enough energy if he doesn't eat breakfast. So she gives him a protein drink in a covered mug with a little opening in the lid. He gets special permission to drink this on the bus. Now he'll arrive at school fueled up and ready to learn.

Like Bella, Danny, Tameka, and Levi, maybe you're particular about what you eat and drink. Sensory issues are at the root of many problems with food. Usually what happens is something like this: You hate the texture (the way something feels) of certain foods in your mouth. You start gagging, or maybe even throw up a little. You remember that reaction. Then, the next time you see or smell the same food, you don't want it anywhere near your mouth! So, understandably, you refuse to eat it. Pretty soon, you resist *other* foods that remind you of the one you hated. That means whole categories of food are sometimes eliminated—no "mushy," no "hot," no "citrus," no "green."

If you're a picky eater, you know it's hard to learn to like things that seem horrible. Believe it or not, though, some food issues can be overcome. Learning to eat different things happens slowly. With lots of practice and patience, kids can learn to eat a wider variety of food—and enjoy it. Really!

How can you make that happen? Keep trying new foods, even if you're scared, disgusted, or convinced you can't do it. You *can* do it. Make it a goal to try one new food each week. If you hate it, okay . . . but don't cross that food off your list forever. A few months later, give that food another try, because you might decide you like it.

Your tastes change as you grow older, which means you'll learn to like more foods as time goes on. The same goes for sensitivities to textures. Over time, they tend to lessen, and that means you'll be able to try more things. An occupational therapist (OT) can help in this area.

However, your *family* is your greatest asset when it comes to changing how you eat. With their support and encouragement, you can make big or small adjustments to your diet. Keep trying and don't give up.

Chapter 22

Keeping It Clean (with Hygiene)

This chapter talks about the things that people often *don't* want to talk about. Embarrassing things, like how to stay fresh and clean. For example, you'll learn some basics about showers and baths, hair care, and hand washing. (All of that is part of hygiene.) But there's something else that's hard to talk about: the idea of looking like you're part of the crowd.

We hope you know that what's *inside* a person counts for way more than what's on the outside. Individuality is a great thing! In a perfect world, people would be accepted for who they are, no matter how they look or what they wear.

But the reality is that people *do* form opinions of you based on how you look. (It's not fair, but it's true.) Looking neat and clean can help you get along better with others. So can wearing clothes and shoes that are similar to what other kids your age wear. You don't have to spend a bunch of money on fashion, or dress in clothes you hate. It's a matter of finding what fits, feels comfortable, and "fits in."

Simple Steps for Success

Generally, kids with ASD show less interest in hygiene compared to other kids their age. Maybe that's true for you (or maybe it's not). If you start following some basic rules of hygiene at an early age, the tasks become easier and more automatic as you get older. Over time, you'll probably start adding more things to these hygiene basics, like shaving, putting on makeup, or even using contact lenses. For now all you need are some simple steps.

Maya's Story

Maya is 12 and tired of hearing about "puberty." Does her mom think that just because Maya has Asperger's she needs to hear about puberty every day? Her mom has explained that puberty means Maya is "growing up," and her body is changing. She's getting taller and needs to use deodorant so she doesn't have body odor. Maya understands this, but her mom seems to think Maya will forget or ignore her advice.

The worst thing for Maya is hearing her mom's comments about her hair. Maya has thick hair that's hard to wash. She used to wash her hair every three or four days, but now her mom says Maya should wash it more often or else it looks greasy.

Greasy? thinks Maya. *What does Mom think—that I rub* butter *in my hair?*

When Maya tries to wash her own hair, it's a big problem. It's really hard to figure out exactly how much shampoo to use. Too little shampoo means barely any lather. Too much shampoo means way too many suds. And rinsing seems to take forever.

Maya has tried adjusting the amount of shampoo she uses so that washing her hair won't be so frustrating. Her mom says, "Just use a *little* shampoo to wash your hair." This is confusing to Maya. How much is "a little"? Can't things be simpler or more clear? Some days, she goes to school feeling like there's extra shampoo in her hair. Her head feels itchy and icky. Other days, her mom says, "Maya, did you *really* wash your hair? Because it doesn't look like it got clean."

This morning, Maya gets up late for school. She runs to the shower and tries to rush, but then everything seems to go wrong. Her mom had bought new shampoo, and it's in a huge, heavy bottle and smells too strong. When Maya opens the bottle, it slips from her hands and shampoo spills all over her.

Her mom calls, "Maya, we're going to be late if you don't hurry up!"

That's when the tears start. Maya hates everything: hair, showers, puberty. She wishes she could just go back to bed. Maya's mom sees how upset she is and helps out. Somehow they get to school on time.

Later, when Maya is back home, her mom says there's a surprise in the shower. Maya runs upstairs with her mom. When she opens the shower curtain, Maya sees a soap dispenser on the wall. It's like the ones near the sinks at school. "I don't get it, Mom," she says.

"Look!" her mom answers. Then she shows her a bottle of Maya's favorite scent-free shampoo and pours the whole thing into the dispenser. "All it takes is two pumps to get the amount you need. Try it."

Maya pumps the dispenser twice. The "right" amount of shampoo—not too much and not too little—appears in her palm.

"Wow, thanks, Mom!"

Now Maya knows that when she washes her hair, all she needs is "two pumps." That's easy to remember. Problem solved.

Bathe or shower each day. Depending on your age and abilities, you might still need some help washing up, or you may be doing just fine on your own. Try to take a bath or shower once a day or every other day, if possible. If you tend to be forgetful or have trouble completing tasks, ask a parent to create a waterproof checklist you can keep nearby when you wash. The checklist can include all the parts to wash, in which order, if you'd like. In the tub or shower, rinse yourself thoroughly to avoid itchy skin. Follow up with moisturizing lotion, if you want to.

Wash your hair as needed. Talk to a parent or another trusted adult about your hair-care needs. A lot depends on how long your hair is and whether it tends to be dry or oily. To keep it simple, you might want to get a shampoo that has a built-in conditioner. Try to notice when your hair looks greasy or flaky. These are signs that you need to wash it more frequently or use a different shampoo. Maybe you wonder if you should use gel or other styling products. You can get advice from a hairstylist or an older sister or brother.

Wash your face. Talk to an adult about how best to take care of your skin. Maybe all you need to do is wash your face with a cleanser. Or maybe you have some acne and need help taking care of pimples. Perhaps your skin is dry and you want to try a moisturizer. Have a parent spend time demonstrating the best way to take care of your skin. Then stick to a daily routine.

Wash your hands often. Keeping your hands clean helps prevent the spread of germs. Each time you wash, use warm water and lots of soap. Scrub for at least 30 seconds. That's long enough to sing the "ABC Song" (remember that?) in your head. Rinse well and dry your hands with a clean towel.

Hand-Washing Hints

Here are five good times to wash your hands:

1. before you eat
2. after using the bathroom
3. after you sneeze, cough, or blow your nose
4. after "gaming" (handheld games, video games, computer, etc.)
5. whenever they're dirty!

Brush and floss your teeth. Keeping your mouth healthy and clean starts with brushing at least twice a day. Two good times are after breakfast and before bed. Brush for two minutes, making sure to brush every tooth and your tongue. You can even buy a special rinse that helps you check out how well you brushed. If your teeth have colored spots after using the rinse, you missed a few places. Consider changing your toothbrush, if needed. Some kids who have ASD love electric vibrating toothbrushes. Others say they "can't stand" them—too much sensory input!

Floss every night, too. Flossing takes some coordination. If it's hard for you, an adult can help. Or, you can try a toothpick-style flossing tool that has a handle to hold onto.

Deodorize as needed. Maybe you already need to use underarm deodorant, or maybe that's still a few years away. Use special foot powder if you sometimes have stinky, sweaty feet. If you hate stuff that has a heavy scent, choose unscented versions of hygiene products.

Take care of your nails. Fingernails and toenails need attention. But they're easy to forget about or overlook. Trim yours with a nail trimmer, file them with a nail file, or ask a parent for help in this area. This helps prevent hangnails and keeps your fingers and toes neater. If your nails are yellowed, you may have a fungus that requires medication. And if you're a nail biter, you might want to ask your doctor or a parent for some advice on how to stop this habit.

For every one of these hygiene tasks, making a checklist can help. Hang the checklist in a handy place, like on the bathroom mirror or behind the door.

Toothbrushing checklist:
- ☐ Use a pea-sized blob of toothpaste.
- ☐ Brush up and down. Use circular motions, like the dentist showed me.
- ☐ Brush for two minutes (use timer).
- ☐ Brush tongue.
- ☐ Rinse and spit.
- ☐ Make sure sink is clean afterward.

All in all, good hygiene leads to better health. So it's worth the extra work.

Looking Good Head to Toe

"Fashion" is tricky to talk about. In today's world, fashion magazines and celebrities often make people think that looks, hair, and clothes are everything. Well, they aren't! So many other things are more important: kindness, courage, confidence, love for others, honesty, a giving spirit. The list goes on and on. You probably have many of these traits yourself. Way to go!

But here's the problem: Many kids, teens, and adults with ASD stand out because of what they wear. And not in a good way. We'd rather you stand out for your individuality, intelligence, sense of humor, or strong character. Those assets of yours will shine even brighter if you blend in when it comes to your clothing.

Does this mean you need to dress like a pop star or model to be accepted? No way! The tips in this chapter aren't meant to turn you into a dress-up doll or Mr. Trendy. You need to be yourself, and you've got to be comfortable. At the same time, it helps to look around and see if some of your clothing choices are giving people an impression you don't intend to give.

Dylan didn't know how to tie his shoes. So he wore sneakers with Velcro when other boys in his class were wearing shoes with laces. For a long time, this didn't bother Dylan a bit. But then he noticed how much he liked some of the other sneaker styles. He wanted a pair for himself. But first, he'd need to learn to tie. Otherwise, what would happen at school if his laces came undone?

Selena loved leggings. They were easy to put on and didn't pinch like jeans. She had a drawer full of blue leggings that she wore winter and summer. One day a boy in her class said, "You wear the exact same pair of pants every day. That's *gross*." Selena knew he was rude, and wrong. She didn't wear the same exact pair—she had lots of different pairs. It wasn't like she pulled them out of the hamper every morning! But still, his comment bothered her.

Lionel hated buttons, snaps, and zippers. He preferred pants that had an elastic waistband, like sweatpants or sports pants. But Lionel often rushed as he got dressed. Then he'd forget to look in the mirror. His pants were usually twisted to the side, or pulled up really high. Some days he wore them backward or inside out.

Ellie was 12 but small for her age. She could still wear clothes in sizes meant for younger children. She loved princesses, so she almost always wore T-shirts and sweatshirts featuring Cinderella or Belle from *Beauty and the Beast*. Other girls in her class laughed at her for this.

Sometimes, it's a good idea to go beyond your usual clothing choices and s-t-r-e-t-c-h yourself to pick something new. Maybe "new" means tennis shoes with laces or a pair of jeans. Maybe it means wearing T-shirts with logos or images. Or making sure you're *not* wearing something that's too tight or small because you've outgrown it.

If you don't care a bit about fashion or clothes, that's fine. Maybe you're mostly concerned with what feels comfortable on your body. But you can be comfy *and* look "cool," too. What about getting someone who's interested in fashion to give you advice? (Tip: Choose someone your own age or just a little older.)

- **Look at magazines or clothing catalogs together.** You're probably a really visual person, so maybe some of the colors, styles, and choices will catch your eye. Ask your "fashion friend" what works and what doesn't. Talk about what might look good on you.

- **Go online.** If you don't like shopping at the mall, you can shop online. (Do this with an adult's permission and supervision.) Look at kids' clothing stores or teen websites for ideas. If a parent orders your clothes online, you get to try them on in private at home, instead of in a public dressing room. Bonus!

- **Notice what other people your age wear.** Are certain brands and styles popular with your classmates or kids in your neighborhood? Find similar clothes at local stores or used-clothing shops. Maybe you have an older sibling or cousin who can hand down clothes to you.

- **Look in your own closet.** You might have more in there than you thought. Sometimes, it's easy to get into a habit of grabbing the first thing you see out of the closet or drawer, or picking something off the pile of folded laundry. If that's what you tend to do, you're probably wearing the same choices day after day. Try something else on instead. You might even ask your "fashion friend" to help you put together new outfits from what you already own.

Check Yourself Out

Before you head out the door each day, give yourself the "once-over":

Is your hair combed?

How are those teeth? Smile and say cheese! (Kidding.)

Is your shirt on the right way? (Not backward or inside out.)

Does your shirt need tucking in?

Does the outfit "go together"? Does it fit the season?

You're wearing clean underwear, right?

Belt buckled? Zipper up? Buttons done?

Are your pants, shorts, or skirt straight?

Do your socks match?

Are your laces tied?

Clothing may seem like an unimportant topic. After all, Einstein wasn't known as a snappy dresser, and look how far he went in life. Many creative people (like artists, writers, and musicians) dress either super-casual or weird-and-wacky—and they do just fine. Besides, you might think, "I'm just a kid in school. Who really cares what I wear for another day of math and gym?" These are all good points.

But one goal of this book is to help you find friends and feel good about yourself. If making some changes in what you wear and how you take care of yourself can help you succeed, then it's worth a try.

The tips in this chapter are a way to help you make little changes day to day. Take them step by step. In time, they may add up to big gains in confidence.

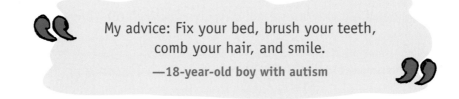

My advice: Fix your bed, brush your teeth, comb your hair, and smile.

—18-year-old boy with autism

Chapter 23

Sleep . . . Zzzzzzz

Sleep time is *growing* time for kids and teens. You need a good night's rest every night to grow up healthy and feel good. But lots of kids on the autism spectrum have a hard time with sleep, for a variety of reasons.

Why do people need sleep in the first place? Lots of important functions take place while the body is at rest. For example:

- **You grow and heal.** Your body repairs and restores itself each night during sleep. As a young person you are growing. A lot of this growing happens at night when special hormones are released.

- **Your brain makes connections.** All the stuff you experience during the daytime is processed and stored in your memory. During sleep, your brain organizes this information and makes important connections with other parts of your brain. This helps your learning and your memory.

- **You save energy.** All day long your senses are on alert. You're seeing, hearing, tasting, touching, and smelling. At night while you sleep and dream, your senses get a much-needed break.

How much sleep is enough? The National Sleep Foundation says kids ages 5 to 12 need 10 to 11 hours of sleep per night. Teens need 8½ to 9½ hours. Not getting enough sleep night after night can lead to problems like these:

- being jittery and hyper
- decreased attention and short-term memory
- poorer performance in school and after-school activities

Plus, you just feel out of sorts when you're not getting enough sleep. That means your body doesn't work as well. You can get sick more easily, and you don't have as much energy. When your body is off-balance, so is your mind. You can't work as hard or think as well. Bad moods are a result, and no wonder! Who can be in a good mood when they're drowsy or feeling lousy?

Bedtime Basics

If you have trouble falling asleep or staying asleep, try some or all of the ideas here, depending on your needs.

Stay awake during the day. That may be hard for you, especially if you're a napper. But even a quick "catnap" can leave you rested enough that you may have trouble falling asleep at bedtime. If you nap, keep it short—have someone wake you up after 20 minutes so you can still fall asleep at bedtime.

Exercise. Physical activity is good for you for many reasons. One of those reasons is that you'll usually sleep better at night if your body is active during the day. Chapter 20 offers lots of ideas for getting exercise. Stay busy and active all day, but don't exercise right before bed. (It might perk you up instead of wearing you out.)

Have a bedtime routine. If you love routines, then setting up one for bedtime shouldn't be too difficult. A helpful routine includes time for relaxing, getting ready (putting on pajamas, washing up, brushing your teeth), and talking quietly with a loved one. Why spend time talking before bed? It gets your worries out and helps you relax. It also strengthens your relationships with people who care for you. If talking is hard, you can hold hands or hug.

Know your bedtime and stick to it. Talk to your dad or mom about what time you should go to bed. (The time depends on your age, what time school starts, how long it takes you to fall asleep and get ready in the morning, and what your parents think is best.) Once you have a bedtime, make sure you're in bed on time every night. This helps set your "body clock" so you're more likely to get sleepy at that time.

Avoid electronics at night. At least one hour before bed, turn off all electronics except for soothing music. That means no more TV, video games, computer time, or loud, upbeat music. (All of these are stimulating—they give your body the "wake-up" signal.) Instead, do quiet activities like doodling, writing, or other suggestions that follow.

Take a long bath or a soothing shower. Hot or warm water can help you feel relaxed and sleepy. You might even want to add bath oil with chamomile or lavender to help you relax. Or, use a body wash that includes "relaxing" ingredients on the label.

Read. Reading is a quiet, soothing activity—unless you're into scary books (which aren't recommended before bed). Keep your favorite books within reach so they're a regular part of your bedtime routine. If reading is hard for you, ask a parent to read aloud to you. Or try books on a CD at a low volume, or choose books that are mostly pictures.

Breathe to relax. On page 180 is a Belly Breathing activity. You can also try the 10-step relaxation exercise on pages 180–181.

Get a rubdown. This is a good choice if you don't mind being touched, and you have a parent who's willing to give you a massage. Maybe you don't like deep pressure—so ask your dad or mom to lightly rub your back or tickle your arms. You can give yourself a foot massage, too. Getting a foot or body rub can relax you and make you feel sleepy. (On the other hand, it might make you feel more awake! Try it during the daytime once or twice to see what effect it has.)

Watch what you eat and drink. If you drink a liquid with caffeine (like soda, coffee, or tea) in the late afternoon or evening, you'll probably have a harder time getting to sleep. The same goes for eating chocolate (which contains caffeine). Some people react to spicy foods. They may have trouble sleeping afterward or get bad dreams. Many people react to sugary foods and drinks, too. They get a "sugar high" that's like fake energy, followed by a "crash" where they feel completely wiped out.

If you have any sleep problems, keep a log of what you eat or drink. That way you can find a pattern. It's also helpful to limit the liquids you drink after dinner. Then you're less likely to have to get up in the night to use the bathroom.

Use an alarm clock. Get up at the same time each morning. Set your alarm for a certain time. When it goes off, try to get up instead of pushing the snooze button a bunch of times. After getting up at the same time for a while, your body might automatically wake up just as your alarm is about to ring.

Darken the room. Maybe you're sensitive to light. Maybe you need a really dark room to sleep in. You can get curtains and room-darkening blinds. If this is true for you, keep all the lights off. Don't use a nightlight if you can help it. You might also need to unplug any electronics that light up. (Find an alarm clock that's not digital so the glowing numbers don't keep you awake.)

Keep it quiet. Ask your family to turn down the volume on any electronics that are still being used after you go to bed. See if they'll talk more softly and avoid making sudden noises, like slamming doors or banging around. If noise is really a problem for you, try some special headphones designed to block out sound. Or get some ear plugs from the drugstore. You may want to try a white-noise machine. It will create a repeating, soothing sound (like waves washing ashore or a train chugging along a track). Or, you can just use a fan.

Get comfortable. What helps you sleep? A pair of warm pajamas? Sleeping in only your underwear? Being tightly wrapped in blankets? Cotton sheets instead of flannel? People prefer different temperatures for sleeping. Check if you're too hot or cold, too weighed down or not snug enough. Try different types of pajamas to see what you like best. Maybe a nightgown gets too tangled, or long johns are too hot or tight. Wear only what's comfortable. Ask a parent to cut the labels off of your pajamas, so they don't rub against your skin.

Think about your pet. Does it help you sleep if your cat is right next to you or if your dog is on the floor by your bed? Then maybe that can be part of your routine. On the other hand, maybe your pet is waking you during the night. You might need to move your hamster or bird cage, for example, or shut your door so your pets can't come in.

Have a plan. What happens if you wake up during the night and have trouble falling back to sleep? Sometimes, just the *worry* of waking up makes sleep more difficult. It helps to have a plan in place. For example, if you wake up you might take a few sips of water, adjust the blankets, or turn over and try a different position. Try picturing and counting sheep in your head or letting your mind wander. If you start thinking stressful thoughts, stop and breathe. Hug your stuffed animals. Think about positive things, like what you're grateful for in life or who you love. Say a prayer. Do some deep breathing.

Stay in your room. Some kids with ASD are very light sleepers. They wake up at night when the rest of the family is sleeping. If this is a problem for you, it's important to have a plan in place, so you're safe at home each night. It's best to stay in your room, even if you're wide awake and everyone else is asleep. Read a book or put on headphones and listen to soothing music. Try to stay calm and relaxed so you have a better chance of getting back to sleep.

One of the best ways you can help yourself get a better night's rest is to let people know how you're doing. Are you often too wound up to settle in to sleep? Do worries keep you awake? Do you get scared of the dark? Do you feel tired during school? Do you usually fall asleep on the bus? Do you crave more physical activity during the day?

First, you need to notice what feels "wrong" to you. Then you can communicate the problem to the adults you trust—a parent, your doctor, a counselor, or a therapist. For more on tuning into feelings or handling emotions, see Chapter 15.

Before You Go

You've reached the end of this book. We hope it has given you some answers to questions you've wanted to ask, and maybe some you hadn't even thought of. This is the kind of book you and your parents can go back to again and again, whenever you need help. Share it with your brothers and sisters so they can understand you better. Share it with friends you think might need help on their own path.

As you get older, each day will bring new experiences—and more questions. Finding the answers won't always be easy. Remember to call on your "team" (Chapter 7). They're there for you in good times and not-so-good times. You can add more team members as the years go on.

Know what this is?

A label. The one-size-fits-all kind. At times, you might feel like a "label" because you have ASD. You might think you *are* your symptoms or your challenges. You are so much more than both!

There is no such thing as one-size-fits-all. Each of us is an individual. *You* are an individual—in life and on the spectrum, too. No one can predict today who you'll be when you grow up.

One thing you might be is a "late bloomer." That means someone whose talents and capabilities are slower to develop. Many people, on the spectrum or not, are late bloomers. They still bloom! So keep learning. Keep reaching.

Yes, you will face frustrations. Life is full of hurts and hardships (for everyone). You'll get through them. And you know what? You'll be stronger for it. The hard times teach us to bend. They also teach us to try to help others through *their* hard times.

As life goes on, you can look forward to many other parts of the human experience: fun new friendships, wild laughter, excellent days, and feelings of "It's great to be alive."

Live life to the fullest. And let us know what happens.

Where to Go for More Info

The number of books and other resources on the topic of ASD is growing by the day. You have many places to turn for help and advice! Below is a list of books and websites/organizations to help you learn more about life on the spectrum. This list is just a start—on your own journey, you'll likely find lots more sources of support.

Books for Kids and Teens

The Aspie Teen's Survival Guide: Candid Advice for Teens, Tweens, and Parents, from a Young Man with Asperger's Syndrome by J.D. Kraus (Future Horizons, 2010). The author, a teen with Asperger's, describes sensory issues, social challenges, and motor-skill difficulties, while offering advice on getting along in school, with friends, and in the confusing world of dating and relationships.

Freaks, Geeks & Asperger Syndrome: A User Guide to Adolescence by Luke Jackson (Jessica Kingsley Publishers, 2002). Luke Jackson, a young man with Asperger's syndrome, describes his symptoms, behaviors, sensory needs, fascinations, family, and friends. His straightforward advice helps kids on the spectrum better understand their condition and themselves.

The Game of My Life: A True Story of Challenge, Triumph, and Growing Up Autistic by Jason "J-Mac" McElwain, with Daniel Paisner (New American Library, 2008). An account of J-Mac's experiences with autism, his love of basketball, and his heart-lifting, highly publicized moments on the court in 2006.

How to Talk to an Autistic Kid by Daniel Stefanski (Free Spirit Publishing, 2011). A boy with autism explains what autism is and how it feels to be different. He offers advice for "typical" kids on the special ways to communicate, socialize, and behave with kids with ASD.

My Brother Charlie by Holly Robinson Peete and Ryan Elizabeth Peete, with Denene Millner (Scholastic Press, 2010). This picture book is a tribute to RJ Peete, who has autism, as well as a story about ASD and family love.

Books for Parents and Caregivers

The Child with Special Needs: Encouraging Intellectual and Emotional Growth by Stanley I. Greenspan, M.D., and Serena Wieder, Ph.D. (Perseus Publishing, 1998). Greenspan was widely known as a leader in the field of helping children with special needs. Here, his award-winning "floor-time" approach is explained step-by-step, encouraging caregivers to use creative play to help children climb the developmental ladder. Includes case histories and compassionate advice about the challenges and rewards of parenting children with special needs.

The Complete Guide to Asperger's Syndrome by Tony Attwood (Jessica Kingsley Publishers, 2007). This book is based on Attwood's extensive clinical experience and longtime support of people with Asperger's syndrome. A definitive guide with chapters on diagnosis, social difficulties and friendship, understanding emotions and Theory of Mind, sensory issues, special interests and obsessions, and much more. Includes first-person accounts and FAQs.

The OASIS Guide to Asperger Syndrome: Advice, Support, Insight, and Inspiration by Patricia Romanowski Bashe, M.S.Ed., and Barbara L. Kirby, founder of the OASIS website (Crown Publishers, 2005). This is a comprehensive resource for parents, teachers, therapists, and others who know and work with kids with Asperger's. The authors share their own experiences and other parents' stories of raising kids on the spectrum. The book includes practical information and emotional support.

Overcoming Autism: Finding the Answers, Strategies, and Hope That Can Transform a Child's Life by Lynn Kern Koegel, Ph.D., and Claire LaZebnik (Viking Books, 2004). The authors describe a state-of-the-art approach to reducing the symptoms of ASD, with a focus on improving communication and social skills while reducing anxiety and self-stimulatory behaviors. Dr. Koegel founded the Autism Research Center at the University of California, Santa Barbara. Her coauthor is a well-known writer and the mother of a son with autism. The authors also wrote *Growing Up on the Spectrum: A Guide to Life, Love, and Learning for Teens and Young Adults with Autism and Asperger's* (2009), which addresses questions from parents and their teens with ASD about going through adolescence and what to expect in the future.

Quirky, Yes, Hopeless, No: Practical Tips to Help Your Child with Asperger's Syndrome Be More Socially Accepted by Cynthia La Brie Norall, Ph.D., with Beth Wagner Brust (St. Martin's Griffin, 2009). A simple A–Z format advises parents, teachers, and other adults who want to help children on the spectrum. Includes basics on teaching kids and teens greetings, cooperating, handling teasing and bullying, and learning manners.

Special Diets for Special Kids by Lisa Lewis, Ph.D. (Future Horizons, 2011). This edition includes volumes one and two of Lewis's original cookbooks, explaining the benefits of a gluten-free, casein-free diet for children with ASD, ADHD, and other conditions. It includes recipes for every meal, snacks, drinks, treats, ethnic foods, and holidays.

Thinking in Pictures and Other Reports from My Life with Autism by Temple Grandin (Vintage Books, 1995). Temple Grandin is a gifted scientist who was diagnosed with autism at a young age. Her book documents her childhood and adult life and includes explanations of her visual thinking, sensory issues, and talent development. Her point of view as a person with autism and a scientist sheds light on the condition and gives readers an insider's view of ASD. Grandin also wrote *Emergence: Labeled Autistic*.

Websites and Organizations

Autism Research Institute

autism.com

Originally founded by Dr. Bernard Rimland, who wrote extensively about autism, the Institute offers information on treatments, support for families and those with ASD, and resources for educators and clinicians.

The Autism Society

autism-society.org

The Autism Society describes itself as "The nation's leading grassroots autism organization, [which] exists to improve the lives of all affected by autism." Its mission is to increase public awareness about the day-to-day issues faced by people on the spectrum, advocate for appropriate services for individuals across the life span, and provide the latest information on treatment, education, research, and advocacy.

Autism Speaks

autismspeaks.org

Founded in 2005 by Bob and Suzanne Wright, Autism Speaks has grown into the nation's largest autism science and advocacy organization. Autism Speaks is dedicated to funding research into the causes of, prevention of, and treatments for autism, as well as increasing awareness and support of ASD.

HollyRod Foundation

hollyrod.org

This foundation was started in 1997 by actress Holly Robinson Peete with her husband—former NFL quarterback—Rodney Peete. Their son RJ was diagnosed with autism in 2000, and their foundation, which once focused on helping those with Parkinson's disease, expanded to include advocating for those with ASD. Efforts of the HollyRod Foundation are providing a better quality of life for individuals with ASD and their families.

The Online Asperger Syndrome Information and Support (OASIS) Center and MAAP Services for Autism and Asperger Syndrome

aspergersyndrome.org

This site provides articles; educational resources; links to local, national, and international support groups; sources of professional help; lists of camps and schools; conference information; recommended reading; and moderated support message boards.

Sharing the Diagnosis with Your Child
(For Parents)

It's not an easy decision to tell your child about the diagnosis. So many questions crop up . . . *How do I tell him? What are the "right" words? Will she understand? Is there a certain age kids should be told? Will telling my child affect his confidence and self-esteem? Where should the conversation take place—at home? During therapy? At the doctor's office? What if the conversation doesn't go well*—then *what?*

One of the reasons we wrote this book was so you could use it as part of the process of getting the conversation started.

There is no tried-and-true way to tell your child about the diagnosis, but you can do several things to make the conversation go more smoothly. First and foremost, know that it's likely your child already has an idea that he or she is "different" in some way. The news may not be as shocking as you think. Kids with autism spectrum disorders realize they struggle in certain areas, but they don't know why. They may think, "I do everything wrong" or "It's all my fault." They may wonder why they're in a special education program or why they see doctors and therapists a lot more often than other kids do. When you talk to your son or daughter about autism or Asperger's syndrome, it's an opportunity for you to give your child not only the reasons but also *reassurance*. Children need to know that having the condition isn't their fault.

The most important thing you can do is to keep the conversation positive. Wait until you yourself are at a point of acceptance. If you're not sure the diagnosis is correct or if you're feeling depressed, angry, or anxious, the timing isn't yet right. Your child will most likely be aware of your confusion and sadness. He or she may return to thinking, "I do everything wrong" or "It's all my fault."

How do you keep the conversation positive? By making it clear that you're there to answer questions, to offer support, and to always be a source of unconditional love. Point out your child's many strengths, rather than focusing on weaknesses. Show empathy. And remember to tell your child, "I'm so proud of you."

Here are tips to start the conversation and keep it going:

Look for signs of readiness. Is your child asking questions such as, "Why do I have to go to therapy?" or "How come other kids aren't like me?" Have you heard your child say something like, "I'm so stupid!" or "I can't do things right"? These are signals that your child already senses a difference.

Choose a good time. You may want to wait until your home is quiet and your child is calm. You could talk during a weekend, when after-school activities and homework aren't a pressing issue. Don't have the conversation on a "bad day"—for example, after your child has had an outburst or a meltdown, scored poorly on a test, or gotten into an argument with a friend. Pick a time when all is (relatively) well.

Have a plan in place. Decide ahead of time who will do the telling. Will it be you? Your spouse or partner? Do you want other trusted people on hand, such as your child's doctor or therapist, or special family members like grandparents and older siblings? Think about who your child is most comfortable around and what role others might play in the discussion.

Make the conversation age-appropriate. You can keep things simple for younger kids or go more in-depth for older ones. Use *The Survival Guide* as needed; read a chapter or two aloud, or show your child that the book is a tool for understanding when he or she is ready to learn more.

Be conscious of how your child responds. If your child shows signs of distress, end the conversation. Let your child know you can talk later, and then give him or her some space and private time. Open the door to questions when your child feels ready.

Know the facts. Autism spectrum disorders are considered medical conditions. Kids who have ASD need help, guidance, and support. Some parents make the mistake of believing that because a diagnosis will lead to a label, that label will then hold their child back in school, in social situations, and throughout life. But failing to acknowledge the condition doesn't change the reality of it. Other parents attempt to soften the truth by telling their child he or she has a learning disorder or a developmental delay. This terminology may give children the impression that they'll outgrow the problem or "get better" if they "do things right." Avoiding the diagnosis or giving it a different name only postpones the process of getting kids the help they need and deserve.

Your child has a better chance of succeeding in life if you face the diagnosis with an open mind, an open heart, and firmer footing on the path ahead.

Sources of Facts and Quotations

Pages 14 and 28: *Freaks, Geeks and Asperger Syndrome: A User Guide to Adolescence* by Luke Jackson. Jessica Kingsley Publishers, 2002, pages 19 and 35, and page 44.

Page 26: *Emergence: Labeled Autistic (A True Story)* by Temple Grandin and Margaret M. Scariano. Warner Books, 1986, page 22.

Page 27: *Autism. An Inside-Out Approach* by Donna Williams. Jessica Kingsley Publishers, 1996.

Page 30: *Autism Spectrum Quarterly*, "An Interview with Rudy Simone," by Liane Holliday Willey, Ed.D., summer 2010, page 45.

Page 34: *The Game of My Life: A True Story of Challenge, Triumph, and Growing Up Autistic* by Jason "J-Mac" McElwain with Daniel Paisner. New American Library, 2008, pages 228–229.

Page 36: *My Brother Charlie* by Holly Robinson Peete and Ryan Elizabeth Peete with Denene Millner. Scholastic Press, 2010, from "Why We Wrote This Book—And How It Can Help You."

Page 38: The information from the study of twins is reported in "Genetics Less Important than Environment in Understanding, Curing Autism, Study Says" by Andy Hinds, July 5, 2011, reporting on a study analyzing the frequency of autism in 192 pairs of twins conducted by the University of California–San Francisco and Stanford and described in the *Archives of General Psychiatry*. Accessed November 18, 2011, at Discovery Communications' TLC Parentables (parentables.howstuffworks.com) under "Health and Wellness."

Page 40: Take a Look! facts from the Centers for Disease Control and Prevention (www.cdc.gov), accessed Nov. 18, 2011; The CDC found that between 1 and 80 and 1 in 240, with an average of 1 in 110, children in the United States have ASD. "About Autism," Easter Seals Metropolitan Chicago (www.chicago .easterseals.com), accessed Nov. 18, 2011; and the April 1, 2011, White House press release "Presidential Proclamation—World Autism Awareness Day."

Page 41: "A Journey Through Autism" by Max LaZebnik, in *The Autism Perspective (TAP)* Magazine, January–March 2005, page 36.

Page 42: *How to Talk to an Autistic Kid* by Daniel Stefanski. Free Spirit Publishing, 2011, pages 30 and 41.

Page 51: *A Friend Like Henry: The Remarkable Story of an Autistic Boy and the Dog That Unlocked His World* by Nuala Gardner. Sourcebooks, 2008, pages 251–252.

Page 56: The "Manners Words" chart is adapted from *Dude, That's Rude! Get Some Manners* by Pamela Espeland and Elizabeth Verdick. Free Spirit Publishing, 2007, page 4. Used with permission.

Page 62: "6 Tips for Being a Good Sport with Family Members" is adapted from *Siblings: You're Stuck with Each Other, So Stick Together!* by James J. Crist and Elizabeth Verdick. Free Spirit Publishing, 2010, pages 98–100. Used with permission.

Pages 64–65: The "STOP THINK GO" strategy is adapted from *Don't Behave Like You Live in a Cave* by Elizabeth Verdick. Free Spirit Publishing, 2010, pages 55–56. Used with permission.

Pages 82 and 153: "Looking You in the Mouth: Abnormal Gaze in Autism Resulting from Impaired Top-Down Modulation of Visual Attention" by Dirk Neumann et al, in *Oxford Journals, Social and Cognitive & Affective Neuroscience,* 2006, Volume 1, Issue 3, pages 194–202.

Page 127: *The Aspie Teen's Survival Guide: Candid Advice for Teens, Tweens, and Parents, from a Young Man with Asperger's Syndrome* by J.D. Kraus. Future Horizons, 2010, pages 151–152.

Pages 179–180: Belly breathing instructions are adapted from *Be the Boss of Your Stress* by Timothy Culbert and Rebecca Kajander. Free Spirit Publishing, 2007, pages 30–31. Used with permission.

Pages 180–181: The relaxation exercise is adapted from *Stress Can Really Get on Your Nerves* by Trevor Romain and Elizabeth Verdick. Free Spirit Publishing, 2000, pages 76–77. Used with permission.

Pages 196–198: The "Check Your Engine" section is adapted from *Don't Behave Like You Live in a Cave* by Elizabeth Verdick. Free Spirit Publishing, 2010, pages 86–92. Used with permission of Free Spirit. The engine concept is introduced in *How Does Your Engine Run?* by Mary Sue Williams and Sherry Shellenberger. Albuquerque: Therapy Works, 1996.

Page 217: Information on how much sleep is enough comes from the National Sleep Foundation.

Index

About the Authors

In her role as a child and adolescent psychiatrist, Dr. Elizabeth Reeve has worked with children, teens, and adults on the autism spectrum for more than 20 years. She is also the mother of a young man with autism. As a parent and physician, she experiences the day-to-day challenges of ASD at home and at work. Dr. Reeve recalls that at various times she was told her own child was "hard of hearing" and "mentally retarded" (although he wasn't), and that he "may never walk" or "could go blind" (wrong again). Today he attends college. The struggles were many, but hard work continues to pay off.

Elizabeth Verdick writes from the perspective of a mother with a child on the spectrum, too. Advocating for her son since he was two years old has been one of the greatest learning experiences in her life. Along the way, she has worked with doctors, behavioral therapists, teachers, school counselors, and speech, occupational, and physical therapists to help her son. As an author of many books for children and teens, she knew she'd someday want to write a book for her son and other kids like him in the hope that it may be a guide to help them not only survive, but *thrive*.

For more autism resources and other great books for kids, visit www.freespirit.com.

Phonics in Proper Perspective

TENTH EDITION

Arthur W. Heilman
Professor Emeritus
Pennsylvania State University

PEARSON

Merrill
Prentice Hall

Upper Saddle River, New Jersey
Columbus, Ohio

Library of Congress Cataloging-in-Publication Data

Heilman, Arthur W.
    Phonics in proper perspective / Arthur W. Heilman.—10th ed.
      p. cm.
    Includes bibliographical references and index.
    ISBN 0-13-117798-2
      1. Reading—Phonetic method.   I. Title.

LB1573.3.H44 2006
372.46'5—dc22   2004061069

Vice President and Executive Publisher: Jeffery W. Johnston
Senior Editor: Linda Ashe Montgomery
Editorial Assistant: Laura J. Weaver
Assistant Development Editor: Kathryn Terzano
Production Coordination: Amy Gehl, Carlisle Publishers Services
Production Editor: Linda Hillis Bayma
Design Coordinator: Diane C. Lorenzo
Cover Designer: Ali Mohrman
Cover Image: Images.com
Production Manager: Pamela Bennett
Director of Marketing: Ann Castel Davis
Marketing Manager: Darcy Betts Prybella
Marketing Coordinator: Brian Mounts

This book was set in Frutiger Light by Carlisle Publishers Services. It was printed and bound by Courier Stoughton, Inc. The cover was printed by Courier Stoughton, Inc.

Pearson Education Ltd.
Pearson Education Singapore Pte. Ltd.
Pearson Education Canada, Ltd.
Pearson Educación de Mexico, S.A. de C.V.

Pearson Education Australia Pty. Limited
Pearson Education North Asia Ltd.
Pearson Education—Japan
Pearson Education Malaysia Pte. Ltd.

10 9 8 7 6 5 4 3 2 1
ISBN: 0-13-117798-2

Preface

The purpose of this book is to provide both the experienced and the prospective teacher with materials that will lead to better understanding of the following:

- The purpose and limitations of phonics instruction as it relates to teaching reading
- Concrete practices to follow in teaching the various steps in phonics analysis
- The rationale that underlies particular instructional practices.

The material in this book reflects several premises:

- Phonics is an important part of teaching beginning reading.
- Teachers should be knowledgeable about the purpose of phonics instruction and its limitations.
- For children to make normal progress in learning to read, they must learn to associate printed letter forms with the speech sounds they represent.
- Beginning reading instruction must not mislead children into thinking that reading is sounding out letters, or learning sight words, or using context clues.

Learning to read involves *all* these skills in the right combination. The optimum amount of phonics instruction for each child is the absolute minimum the child needs to become an independent reader. Excessive phonics instruction will usurp time that should be devoted to reading, can destroy children's interest in reading, and may lead critics to attack phonics instruction rather than bad phonics instruction.

For this edition, a focus has been put on revising chapter 4, "Moving Into Reading," which attempts to put the learning of sight words in proper perspective. A hundred-plus English words are the gatekeepers that expedite or stifle early readers in their quest for literacy. These have been called *service words, glue words,* and *blue-collar working words.* These are words that occur most frequently in spoken and written English. If a book or other unit of print contains a hundred thousand words, forty to fifty thousand will be the blue-collar working words used over and over. Readers must instantly recognize these words or be left behind.

For the tenth edition, I would like to thank the following reviewers who provided valuable comments and suggestions: Marilyn L. Haller, Oklahoma Baptist University; Cindy Hendricks, Bowling Green State University; Kathryn A. Lund, Arizona State University; Ray Ostrander, Andrews University; and Mary Shake, University of Kentucky.

Contents

Chapter 1

PHONICS: PURPOSE AND LIMITATIONS

*T*he purpose of phonics instruction is to teach beginning readers that printed letters and letter combinations represent speech sounds heard in words. In applying phonic skills to an unknown word, the reader blends a series of sounds dictated by the order in which particular letters occur in the printed word. One needs this ability to arrive at the pronunciation of printed word symbols that are not instantly recognized. Obviously, if one recognizes a printed word, he should not puzzle over the speech sounds represented by the individual letters.

"Arriving at the pronunciation" of a word does not mean learning *how* to pronounce that word. In most reading situations, particularly in the primary grades, the readers know the pronunciation of practically all words they will meet in their reading. What they do not know is that the printed word symbol *represents* the pronunciation of a particular word they use and understand in oral language. Through phonic analysis they resolve this dilemma.

THE STUDY OF PHONICS

Phonics is not a *method* of teaching reading, nor is it the same as phonetics. Phonics is one of a number of ways a child may "solve" words not known as sight words. Phonics instruction is concerned with teaching letter-sound relationships *only as they relate to learning to read.* English spelling patterns being what they are, children will sometimes arrive at only a close approximation of the needed sounds. They may pronounce *broad* so it rhymes with *road,* or *fath* (in father) so that it rhymes with *path.* Fortunately, if they are reading for meaning, they will instantly correct these errors. After a few such self-corrections, they will never again make these particular mistakes.

Phonetics is much more precise. It is the scientific study of the sound systems of language. Phoneticians are scientists. They know much more about speech sounds and spelling patterns than is necessary for children to know while learning to read, or for teachers to teach when the goal is teaching reading.

Linguists rightfully urge reading teachers not to confuse phonics with phonetics. Phonetics is a science; the teaching of reading is not. While it is true that phonics is based on phonetics, linguists should not be distressed when they observe a phonics instruction program that does not include certain known phonetic data. First and second graders do not need to be exposed to all the phonetic data that have been assembled. Learning to read is a complicated process, and it need not be complicated further simply because a vast body of phonetic data exists. In teaching reading, one must hold to the scientific principle that instruction must follow the most economical path to its chosen goal. A guideline for instruction is that *the optimum amount of phonics instruction a child should be exposed to is the minimum the child needs to become an independent reader.* This is certainly not the way to become a linguist, but it is good pedagogy for beginning reading instruction.

Terminology

In recent years, noticeable confusion has accompanied discussions of reading because the meaning of some of the terms used has been vague or misleading. To eliminate further confusion, we will briefly define a few basic terms.

Alphabetic principle.   Graphic symbols have been devised for representing a large number of spoken languages. Three types of writing (picture, ideographic, and alphabetic) represent the English words or concepts *car, carp,* and *carpet* in Figure 1–1.

The picture and ideographic writing are purely arbitrary. The ideographs are not taken from an established language. The most important feature of the ideographic writing is that there are no common features in the three symbols. The alphabetic writing is also arbitrary, but it is based on the alphabetic principle: the letter symbols and

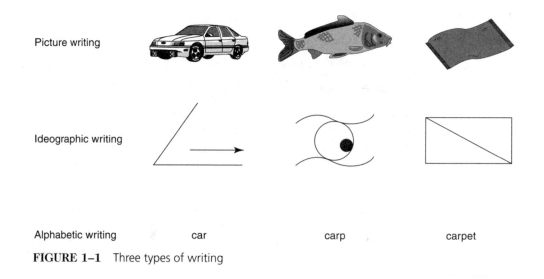

Picture writing

Ideographic writing

Alphabetic writing   car   carp   carpet

FIGURE 1–1   Three types of writing

their order of occurrence have been universally agreed upon since they are taken from English writing. The first three letter symbols in each word are identical. They signal the reader to blend the same three speech sounds (phonemes) if the goal is to arrive at the spoken word that the various letter configurations represent. In the case of *carp* and *carpet,* the reader must blend still other phonemes.

There are many other spoken words in which one hears the same three phonemes in the same sequence. The graphic representation of these speech sounds will be the same in a number of printed words: *carnival, cardinal, card, cartoon.* In English writing, however, one may see the graphic symbols *car* and find that they represent different phonemes from the ones under discussion (*carol, care, career, caress, caret*).

Digraph.   A digraph is a combination of two letters that represent one speech sound (consonant examples: *church, show, thank;* vowel examples: b*ee*t, c*oa*t, m*ai*l).

Diphthong.   A diphthong is a vowel blend: two adjacent vowels, each of which is sounded (*ou* in h*ou*se, *oi* in *oi*l, *oy* in b*oy,* *ow* in h*ow*).

Grapheme.   A grapheme is a written or printed letter symbol used to represent a speech sound or phoneme.

Grapheme-phoneme relationship.   This term refers to the relationship between printed letters and the sounds they represent; it also covers the deviations found in such a relationship. Thus, while English writing is based on an alphabetic code, there is not a one-to-one relationship between graphemes (printed symbols) and the phonemes (speech sounds) they represent. Some printed symbols represent several different sounds (*car, caress, cake*), and one speech sound may be represented by many different letters or combinations of letters (which we will discuss later in this chapter). To a great extent, this problem stems from the spelling patterns of words that have become established in English writing.

Morpheme.   This is the smallest meaningful unit of language. The word *cat* is a morpheme whose pronunciation consists of three phonemes. If one wishes to speak of more than one cat, the letter *s* forming the plural *cats* becomes a morpheme, since it changes the meaning (as does the possessive *'s* in the *cat's* dinner).

There are two classes of morphemes, free and bound. The former functions independently in any utterance (*house, lock, man, want*). Bound morphemes consist of prefixes, suffixes, and inflectional endings and must combine with other morphemes (*houses, unlock, man's, wanted*).

Onset.   An initial consonant or consonant cluster is an onset. In the word *name, n* is the onset; in the word *blame, bl* is the onset.

Phoneme.   A phoneme is the smallest unit of sound in a language that distinguishes one word from another. Pronouncing the word *cat* involves blending three phonemes: /k / /æ/ /t /.

Phonemic awareness. This term refers to the knowledge or understanding that speech consists of a series of sounds and that individual words can be divided into phonemes.

Phonemic segmentation. Breaking a syllable or word into its constituent phonemes [top = /t/ /o/ /p/].

Phonetic method. This is a vague term that once was used to indicate instruction that included phonics, emphasized phonics, or overemphasized phonics. Eventually it acquired the polar connotation of "pro-phonics" and "anti-sight-word method." (We will discuss this dichotomy in Chapter 2.)

Phonetics. This term refers to the segment of linguistic science that deals with (a) speech sounds; (b) how these sounds are made vocally; (c) sound changes that develop in languages; and (d) the relation of speech sounds to the total language process. All phonics instruction is derived from phonetics, but phonics as it relates to reading utilizes only a relatively small portion of the body of knowledge identified as phonetics.

Phonic analysis. This is the process of applying knowledge of letter-sound relationships, that is, blending the sounds represented by letters so as to arrive at the pronunciation of printed words.

Phonics instruction. Phonics instruction is a facet of reading instruction that (a) leads the child to understand that printed letters in printed words represent the speech sounds heard when words are pronounced; and (b) involves the actual teaching of which sound is associated with a particular letter or combination of letters.

Rime. A rime is the vowel or vowel and consonant(s) that follow the onset. In the word *name, ame* is the rime.

Schwa. The schwa sound is a diminished stress, or a softening of the vowel sound. Schwa is represented by the symbol ə (bedlam = bed' ləm; beckon = bek'ən). Any of the vowels may represent the schwa sound.

Sight vocabulary. A sight vocabulary includes any words a reader recognizes instantly, without having to resort to any word-recognition strategies.

Sight-word method. The term *sight-word method* is an abstraction rather than a description of reading instruction. Some beginning reading materials developed prior to the mid-1950s, however, advocated teaching a limited number of sight words before phonic analysis was introduced. The term *sight-word method* became common even though it actually described only this initial teaching procedure. Gradually the term was used to imply the existence of an instructional approach that allegedly proscribed phonics and advocated teaching every new word by sight only.

Word analysis. This is an inclusive term that refers to all methods of word recognition. Phonics is one such method.

Limitations of Phonics

Phonics instruction does have limitations. Knowing this fact helps us avoid expecting too much of our lessons. It also helps us see why children need other related word recognition skills.

VARIABILITY OF LETTER-SOUNDS IN ENGLISH

proof of not using phonics alone as your only word work

The greatest limitation of the use of phonics is the spelling patterns of many English words. Although written English is alphabetic, the irregular spellings of words prevent anything like a one-to-one relationship between letters seen and sounds heard. Some of the reasons for, and examples of, this problem include the following.

1. Many English words have come from other languages such as Latin, Greek, French, and German (*waive, alias, corps, debris, alien, buoy, feint, bouquet*). The spelling of these words is often confusing.
2. A given letter, or letters, may represent different sounds in different words: c*ow* = ow, l*ow* = ō; c*an* = ă, c*ane* = ā, *cap* = k, *city* = s; bu*s* = s, hi*s* = z, mea*s*ure = zh.
3. The following illustrate some of the variability found in English words. Some words (homonyms) are (a) pronounced the same, (b) spelled differently, and (c) each is phonetically "lawful."

weak—week	meat—meet	heal—heel	beat—beet
peal—peel	real—reel	peak—peek	steal—steel

In these examples, the generalization that applies to both spellings is *when there are two adjacent vowels in a word, usually the first is long and the second is not sounded.*

One word in each of the following pairs is governed by this phonic generalization; the other is not.

vain	rain	peace	wait
vein	reign	piece	weight

4. In hundreds of English words, a letter or letters may represent no sound.

nig̸ht	comb̸	of̸ten	w̸rong

5. A word may have one or more letters not sounded that differentiate it from another word pronounced exactly the same.

new	our	plum	cent	no
knew	hour	plumb	scent	know

6. The long sound of vowels may be represented by any of these and other combinations in words.

	day	they	fate	sail	reign	great
ā =	ay	ey	a(e)	ai	ei	ea
	feet	meat	deceive	brief	ski	key
ē =	ee	ea	ei	ie	i	ey
	my	kite	pie	height	buy	guide
ī =	y	i(e)	ie	ei	uy	ui
	show	hold	boat	note	go	sew
ō =	ow	o(+ ld)	oa	o(e)	o	ew
	flew	view	tube	due	suit	you
ū =	ew	iew	u	ue	ui	ou

One of the problems in teaching letter-sound relationships is that dozens of "rules" or "generalizations" have been developed to help learners arrive at the pronunciation of words they do not recognize. The following discussion focuses on three of the most widely used generalizations and their limited efficacy resulting from numerous exceptions.

1. *When two vowels are side by side in a word, the first usually has its long sound and the second is not sounded.*

   Rule applies: boat, rain, meat, week, soap, sail, need
   Exceptions: been, said, chief, dead, field, head, their

2. *When a word has two vowels, the second being final e, the first usually has its long sound and the final e is not sounded.*

   Rule applies: ride, pale, hate, bite, dime, hide, cane, cute
   Exceptions: love, done, have, come, give, none, once

3. *A single vowel in medial position in a word or syllable usually has its short sound.*

Extensive research has shown that the first two rules apply less than 50% of the time in high-frequency words. The third generalization can be useful to children learning to read. It applies to enough high-frequency words to justify calling it to students' attention. However, there is no phonetic rule that will apply to all words that meet the criteria the rule sets forth. The following illustrates how, when a rule does not apply to a number of words, a new rule emerges to cover this situation.

Exception A: *hold, cold, bold, gold; bolt, colt*
New rule: The single vowel o, followed by *ld* or *lt*, has its long sound.

[handwritten margin notes: "Only 50% h.f. words" pointing to rules 1 and 2; "justified to teach" pointing to rule 3]

Exception B: *car, fir, fur, her, for, part, bird, hurt, perch, corn*
New rule: A vowel followed by *r* has neither its long nor short sound—the vowel sound is modified by the *r.*

Exception C: *wild, mild, child; find, kind, mind, blind*
New rule: The vowel *i* before *ld* or *nd* is usually long.

Exception D: *fall, call, ball; salt, malt, halt*
New rule: The vowel *a* followed by *ll* or *lt* is pronounced like *aw* (ball = bawl).

Exception E: *high, sigh; light, night, bright, flight*
New rule: The vowel *i* in *igh* and *ight* words is usually long.

Other exceptions: *sign* = (i); *was* = (u); *both* = (ō); *front* = (u)

These examples deal only with monosyllabic words containing a single vowel in a medial position. There are also a number of consonant irregularities, discussed in Chapter 5, but none of these represent the large number of sounding options that are characteristic of vowels. The exceptions to the basic rule are only the major ones that might logically be dealt with in teaching reading, and the words listed represent only a small fraction of those that could be cited. As rules become more involved and cover fewer and fewer actual words, one might question the relationship between learning these rules and learning the process called reading.

For many years, teachers have had considerable data available that focus on the frequency with which various phonic rules apply to words children will meet in their primary and elementary school experiences. Studies by Oaks (1952), Clymer (1963), Bailey (1967), Emans (1967), Burmeister (1968), and Burrows and Lourie (1963) are in agreement in their findings that there are a significant number of exceptions to generalizations covering vowel sounds.

The educational issue is not arriving at a universally agreed upon list of rules to be taught. The real problem, which is much more complicated, is what happens to learners under various types of instruction that focus on rules. What types of attack strategies do children develop? There is little information to guide teachers. Those who have worked extensively with impaired readers have undoubtedly encountered some children who are rule oriented. Some of these children persist in trying to make the rule fit even when the word they are attacking is an exception. Others can cite the rule and still are unable to apply it to words that it covers.

Despite the absence of data that might serve as a guide for teaching phonic generalizations, teachers must decide on the teaching strategies they will use. They may choose instructional materials that make a fetish of memorizing phonic generalizations. They might, however, present a series of words governed by a particular rule and invite children to formulate a generalization. The latter course seems preferable, not just because it fits under the rubric *discovery method,* but because it permits children to work with concepts they can understand. Furthermore, it relieves the learning situation of a certain degree of rigidity and reduces the finality that is usually associated with a rule.

SELECTED READINGS

Bailey, M. H. (1967). The utility of phonic generalizations in grades one through six. *The Reading Teacher, 20,* 413–418.

Burmeister, L. E. (1968). Vowel pairs. *The Reading Teacher, 21,* 445–452.

Burrows, A., & Lourie, Z. (1963). When two vowels go walking. *The Reading Teacher, 17,* 79–82.

Clymer, T. (1963). The utility of phonic generalizations in the primary grades. *The Reading Teacher, 16,* 252–258.

Emans, R. (1967). The usefulness of phonic generalizations above the primary grades. *The Reading Teacher, 20,* 419–425.

Oaks, R. E. (1952). A study of the vowel situations in a primary vocabulary. *Education, 72,* 604–617.

Chapter 2

Phonics: History and Controversy

A merica is in the latter stages of repealing the dream of universal free education and the goal of educating all children to the maximum of their ability. Neither educators nor their critics believe the schools can educate all of the children that our society delivers to the schools. For decades, criticism of American education has focused on reading, or more precisely, on the phonics component of that instruction.

Should educators, and specifically reading teachers, be conversant with past instructional methods and materials? It might be difficult to establish that knowledge of this history is essential for successful teaching of reading. However, such knowledge can be helpful in understanding some of the problems, attitudes, and misunderstandings that have been and still are associated with American reading instruction. The instructional programs and philosophies presented in the following discussion—both for and against phonics—were all devised by adults, allegedly with the best interests of children in mind. However, hindsight suggests the danger of permitting the beliefs of single-minded crusaders to go unchallenged.

EARLY TRENDS

During the latter part of the 19th century, beginning reading instruction stressed the teaching of the ABCs. Children were taught to recite the names of the letters that made up unknown words met in reading. It was believed that letter naming would provide the necessary phonetic clues for arriving at the spoken word the printed symbols represented. In essence, this was a spelling approach, since letter names often have little resemblance to speech sounds represented by letters (come = see oh em ee = kum). This approach, abandoned because it didn't work, was revived in 1961 by Leonard Bloomfield.

Prior to 1900, and continuing for over a decade, emphasis shifted from drill on letter names to drill on the sounds of the various letters. Rebecca Pollard's *Synthetic Method,* introduced in 1889, advocated reducing reading to a number of mechanical procedures, each of which focused on a unit smaller than a word. Reading became very mechanistic and, when mastered, often produced individuals who were adept at working their way through a given word. The result among both teachers and pupils was that reading became equated with "facility in calling words." A few of the recommended procedures of this method include the following.

1. Drills in articulation were to precede any attempt at reading. The child was to drill on the "sounds of letters." Then the child would be able, it was reasoned, to attack whole words.
2. Single consonants were "sounded." Each consonant was given a sound equivalent to a syllable. Thus, *b, c, d, p, h,* and *t* were sounded *buh, cuh, duh, puh, huh,* and *tuh.*
3. Drills on word families were stressed without regard for word meanings. Sometimes children memorized lists of words ending in such common family phonograms as *ill, am, ick, ate, old,* and *ack.*
4. Diacritical markings were introduced in first grade, and children drilled on "marking sentences." For example: The ghōst wăs a cŏmmŏn sīght near the wrĕck. He knew the īsland was ĕmpty.

This and similar approaches had a number of weaknesses, including the following.

1. The sounds assigned to consonant letters were arbitrary.
2. Letter sounds were overemphasized and taught in isolation (*buh-ah-tuh* = *bat*).
3. This was true also as drill on vowel letter sounds was combined with initial consonant sounds (*ba, da, ha, ma, pa, ra*).
4. Drill instruction was not related to actual words or to actual reading.

It is easy to see that this type of instruction placed little emphasis on reading as a meaning-making process. As children performed these ritualistic drills, they developed an inappropriate concept of reading that negatively influenced their reading behavior.

While these so-called phonics instructional practices were indefensible, the response to these excesses was equally unrealistic. The revolt against the say-the-letters-ignore-the-meaning era resulted in behavior that seemed to suggest that children might learn to read if *words* were bypassed and instruction began immediately with larger units of print. These were called "meaning-bearing units," and it was suggested that beginning instruction focus on sentences, stories, and real literature.

In the book *American Reading Instruction* (1934), Nila B. Smith describes this period. Her book is the source for the several publications cited in the following brief discussion.

In 1895, George L. Farham published *The Sentence Method of Teaching Reading* (cited in Smith, 1934, p. 140). This approach advocated using whole sentences or even stories as a starting point. The teacher would read these "whole messages" to the class and repeat them many times. The children would then recite the material several times. The goal was to have children learn these passages. If they were successful, these activities were somehow equated with reading. Children were not taught to identify any of the words, except perhaps by their visual patterns. Thus, nothing they learned could transfer to the next reading experience if other words were involved. This approach became more aptly named when Charles McMurray, in 1897, published *The Method of Recitation* (cited in Smith, 1934, p. 117).

When support for the sentence-and-story-recitation methods waned, there emerged a movement to use literature as the reading curriculum. A number of reading textbooks published in this era are cited by Smith (1934, p. 122):

Stepping Stones to Literature (1897)

Graded Literature Series (1899)

Special Methods in Reading of Complete English Classics (1899)

The latter text suggested that materials such as *Snow Bound, The Great Stone Face,* and *Julius Caesar* be read and studied as complete works. In agreement, Charles W. Eliot, then president of Harvard University, suggested that existing reading textbooks be removed because they were not *real* literature, just excerpts from literature. Smith (1934) wrote, "We found that between the approximate dates of 1880 and 1918 educators considered the supreme function of reading instruction to be that of developing appreciation for and permanent interest in literature" (p. 185).

The era of literature emphasis just sketched had an elitist component. This reading curriculum might possibly have made sense for that minority of young people destined for more advanced education, college, and the professions. The socioeconomic status of this group was a guarantee that they would acquire (in or out of school) the prerequisite of actually knowing how to read. The problem was that the majority of children in the public schools were not learning reading skills adequate to follow the literature curriculum.

REALITY CHECK: BASAL PROGRAMS

There were a number of changes taking place in American society that raised serious questions about the utility of literature as the reading curriculum. Compulsory education laws kept children in school longer, and students' inability to read caused the schools problems. Also, the workplace was demanding a higher level of literacy. Thus, the inability to read was noticed and became an issue in both the school and the larger community.

The result was a challenge to the magnificent obsession that exposure to literature (sans reading ability) could result in students reading literature. The alternative was to teach children to read—then teach the literature. Instruction would have to change. It would be slower, more obvious, and more direct. Actual teaching materials could not continue to be adult-critiqued literature. To borrow a future criticism, there had to be a "dumbing down" of the reading curriculum. This was accomplished with the emergence of a new wave of basal reading materials.

Graded materials for primary-level instruction (grades 1–6) had been available for more than a century. However, these new materials were definitely a break with tradition. The chief difference was the dual thrust of reading textbooks accompanied by increased emphasis on workbooks that emphasized, taught, and reviewed reading skills. Several characteristics of these materials should be noted.

1. The difficulty level of the reading materials was held to an absolute minimum by severely controlling and limiting the introduction of printed words. After

months of instruction, children were still dealing with stories limited to a vocabulary of 60 to 80 words.

2. This very limited vocabulary necessitated interminable repetition of words in the text materials. This was deadly for students, teachers, parents, and society. Nevertheless, the basals remained the materials of choice for several decades.

3. Basal programs were able to temporarily avoid entanglement in the polar positions regarding teaching phonics. There is no evidence of a deliberate effort to foster the appearance of neutrality in regard to phonics instruction. However, the actual reading textbooks contained little or no overt teaching of letter-sound relationships, while the workbook segments of the programs taught and reviewed phonics skills at every level. Thus, whatever position one preferred in regard to teaching phonics could be accommodated by how one chose to use and emphasize various parts of these programs.

Teachers were poorly served by this laissez-faire attitude toward phonics. There was little guidance in regard to the introduction, emphasis, or methodology involved in teaching phonics. For some teachers, this instruction became less deliberate and less systematic. Many children experienced difficulty in becoming independent readers. In other classrooms, the workbooks became a substitute for teaching. There, mindless repetition of seatwork posing as reading turned children away from reading.

Teacher indecision about instructional practices left fertile ground for the reemergence of an old idea. During the 1850s and later, the conventional wisdom had been that beginning reading instruction should focus on children learning to recognize whole words. This practice could lead to success for a limited time. Children could learn to differentiate among a number of words relying on visual cues only. However, progress in learning broke down when children started to meet an avalanche of unknown words that were very similar in their visual patterns. The word method then gave way to the sentence method and the literature emphasis mentioned previously. The ambivalent attitude toward phonics instruction opened the door to a new version of the whole-word approach.

Sight-Word Method Versus Phonetic Method

Gradually, the conventional wisdom decreed that children should learn a number of sight words prior to receiving any phonics instruction. This philosophy, then reflected in many of the basal materials that were used in the schools, had a tendency to delay phonics instruction. Somehow this instructional philosophy became labeled the "sight-word method."

It is probably safe to surmise that the term *sight-word method* led some people to believe that there was such a method. Since the term omits any reference to phonics, some people might have inferred that phonics was meant to be excluded. At the other end of the continuum, the same type of illogical labeling was taking place. A belief that letter-sound relationships should be taught made one an advocate of the *phonetic method*. Gradually, these two terms took on an either-or connotation, and these were the only positions available. One was either pro-phonics and opposed to teaching sight words or vice versa.

Although these labels could not, and did not, describe any instructional programs in the schools, they completely dominated the debate on reading instruction. Hundreds of research articles, most of them of dubious quality, divided quite evenly on espousing either the phonetic or sight-word method. Thus, the 20-year period preceding the 1950s did not witness any significant modifications in either instructional materials or methodology. All of the widely used basal reading programs were quite similar.

During this period, some children learned to read, some were definitely impaired readers, and very few loved to read. At reading conferences and conventions, teachers constantly asked, "How do you motivate children to read?" This question persisted because it never received a serious answer. There was no responsible answer as long as the then-existing reading curriculum was in place. Children were being asked to read bland, unchildlike materials while instruction moved them much too slowly toward becoming independent readers. Few suspected that things were about to get worse.

CRITICISM LEADS TO NEW PHONICS MATERIALS

As criticism of children's reading ability increased, hostility to existing instructional materials mounted. The 1950s featured more focus and debate on reading instruction and more calls for change than there had been in any previous period. The major catalyst for change was a book written with the fervor that only a true believer could muster: in 1955, Rudolph Flesch published the book *Why Johnny Can't Read*.

Flesch's book came on the scene at exactly the right time. It was simplistic, but written with enough unabashed authority that it was hailed as a panacea. *Why Johnny Can't Read* was one dimensional in that lack of phonics instruction was the alleged problem, and more phonics was the only acceptable solution. There was, Flesh claimed, a conspiracy within the reading establishment to prevent the teaching of phonics. Institutions involved with teacher preparation were a part of, and a moving force behind, this conspiracy. Having identified the problem, Flesh advanced a solution: Teach phonics my way and there will be no failures in learning to read. This publication eventually triggered a strong swing of the pendulum back to phonics instruction.

While Flesch was instrumental in arousing interest in phonics, his suggestions relative to teaching were quite primitive. His material consisted mostly of lists of words presenting different letter-sound patterns. Drill on these word lists was the extent of his instructional program. It was impossible for teachers to use these lists as a basis for instruction.

However, this instructional vacuum was soon filled with a number of new methods and materials that were developed and vigorously promoted. A number of supplementary "phonics emphasis" materials such as flash cards, workbooks, and tape recordings were offered as add-ons for any existing programs. In addition, whole new instructional programs with their own teaching materials were developed, including *Programmed Reading* (n.d.), *Words in Color* (Gattengo, 1962), and the *Initial Teaching Alphabet (ITA)* (Downing, 1963).

This new emphasis on code-cracking (phonics instruction) also spawned a set of instructional materials that were alleged to focus on cracking the code. However, their main thrust was total opposition to teaching any real phonics or letter-sound relationships. To illustrate the scope, philosophy, and inherent weaknesses of these new programs, two will be briefly summarized here. These are the *ITA*, which represented a strong phonics emphasis, and the *Linguistic Regular Spelling* program, which proscribed the teaching of phonics.

THE INITIAL TEACHING ALPHABET (ITA)

The Initial Teaching Alphabet was developed in England by Sir James Pitman in order to achieve a more uniform letter-seen–sound-heard relationship in English writing. This was first called the Augmented Roman Alphabet, since it consisted of 44 rather than 26 letter symbols (Figure 2–1).

FIGURE 2–1 Pitman's Initial Teaching Alphabet (ITA)

Source: From Richard Fink and Patricia Keiserman, *ITA Teacher Training Workbook and Guide* (New York: Initial Teaching Alphabet Publications, 1969). Reprinted by permission.

The use of 44 symbols permits a much closer approximation of a one-to-one relationship between printed letters and the sounds they represent. Obviously, teaching with the ITA involved the development and use of reading materials printed in the ITA. Since the materials were concerned only with initial instruction, learners had to transfer from the ITA materials to materials printed in regular orthography sometime near the end of first grade.

The ITA Instructional Program

The ITA involved more than just the use of a modified orthography. Several salient instructional features were an integral part of its methodology.

1. Children were not taught letter names, but they were taught that each ITA symbol represented a particular sound. Early instruction consisted of systematic teaching of these symbol-sound relationships.
2. From the very beginning of instruction, children were taught to write using the ITA symbols. Writing, which involves spelling of words, reinforced the phonics instruction (letter-sound relationships).
3. In ITA instruction, children learned only the lowercase letters. Capitals were indicated simply by making the letter larger. Thus, the child did not have to deal with two different symbols for the same letter (Aa, Bb, Cc, Dd, Ee, Ff, Gg, Hh) in the initial stages of learning to read and write. In essence, what this practice did was to delay for a time the child's need to master both sets of symbols.
4. Promotional materials for the ITA claimed that there was a high degree of compatibility between ITA and traditional spellings. A fact ignored was that ITA materials frequently resorted to phonetic respelling of irregularly spelled words.

ITA: Postponing the Difficult

As the title *Initial Teaching Alphabet* implies, this was an approach that focused on beginning reading only. Beginning reading tasks were simplified in several ways.

1. Capital letter forms were not introduced.
2. Irregularly spelled words were respelled.
3. All long vowel sounds were represented by two adjacent vowel letters.

Particular attention had to be paid to the various respellings, which resulted in a high degree of consistency between letters seen and sounds heard. This would have had great virtue if it had represented a real spelling reform. However, at the time of transfer, children had to face the reality of irregular spellings while having been taught that words could be sounded by blending the sounds of the letters seen. This mindset that was developed during initial teaching could easily inhibit growth when irregular spellings were met in great profusion in traditional orthography. Table 2–1 illustrates respellings that have nothing to do with the modified alphabet.

Some of these respellings change the visual pattern of words quite drastically, which does not facilitate transfer to traditional print and spelling. While this practice might have resulted in a rapid start in beginning reading, it had minimal effects on

TABLE 2–1   *Initial Teaching Alphabet Respellings*

enough – – – – – enuf	anyone – – – – – enywun	said – – – – – – sed
once – – – – – – wuns	large – – – – – – larj	next – – – – – – nekst
lovely – – – – – – luvly	many – – – – – – meny	George – – – – – Jorj
crossed – – – – – crosst	some – – – – – – sum	one – – – – – – wun
six – – – – – – – siks	money – – – – – muny	couple – – – – – cupl
glove – – – – – – gluv	laugh – – – – – – laf	none – – – – – – nun
wax – – – – – – – waks	ought – – – – – – aut	someone – – – – sumwun
yacht – – – – – – yot	tough – – – – – tuf	trouble – – – – – trubl

TABLE 2–2   *Initial Teaching Alphabet Two-Vowel Generation*

also – – – – – – – auls œ	night – – – – – – niet	find – – – – – – f iend
their – – – – – – – thær	so – – – – – – – s œ	seized – – – – – s ee zd
there – – – – – – thær	idea – – – – – – ie dee a	wife – – – – – – w ie f
I – – – – – – – – – ie	most – – – – – – mœst	walked – – – – – w au kt
knows – – – – – n œs	came – – – – – – c æm	ate – – – – – – æt
fire – – – – – – – fie r	lace – – – – – – l æ s	owe – – – – – – œ
my – – – – – – – m ie	phone – – – – – f œ n	page – – – – – pæj
sight – – – – – – sie t	weigh – – – – – w æ	gave – – – – – g æ v
giant – – – – – – j ie ant	nice – – – – – – n ie s	people – – – – p ee pl
eyes – – – – – – ie s	five – – – – – – f ie v	life – – – – – – l ie f

children cracking the main code. They eventually had to deal with irregular words when they transferred to traditional orthography.

In addition to the phonetic respellings, which did not involve any of the new ITA characters, many spelling changes involved a reshuffling of vowels. The vowel changes and transpositions were made so that the spelling would follow the "two-vowel generalization": when two vowels come together, the first has its long sound and the second is silent. Some examples of this are presented in Table 2–2.

Transfer from the ITA to Traditional Orthography

Concurrently with the introduction and use of the ITA in America, there were assurances from many quarters that transfer from the ITA to traditional print would not pose a problem. This optimism was allegedly grounded on reports from England. While John Downing of England was actively promoting the experimental use of the ITA in America, his 1963 publication, *Experiments with Pitman's Initial Teaching Alphabet in British Schools,* contained a note of caution on the issue of transfer:

> If teachers' *opinions* are supported by the results of the objective tests conducted last month [March 1963], we may feel encouraged in *our hopes* that all children will pass through the transfer stage with success, but *we must urge the greatest caution in drawing final conclusions or taking action on the basis of this preliminary trial.* (p. 125)

Downing's caution was vindicated by the outcome of studies in England and America. In the December 1967 issue of *Elementary English,* Downing stated,

> Although teachers' subjective impressions of the transition stage have suggested that it is smooth and effortless, test results show that i.t.a. students from about mid-second year until about mid-third year do not read t.o. [traditional orthography] as well as they read i.t.a. a few weeks or even months previously. . . . More specifically, the British experiments show that children are not transferring from i.t.a. to t.o. in quite the way originally predicted. (p. 849)

Reading achievement resulting from the use of the ITA failed to establish this medium as superior to traditionally printed materials in which methodology also stressed systematic phonics instruction.

THE LINGUISTIC (REGULAR SPELLING) APPROACH

Of all the newer methods that emerged in the post-Flesch period, the linguistic approach may well be the strangest. These materials were first published by Leonard Bloomfield in 1942. For the next decade, Bloomfield and his colleague, Clarence L. Barnhart, collaborated in efforts to have the materials adapted and used in mainstream reading instruction. However, during this time they received little if any favorable response or acceptance.

After Bloomfield's death and the increasing emphasis on teaching phonics, Barnhart published *Let's Read: A Linguistic Approach* in 1961. The materials contained therein had no roots in any branch of linguistic science. However, Bloomfield was a noted linguist and the term *linguistics* was popular and frequently invoked by critics of reading instruction. Thus the subtitle, *A Linguistic Approach.*

The irony of *Let's Read* is that it was published as part of the *Why Johnny Can't Read* revolution, the main thrust of which was the relentless, hard-nosed teaching of phonics or code-cracking. Somehow, *Let's Read* was able to pose as code-cracking material even thought the teaching of phonics or letter-sound relationships was proscribed.

The most tenable hypothesis as to how this could have happened was that the material so closely resembled a previously used phonics instructional approach that the two were confused. This was especially the case in regard to the systematic teaching of a series of words that each ended with the same phonogram. This was called the "word-family" approach, and the word families were identical to the spelling patterns stressed in the regular spelling approach. Some examples are *cat, hat, mat, fat, bat* and *can, man, tan, fan, ran.* The teaching methodologies involved in the two approaches, however, were antithetical. In the word-family method, children were taught to think and say the sound represented by the first letter. This sounding clue helped them distinguish between the sounds of the words *cat, hat,* m*at,* f*at,* b*at,* s*at,* p*at,* and r*at.* In the regular spelling methodology, children had to learn each word configuration by memory.

The Regular Spelling Instructional Program

Vocabulary control (regular spelling concept).   The major premise of these materials was that initial instruction should be based exclusively on a unique vocabulary-control principle. This principle was that in early reading instruction, the child should meet only those words that have "regular spellings," a term used to designate words in which printed letters represent "the most characteristic sound" associated with each letter.

The word *cat* would meet this criterion, but the word *cent* would be irregular because the *c* does not represent the characteristic *k* sound but rather the sound usually represented by *s.* The spelling of *bird* is irregular because the *i* represents a sound usually represented by *u* (burd) as does the *o* in *come* (kum).

Initial teaching (letter names, not letter sounds).   In the regular spelling approach, the child was taught letter recognition and letter names (aye, bee, see, dee, ee, eff). After the letters are learned in isolation they are combined into words:

> The child need not even be told that the combinations are words; and he should certainly not be required to recognize or read words. *All he needs to do is read off the names of the successive letters, from left to right.* (Bloomfield and Barnhart, 1961, p. 36)

Then the child is ready to begin working his way through a series of words that end with identical letter-phoneme patterns (*can, fan, man, tan*). Bloomfield and Barnhart (1961) suggested that teaching should proceed as follows.

1. Print and point to the word CAN.
2. The child is to read the letters "see aye en."
3. The teacher states "Now we have spelled the word. Now we are going to *read* it. This word is can. Read it *can.*"
4. Present another word from the "an family" such as *tan.* (p. 41)

The aim of this teaching method was to have the child distinguish between various words that differ only in the initial grapheme-phoneme. However, the child was never taught the association between the initial letter and the sound it represents in words. There is no question but that a child must learn this relationship in order to become an independent reader.

Meaning waived in beginning instruction.   Unfortunately, many of the English words we use most frequently in building even the simplest of sentences have irregular spellings. Some examples include *a, the, was, once, of, any, could, love, too, their, do, said, one, who, some, only, gone, live, father, give, many, are, would, come, head, both, again, been, have, they, there, to, get,* and *should.* Typical English sentences are difficult to build when one decides to use only words that follow regular spelling patterns. For example, in Bloomfield's and Barnhart's (1961) material, after the teaching of 66 words (roughly equivalent to several preprimers in a representative basal series), one finds only the most contrived sentences and absolutely no story line.

> Pat had ham.
> Nat had jam.
> Sam had a cap.
> Dan had a hat.
> Sam ran.
> Can Sam tag Pam?
> Can Pam tag Sam? (p. 65)

After 200 words had been learned, the child read these sentences.

> Let Dan bat.
> Did Al get wet?
> Van had a pet cat.
> Get up, Tad!
> Let us in, Sis!
> Sis, let us in!
> Let Sid pet a pup. (Bloomfield and Barnhart, 1961, p. 87)

If letter-sound relationships were learned, the child could then use this learning in future reading tasks. For instance, learning the sound that *b* represents in the word b*at* would transfer to the *b* in other word families such as b*et,* b*it,* b*ut,* b*ad,* b*ud,* b*id,* b*ug,* b*un,* b*us,* b*ag,* b*ig,* and b*ed.* More important, the knowledge the sound *b* represents would also function in words with irregular spellings because the sound represented by *b* remains consistent in hundreds of these words (barn, ball, bath, bird, bold, busy, burn, both, bow).

Only 38% of the *Let's Read* program consisted of regularly spelled words. It is clear that what was learned in the initial instruction was not expected to transfer to the remaining two thirds of the program. Bloomfield and Barnhart (1961) revealed the Achilles heel of the material when they stated,

> When it comes to teaching irregular and special words, each word will demand a separate effort and separate practice. (p. 206)

No guidelines or blueprint for such instruction was provided. Initial instruction soon exhausted the easier aspects of learning to read. Then children and teachers were abandoned when the more difficult aspects of learning to read could no longer be avoided.

THE INDIVIDUALIZED READING AND LANGUAGE EXPERIENCE APPROACHES

While the highly structured beginning reading programs just discussed were seeking converts, there also emerged a philosophy of reading instruction that sought to curtail or abolish much of the structure and routine associated with the basal programs. This new philosophy operated under the twin banner of the *Individualized Reading*

Movement and the *Language Experience Approach.* The chief premises of these new approaches included the following.

1. Reliance on basal reader materials was to be avoided. These were considered to be too restrictive, dull, and uninspiring.
2. Trade books (children's literature) were to be plentiful in every classroom.
3. Children were to select the reading materials they wished to read.
4. Both reading and writing were to be incorporated into the reading instruction curriculum. They were considered to be complementary parts of language acquisition.
5. Children were to write, or dictate to the teacher, their own experiences or stories. These reading materials were to remain available in the classroom as long as the materials had motivational value.
6. Teachers were to schedule a time period for any child who could profit from a teacher-pupil conference.
7. Workbooks and their repetitive teaching of skills were frowned upon.

This new emphasis on children reading children's literature was a significant departure from the turn of the century's emphasis on literature. Then, the focus had been on adult classics that had been authenticated by adults as having "cultural value." The emphasis on children's literature as an integral part of the reading-instruction curriculum was a significant development. This was a reform that contained the potential for an educational revolution.

WHOLE LANGUAGE

The individualized reading approach's break with traditional instruction and its emphasis on integrating writing and reading instruction became the foundation for the whole-language movement. Whole language is not an instructional program, and its proponents do not claim that it is. It has been called a philosophy, a dynamic system of beliefs, a child-centered curriculum, and a means for empowering children. Goodman (1992), describing the status of whole language, writes, "Whole language is producing a holistic reading and writing curriculum which uses real authentic literature and real books" (p. 196).

Both supporters and critics agree that the concept of whole language is vague. One is invited into a seemingly attractive territory for which there is as yet no map. Its position is reminiscent of descriptions of individualized reading made in the mid-1970s:

> Paradoxically its greatest potential strengths and weaknesses stem from the same factor. There is no concise definition of "what it is" and thus no blueprint for 'how to do it'. . . . In one sense, individualized reading focuses on the child-as-a-reader more than the teacher-as-a-teacher. (Heilman, 1977, pp. 306–308)

Goodman (1992) has written that "whole language aims to be an inclusive philosophy of education" (p. 196). Actually, it has not been totally inclusive. There is a litmus test that proscribes the direct teaching of *reading skills* (which is a code-word for *phonics*). This cannot be explained away as being a gratuitous diversion: It is the chief article of faith of true believers in whole language. Whole language can fit comfortably at every level of the curriculum except for the period called "learning to read." Here one must develop the skills needed to move into a literature curriculum.

Whole language is the latest version of that magnificent obsession that children might be successful in reading literature prior to solving the written code. What sustains this recurring dream? Is it based on the fact that learning the code is not a totally pleasant experience? Adult critics have noticed this as they observe children learning to read. When these adult, expert readers read, they are immersed in and sustained by the power and beauty of language. They say, "Let beginning reading be like this. Let beginning readers become involved with the beauty of language that resides in literature." To believe that this can occur, it is necessary to blur the difference between reading and learning to read. However, reading and learning to read are not synonymous. Learning to read is the price we pay in order to read literature.

Relative to this discussion, Jerome Bruner, a psychologist who helped develop the cognitive approach in the 1950s, made a significant observation and shared it with reading teachers. He said, "Learning to read is not a self-sustaining activity" (1972). He knew that learning to read is not the same activity that expert readers experience when they read. For learners, some of the joy is missing. The power and beauty of language is held hostage by the unknown words that interrupt the melody of language.

While learning to read may not be a self-sustaining activity, it is an activity that must be sustained until children make it to the next level, which is reading. Readers, by definition, can deal independently with the printed page. Children at all levels of reading ability will meet some words that they do not instantly recognize. But if they have mastered the code, they will be able to solve the identity of most of these words. Once children reach this point on the learning-to-read continuum, they are ready for the whole-language curriculum.

SELECTED READINGS

Bruner, J. S. (1972). Address to the International Reading Association Convention. Detroit.

Downing, J. A. (1963). *Experiments with Pitman's initial teaching alphabet in British schools.* New York: Initial Teaching Alphabet Publications.

Downing, J. A. (May, 1965). Common misconceptions about i.t.a. *Elementary English, 42,* 492–501.

Downing, J. A. (December, 1967). Can i.t.a. be improved? *Elementary English, 44,* 849–855.

Flesch, R. (1955). *Why Johnny can't read.* New York: Harper.

Fink, R., & Keiserman, P. (1969). ITA Teacher trainng workbook and guide. New York: Initial Teaching Alphabet Publications.

Fries, C. C. (1963). *Linguistics and reading.* New York: Holt, Rinehart, & Winston.

Gattengo, C. (1962). *Words in color.* Chicago: Learning Materials.

Goodman, K. S. (1992). I didn't found whole language. *The Reading Teacher, 46,* 188–198.

Heilman, A. W. (1977). *Principles and practices of teaching reading.* 4th ed. Columbus, OH: Merrill.

Pollard, R. (1889). *Pollard's synthetic method.* Chicago: Western Publishing House.

Smith, N. B. (1934). *American Reading Instruction.* New York: Silver Burdett.

•

Chapter 3

PREREQUISITES FOR PHONICS INSTRUCTION

PHONOLOGICAL AWARENESS: THE FIRST PREREQUISITE FOR PHONICS INSTRUCTION

Children enter the world as auditory learners. Children who develop their language with normal hearing ability attend to sounds all around them: caregivers "oohing" and "ahhing," as well as the ongoing repetition of songs, rhymes, and important names in their lives. This ongoing auditory language-rich stimulation is a necessary ingredient for developing phonological awareness. Phonological awareness is the ability to think about all the possible sounds in a word: syllables, onset, rime, and phonemes. For example, the word *crack* can be heard as a one-syllable word: crack. Crack can also be heard in its onset and rime form: cr-ack. Or crack can be heard as individual phonemes: c-r-a-ck.

Early in a child's development, phonological awareness occurs subconsciously. As the child learns language, he or she will subconsciously play with syllables (ma-ma, da-da), onsets and rimes (Holly, bolly, dolly, molly, wolly), and phonemes—usually with the loudest or last sound (hat,t,t,t,t,t). As the child becomes more phonologically aware, the play becomes more purposeful and the child develops an understanding that:

- words can rhyme.
- words can have one or more syllables.
- words are in sentences.
- words can begin and end with the same sounds.
- words are made up of small sounds called phonemes (this is the beginning of phonemic awareness).

There are many informal, play-like language activities that can purposely help children to analyze and articulate the sounds heard in their world. These activities should be orally directed and initiated—it is not necessary to have any print available.

1. Sound Ordering Activity

- The teacher determines three common sounds to make in the classroom. These sounds need to be familiar to the students (ringing bell, blowing whistle, knocking on the door).
- Ask the students to listen and watch carefully as you make each sound and name the object that makes the sound.
- Explain to the students that they will be asked to close their eyes and listen for the sounds. The goal is to try to listen carefully so that all students can recall the order that the sounds were made.
- Ask the students to close their eyes. You make the three sounds.
- Students open their eyes and try to recall the sounds in order.
- Guide their response by using three blank Post-it® Notes (sound notes) arranged in a line on the board. Which sound do they recall hearing? They recall hearing the bell. Was that the first sound, the middle sound, or the final sound? By using these prompts, you are helping the students to develop an ordering skill that will be very helpful when analyzing sounds (phonemes) in words for phonemic awareness.
- Once the students have ordered the sounds, you can draw simple illustrations on the Post-it Notes.
- Ask a student to point to each Post-it Note as you make the sounds.

Extension Activity: On another day, ask a student to secretly reorder the Post-it Notes. These notes should be kept out of sight from the remainder of the class. You direct the class as detailed previously. Place new blank Post-it Notes (sound notes) on the board. Make the sounds as determined by the student. The goal is to have the remaining members of the class determine the new order of sounds. The student selected to secretly reorder the sounds receives guided support from you in determining if the students can recall the correct order.

Further Extensions: While out on a walk, stop and listen to the sounds for a few moments. Try to order the first three sounds you hear during that brief pause.

2. Word Ordering Activity

Say a familiar short poem to the students. For example, say the following,

> Peas porridge hot
> Peas porridge cold,
> Peas porridge in the pot
> Nine days old.

- Ask the students to recite it after you.
- Tell the students, "I want you to listen carefully to the first line of the poem: 'Peas porridge hot.' Repeat it after me. What is a word that you remember saying? Was that the first word, second word or last word?"

- Place three blank Post-it Notes (word notes) on the board and point to them saying, "Peas porridge hot." Help the students to locate the Post-it Note (word note) that corresponds to the word they remember hearing.
- Once all the words have been recalled and ordered, recite and say "Peas porridge hot" together and point to the Post-it Notes as you say the words. (Remember, this is an auditory activity so print is not necessary. You are helping the students to recall a three-word phrase, order the three words, and see the words as distinct sounds in the phrase.)

Extension Activity: Develop a three- or four-word sentence about school. This can be done together as a class activity.

- Once you have come up with the sentence, place Post-it Notes on the board as you recite the sentence together. For example, "We like recess."
- Recite the sentence together and point to the blank Post-it Notes in correct sentence order, moving from left to right as you say each word.
- Ask the students to point to the Post-it Note that represents "We." This is called the first word. Ask them to point to the note for "recess." This is the second word. What Post-it Note represents "recess?" What would we call that word? This is the third word.
- Count the words and read the sentence together once again.

3. Direction Ordering Activity

List three simple directions that involve a series of tasks. For example, explain to the students that when they enter the classroom each day, they must sign-in at their table, pull out their notebooks, and select a book for silent reading.

- Place three Post-it Notes (direction notes) on the board.
- Ask the students to recall one of the directions.
- Is it the first direction, the second direction, or the last direction?
- Work at recalling the other directions and ordering them.
- Once the directions have been recalled and ordered correctly, recite them together.
- Draw simple illustrations on the Post-it Notes to help the students recall the directions as prompts for their independent work time.

4. Rhyming Activity: Beginning Play with Onsets and Rimes

Immerse the students in rich poetry and song that is filled with rhyming words. Talk about the words that have an ending (rime) that sounds the same. Play with these words by placing beginning sounds on the end and determining if these are sensible words or nonsense words. For example, "Miss Mary Mack" is a wonderful rhythmic poem that can be used to illustrate this activity. Say it several times with the students so that they are familiar with the poem and can easily recite it with you.

> "Miss Mary Mack, Mack, Mack
>
> All dressed in black, black, black
>
> With silver buttons, buttons, buttons,
>
> All down her back, back, back."

- After reciting it a number of times, ask the following: What words in this poem have the same ending sound? (As much as possible, give the students appropriate thinking time so that these responses are student-generated and teacher-guided.) For example, mack, black, back. These words rhyme.
- Now, listen carefully to how these words sound together: Mack, buttons. What do you notice about these words? (They do not rhyme. Their ending sounds are different.)
- Let's make other words that rhyme with Mack, black, and back. (Again, give the students appropriate thinking time so that these responses are student-generated and teacher-guided.) For example, tack, sack, gack.
- Is tack a real word that makes sense and sounds right? Have you ever heard of a tack?
- Is sack a real word that makes sense and sounds right? Have you ever heard of a sack?
- Is gack a word that makes sense and sounds right? Have you ever heard of a gack?

5. Ordering Words into Sentences Activity

Select sentences from rhythmic, familiar, patterned reading text. For example, a sentence that appears repeatedly in a familiar book that the students know well: "The people ran and ran!"

- Read the sentence and place Post-it Notes (word notes) on the board (one for each word).
- Recite the sentence together and point to the Post-it Notes (word notes).
- Ask the students to count the Post-it Notes and determine how many words are in the sentence.
- Locate the first word and say it.
- Locate the last word and say it.
- Change the text to include an animal name. "The horses ran and ran."
- Locate which Post-it Note will represent "horses."
- Locate the Post-it Notes that represent "ran."
- Change the word "ran" to "ate." "The horses ate and ate."
- Locate "horses."
- Locate "ate and ate."

6. Syllable Activity

Gather the students in a circle on the floor. Using the children's names, clap the number of syllables in each child's name as you say it. This can be done in a round-like fashion.

- As you clap his or her name, give each student the correct number of note cards to correspond to the number of syllables in his or her name.
- These cards are placed on the floor in front of them and are used as syllable prompts for clapping syllables the second time around.
- After all the names have been clapped and each child has the correct number of note cards, softly work around the circle saying their names, clapping the syllables and counting the note cards. For example:

   "Sar-ah." Clap, clap. Two syllables.

   "Sam." Clap. One syllable.

   "Ro-ber-ta." Clap, clap, clap. Three syllables.

- Take time to discuss the idea that all words and names can have one syllable, two syllables, three syllables, or more.

Extension Activity: Take the cards and sort them on a bulletin board according to those names that have one syllable, two syllables, three syllables, and so forth. These can be arranged in a chart-like fashion with a small photograph of each child next to his or her corresponding syllable note cards. Students are encouraged to take a pointer and count, or clap, the syllables on their own.

7. Onset and Rime Activity

As with all the previous activities, the following will continue to be auditory-based with no use of letters or words. The goal of all these activities is the ongoing discussion about sounds: the type of sound (sound in the room, words in a phrase, words in a sentence, or syllables in a word), the location of the sound (first, middle, or last), and what makes that sound (object, word, syllable). This next activity reflects a higher level of phonological awareness: onsets and rimes.

- This activity can be used with poetry, songs, names, and environmental print. It is recommended to select a one-syllable word that can have several possibilities of sensible onsets. For example, if you have a student in your classroom with the name "Pam," use her name. You can also bring in a piece of environmental print that has a familiar one-syllable label: CREST.
- Say "Pam" and clap out the syllables (one clap).
- Explain that you are going to listen for smaller sounds in Pam's name and that you are most interested in using her name to rhyme with other words.
- Place two Post-it Notes (sound notes) on the board and say P-AM. Point to the first note for /P/, and the second note for /AM/. Remind the students that you are talking about something different than syllables.
- Ask the students to locate the note for /P/. Is this the first sound or the last sound in PAM?

- Ask the students to locate the note for /AM/. Is this the first or last sound?
- Point to the /AM/ Post-it Note. What is this again? Can you think of any words that would rhyme with the /AM/ sound in PAM?
- As students come up with words, slowly sound them out accordingly: S-AM, H-AM, SL-AM, J-AM. While you do this, point to the correct blank Post-it Notes. If a student responds with a word that does not share the rhyme, but shares the onset /P/, point out that they are hearing the first sound in PAM.

8. Phoneme Activity: Preparation for Phonemic Awareness

Using a familiar one-syllable, three-sound word, place three Post-it Notes on the board. These must be arranged in left to right progression, with a small space between each note. It is important to select a word that is familiar to the students: a student's name; a familiar word from a song, poem, or text; or environmental print. For example, if you have read a familiar text about a CAT, this would be an excellent word to select.

- I would like to take some time to talk about the smallest sounds in CAT. CAT has a syllable sound. Let's clap it. CAT. CAT has one syllable.
- CAT has two smaller sounds that we can hear as /C/ /AT/. These are the two sounds in CAT that we can use to make silly words and real words for rhyming play.
- CAT also has three very small sounds. Let's see if we can hear any of the smallest sounds in CAT.
- Listen and watch as I point to our sound notes (Post-it Notes) and then we will talk about what you remember hearing.
- Say /C/ softly and carefully, and point to the first note, /A/ and point to the middle note, /T/ and point to the final Post-it Note. (Be very careful to say the sounds softly and not stretch them out into a syllable formation. It is helpful to whisper the sounds and try to keep them as short as possible.)
- What sound do you remember hearing? (Please give the students appropriate thinking time so that these responses are student-generated and teacher-guided.) Did you say that you heard a /T/?
- Where do you think you heard it in the word CAT? Point to the notes and say /C/ softly, and point to the first note, /A/ and point to the middle note, /T/ and point to the final Post-it Note. Can you tell which sound note is the /T/ sound?
- Now locate the next sound (most often the /C/). Unless you have a speller in your classroom, the vowel sound will not be discriminated by most of your students. Talk about how hard it can be to hear this sound and describe it and locate it as the middle sound.
- Say all the sounds in order and point to the Post-it Notes (sound notes).
- Play this activity several times a week with fun, meaningful words.

PHONEMIC AWARENESS: THE SECOND PREREQUISITE FOR PHONICS INSTRUCTION

A second important prerequisite for phonics instruction is phonemic awareness. This term refers to the knowledge or understanding that speech consists of a series of sounds and that individual words can be divided into phonemes. Phonemic awareness is the ability to identify and manipulate these sounds (phonemes). Once a child develops an awareness of the smallest sounds in a word, he or she is able to understand that:

- words have small sounds that can be pulled apart and put back together.
- sounds in words have a specific order (first sound, middle sound, final sound).
- sounds in words can be counted.
- sounds in words can be moved, removed, or replaced to make new words.
- several sounds can be represented by different letters.

DEVELOPING PHONEMIC AWARENESS

In learning speech, individual phonemes are slighted. Preschool children have developed expertise in differentiating words as speech units. They tend to hear syllables and shorter words as auditory wholes. That is, when they hear or say the word *stand,* they are unaware that what they say or hear is speech-flow consisting of a blend of five speech sounds (phonemes). In order to learn to read the printed code, they must become proficient in segmenting syllables into their constituent phonemes. This ability has been found to be an accurate predictor of success in early reading achievement.

There are many instructional procedures that can enhance children's development of phonemic awareness. Regardless of their educational experience, children will learn and progress at vastly different rates. It is no longer questioned that the earlier children master this skill, the more rapid is their progress in learning to read.

Phonemic awareness skills are rarely well developed while children are learning speech prior to entering school. These skills should be taught both before and along with early reading instruction. They are developmental in nature, which suggests that regardless of what has been mastered, there is more to be learned. The following are oral language activities that do not involve children with print.

HEARING SPEECH SOUNDS IN WORDS

1. Explain that words are made up of one or more sounds. Inquire if anyone can name a word that has only one sound. Eventually choose *I* as a word that has only one sound. Have children pronounce *I*.

> "Now I say the word *hi*. How many sounds in *hi*?
>
> Yes, we hear two sounds in *hi,* one sound in *I*.
>
> The sound *a* is a word in a sentence like 'There is *a* cow!'
>
> Do cows eat *a*? What do cows eat?
>
> Yes, cows eat *hay*.
>
> Do you hear two sounds in *hay*?"

(If someone interjects that there are three letters in the word *hay,* congratulate her and agree, but point out we *hear* just two speech sounds (*h/a/*).

Variation: "How many sounds do we hear in the word *zoo*?

> Yes, two in *zoo*.
>
> How many in *zoom*?
>
> > in *moo*?
> >
> > in *moon*?
>
> Children may enjoy a little doggerel.
>
> Two in *zoo,* three in *zoom*.
>
> Still two in *moo,* and three in *moon*.
>
> But four we hear when we say *spoon!*"

2. Same or Different

Pronounce pairs of words. In some pairs, have both words contain the same number of speech sounds. In other pairs, have the words differ in the number of speech sounds they contain. Children respond *"same"* or *"different"* following each pair.

owl - fowl (d)	rain - train (d)	come - hum (s)
ask - try (s)	go - sun (d)	jump - fire (d)
goose - moose (s)	sled - flag (s)	nail - snail (d)
play - say (d)	sled - led (d)	spot - stop (s)

3. Next Difficulty Level

Use the same or similar data found in Activity 2. Pronounce each pair of words. Children identify the number of speech sounds heard in each word, i.e., "Four sounds in *sled;* three sounds in *led.*"

Variation: "I will say two words. Only one of them will be made up of three speech sounds. Repeat the word that has three sounds."

3	3	3	3
(too — took)	(see — set)	(sat — at)	(ate — hat)
3	3	3	3
(hid — he)	(fast — man)	(seek — sheep)	(stop — play)

✍ INITIAL SOUNDS IN WORDS

1. Children listen to the pronunciation of a series of words, all of which begin with the same sound: *make, most, must, made, mine, meet.* Children then volunteer other words that begin with the /m/ sound: *mile, music, month, mail, mop, mask.*

2. Collect a number of pictures from workbooks, catalogues, or magazines. Select several pairs of pictures whose naming words begin with the same sound. Attach each picture to a separate piece of cardboard to make handling easier. Children then group pictures according to their initial sound (ball-boat; house-horse; fence-feather; pig-pumpkin; log-ladder). As the children progress, the difficulty level of the exercise can be increased by including three or more pictures whose names begin with the same sound. Of course, the objects in the pictures should be known by the children.

3. Rimes in search of an onset.

   Review: In the word *cap*, *c* is the onset; *ap* is the rime.

   Explain that each sentence you read will end with two speech sounds that do not make a word. Children are to add one sound in front of these sounds to make a word.

   Examples: "He was chewing _um." Children say, "Gum."
   "The car was stuck in the _ud." Children say, "Mud."

How fast can he _un?	(r)
A baby goat is a _id.	(k)
The boy's name is _om.	(T)
False hair is a _ig.	(w)
Never play with a _un.	(g)
That pot has no _id.	(l)
The guide looked at the _ap.	(m)
He caught the fish in a _et.	(n)
The light was very _im.	(d)
The squirrel ate the _ut.	(n)

   Variation: "Add a sound in front of the word I pronounce to make a new word."
   at converts to (b*at*, r*at*, h*at*, p*at*, m*at*)
   an converts to (f*an*, m*an*, t*an*, r*an*, c(k)*an*)

it converts to (h*it*, l*it*, p*it*, w*it*, s*it*)

am converts to (j*am*, d*am*, h*am*, S*am*)

in converts to (w*in*, f*in*, t*in*, b*in*, s*in*)

all converts to (b*all*, c*all*, h*all*, f*all*, t*all*)

eat converts to (h*eat*, b*eat*, m*eat*, s*eat*, n*eat*)

4. Delete the initial sound and make a new word.

"I will say a word. If you say all but the first sound in that word, you will make a different word."

Examples: If I say *cup*, you say _____? up

If I say *bus*, you say _____? us

Teacher		Student	Teacher		Student	Teacher		Student
pan	-	an	hit	-	it	beat	-	eat
win	-	in	ham	-	am	hand	-	and
can	-	an	spin	-	pin	tin	-	in
sand	-	and	small	-	mall	spill	-	pill
twin	-	win	howl	-	owl	jam	-	am

WORKING WITH RHYMES

The purpose of the following activities is to provide practice in discriminating speech sounds in words, specifically rhyming elements. In addition, the exercises focus on developing other skills such as listening (limiting responses to one category: e.g., numbers, colors, or animals), following directions, and noting stress and intonation patterns.

1. Thinking of Rhyming Words

Explain that you are going to read some sentences. Children are to listen carefully so they can supply words that rhyme with the last word in each sentence. The last word in the sentence should be stressed; in some classroom situations, it may even be advisable to repeat it.

1. Be sure to wear a hat on your *head.* (red, bed, Ted, said)
2. We will take a trip to the *lake.*
3. John, you may pet the *cat.*
4. They all said hello to the *man.*
5. Have you ever seen a *moose?*
6. We watched the bird build its *nest.*
7. Let's all count to *ten.*
8. Mary walked in the rain and got *wet.*
9. Sunday, we went to the *beach.*

Variation: Prepare sentences in which the final word is omitted. In reading the sentence, emphasize one word. A child completes the sentence by giving a word that rhymes with the word that is emphasized. This procedure also teaches the concept of stress as part of intonation patterns.

1. A *frog* sat on a _____. (log)
2. Mary will *bake* a chocolate _____. (cake)
3. Please do not bounce the *ball* in the _____. (hall)
4. On his finger the *king* wore a _____. (ring)
5. Kate will *wait* by the _____. (gate)
6. Keith swept the *room* with a nice new _____. (broom)

2. Number Rhymes

Explain that you will pronounce and emphasize two words that rhyme with a number word. The children are to supply the rhyming number word to finish each sentence.

1. *Blue* and *shoe* rhyme with _____. (two)
2. *Gate* and *hate* rhyme with _____. (eight)
3. *Fix* and *mix* rhyme with _____. (six)
4. *Drive* and *hive* rhyme with _____. (five)
5. *Gun* and *run* rhyme with _____. (one)
6. *Tree* and *see* rhyme with _____. (three)
7. *When* and *then* rhyme with _____. (ten)
8. *Pine* and *line* rhyme with _____. (nine)
9. *Door* and *more* rhyme with _____. (four)
10. *Eleven* and *heaven* rhyme with _____. (seven)

To provide practice in speaking in sentences, have one volunteer say the entire sentence after each rhyme: "*Gate* and *late* rhyme with *eight*."

Variation: This activity is similar to the preceding one except that the last word you speak is the clue to the rhyming word.

Teacher: "Give me a number that rhymes with _____."

1. *fun* (one)
2. *fix* (six)
3. *fine* (nine)
4. *floor* (four)
5. *bee* (three)
6. *hen* (ten)
7. *late* (eight)
8. *do* (two)
9. *alive* (five)
10. *heaven* (seven)

3. Color Names to Complete a Rhyme

Teacher: "Name the color that rhymes with _____."

1. *head* and *bed* (red)
2. *clean* and *queen* (green)
3. *tray* and *play* (gray)
4. *do* and *you* (blue)
5. *track* and *back* (black)
6. *town* and *gown* (brown)
7. *man* and *ran* (tan)

    8. *sight* and *kite* (white)
    9. *think* and *sink* (pink)
  10. *fellow* and *Jell-O* (yellow)

4. Animal Names to Complete a Rhyme

Teacher: "Name an animal that rhymes with _____."

1. *hat* (rat, cat)		**6.** *near* (deer)
2. *log* (dog, frog)		**7.** *jeep* (sheep)
3. *house* (mouse)		**8.** *cantaloupe* (antelope)
4. *boat* (goat)		**9.** *big* (pig)
5. *mitten* (kitten)		**10.** *box* (fox)

5. Rhyming Words and Following Directions

Each participant should have two 3″ × 5″ cards with the word *yes* printed on both sides of one card, and *no* printed on both sides of the other. Read statements similar to those below. If the two emphasized words rhyme, children hold up the *yes* card; if the words do not rhyme, they hold up the *no* card.

    1. I say *fox* and *box.* (yes)
    2. I say *coat* and *road.* (no)
    3. I say *found* and *ground.* (yes)
    4. I say *man* and *men.* (no)
    5. I say *car* and *cart.* (no)
    6. I say *feet* and *meet.* (yes)
    7. I say *book* and *look.* (yes)
    8. I say *glass* and *dress.* (no)
    9. I say *bug* and *rug.* (yes)
  10. I say *chair* and *church.* (no)

6. Forming Rhymes with Letter Names

Teacher: "Name a letter (or letters) that rhymes with _____." Or, "What letter(s) rhymes with _____?"

    1. *say* and *day* (a, k, j)
    2. *me* and *tree* (b, c, d, e, g, v, t, z, p)
    3. *sell* and *bell* (l)
    4. *hen* and *ten* (n)
    5. *high* and *sky* (i, y)
    6. *far* and *car* (r)
    7. *true* and *blue* (u, q)
    8. *them* and *gem* (m)
    9. *no* and *grow* (o)
  10. *dress* and *less* (s)

HEARING FINAL SOUNDS IN WORDS (NONRHYMING)

Besides practice on initial sounds and rhyming elements, children need auditory practice in matching and differentiating the final sound in words (nonrhyming elements). It is easier for children to note that *cat* and *rat* end with the same sounds than it is to note that *cat* and *tent* end with the same sound.

1. Pairs of Words

Pronounce pairs of words, some of which end with the same sound. If the two words end with the same sound, the children respond "same"; if the final sounds are different, they say "different."

1. *net* and *but* (same)
2. *fan* and *fat* (different)
3. *fog* and *pig* (same)
4. *hen* and *man* (same)
5. *six* and *tax* (same)
6. *bus* and *gas* (same)
7. *hat* and *hid* (different)
8. *leg* and *let* (different)
9. *rub* and *rug* (different)
10. *lip* and *tap* (same)
11. *hop* and *hot* (different)
12. *log* and *bug* (same)

MOM AND POP WORDS

Invite children to listen carefully as you pronounce a number of words. Explain that some of these words will begin and end with the same sound while others will not.

Example: *pup*   "Does *pup* begin and end with the same sound?" (yes)

   bed   "Does *bed* begin and end with the same sound?" (no)

"Now, when I say a word, you repeat it. If the first and last sounds are the same, say *yes*. If they are not the same, say *no*."

tent (yes)	tube (no)	soon (no)	toast (yes)	did (yes)
dad (yes)	pep (yes)	mom (yes)	bud (no)	trip (no)
noon (yes)	top (no)	bed (no)	toot (yes)	pop (yes)

DELETE A FINAL PHONEME (THE WORD YOU MAKE IS?)

Select a series of words that form a different word when the last sound is deleted. Children listen carefully as each word is pronounced. Then they repeat all but the last sound, which results in a different word.

Examples: If I say *card,* you say _____. (car)

When I say *seem,* you say _____. (see)

and (an)	farm (far)	tent (ten)	howl (how)	Anna (Ann)	seek (see)
boot (boo)	meat (me)	ant (an)	farms (farm)	start (star)	mend (men)
wind (win)	wasp (was)	zoom (zoo)	seal (sea)	hump (hum)	team (tea)

There are many ways to help children develop phonemic awareness. Some that are experienced by children before they enter school are continued well into reading instruction. These include contact with nursery rhymes, children's songs, alphabet books and songs, children's educational TV, and Dr. Seuss and other "I-Can-Read" books.

VISUAL DISCRIMINATION: THE THIRD PREREQUISITE FOR PHONICS INSTRUCTION

Children will have had innumerable experiences in making visual discriminations before they enter school and are called upon to make the much finer discriminations required in reading. The school will then provide many readiness activities that foster visual discrimination skills. Some of these may be only vaguely related to learning to read—matching objects and geometric forms, noting missing parts of pictures, and the like.

Other activities will relate more closely to the tasks required in reading. Studies have established that the ability to name the letters of the alphabet is one of the best predictors of a child's success in beginning reading. However, naming letters is a memory-association skill and is really not the crucial issue. The importance of being able to name letters is that it establishes that the child can discriminate visually among the various letter forms. Children have an almost uncanny ability to learn names or labels. Thus, teaching letter names is not the primary goal, but the ability to name letters is the criterion for establishing visual discrimination of graphic forms.

MATCHING AND NAMING LETTER FORMS

1. Match Letters

Duplicate exercises similar to the following illustration. The children circle or trace each letter on the line that is exactly like the stimulus on the left.

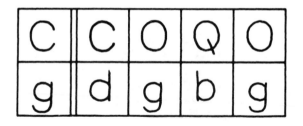

2. Flash Card Drill

a. Prepare large flash cards for each letter of the alphabet. Hold up a card and select a volunteer to name the letter or have the group name the letter in unison.

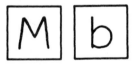

b. Prepare smaller letter cards for each participant with the same letter form on the front and back of the card.

Hand out identical card groups of three or four to all participants, who spread the cards on their desks. Give directions: "Hold up the letter *m.*" Observe children who are having difficulty and provide added practice for these students.

3. Build a Pile

a. This is a game for two or more children. Use a pack of letter cards, each of which has a letter form on one side only.

b. The cards are placed face down and the first player draws a card. He shows the card, and if he names the letter he places it face down in his pile.

c. When a player fails to name the letter, the next player may try to name it and place it in her pile. Then she draws a card.

d. At the end of the game, the player with the most cards wins.

4. Two-letter Sequence

Duplicate a series of two-letter words. Instruct children to circle each word that is exactly like the stimulus at the left.

it	at	in	up	it
on	of	on	no	on
is	as	us	is	so

5. Three-letter Sequence

For added difficulty, use the same directions as for two-letter sequence using three-letter words.

sat	hat	sat	say	sad
can	cat	pan	can	cap
dug	dug	bug	dog	dug

MATCHING CAPITAL AND LOWERCASE LETTERS

1. The children draw a line from the capital letter at the left of the box to the matching lowercase letter at the right of the box.

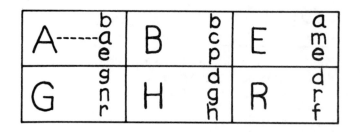

2. Duplicate a page of boxes, each containing two letter forms. The children circle each pair of letters that contains both a capital and lowercase form of the same letter.

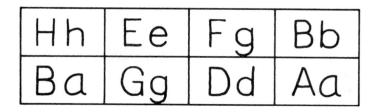

3. Prepare a series of cards similar to those used for the Flash Card Drill. (Each participant has lowercase letter cards for each letter in the exercise.) Place one capital letter form on the chalk tray. Call on a volunteer to place the matching lowercase letter below the capital form shown. Continue through the cards.

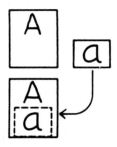

4. a. Duplicate Tic-Tac-Toe pages of squares composed of three-by-three smaller squares.

b. Each set should have a capital letter in the center square and a variety of lowercase letters in all other squares. These should be arranged so that one line contains the capital and two lowercase forms of the same letter.

c. Have the children draw a line through the three squares that contain the same letter form.

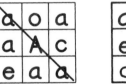

TRACING LETTER FORMS

1. Print a large letter form on the chalkboard. Trace the form and say the letter name while children trace the form in the air and repeat the letter name.

2. Prepare duplicated pages showing a heavy-line letter form on the left and dotted letter outlines on the balance of the line. Children trace over the dots to form the letters.

3. Duplicate a page of letter stimuli as shown. The children trace each letter outline that will result in the same letter as the stimulus at the left.

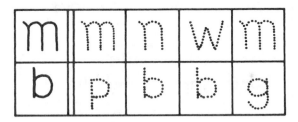

4. Prepare duplicated pages of letters as shown. After tracing the first letter outlined, the children print the letter in each of the remaining boxes on the line.

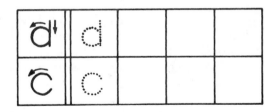

5. Prepare a page of letter symbols, each of which is followed by a partially completed letter. The children are to add the part that is missing in order to complete the letter shown at the left.

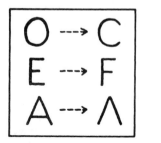 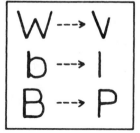 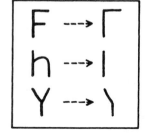

DISCRIMINATION OF WORD FORMS

In this task, children do not have to be able to name the words; they simply underline every word in the box that is the same as the stimulus word at the left. Exercises progress from gross differences to minimum differences.

lake	small	the	lake	name
word	take	word	each	word

ball	ball	fill	bat	ball
come	call	come	come	love

cat	can	cat	rat	cat
hand	band	sand	hand	hand

SUMMARY

This chapter focused on developing skills essential for beginning phonics instruction. These include developing phonemic awareness through activities such as counting speech sounds heard in words, isolating initial and final consonant sounds, adding and deleting phonemes to produce different words, and working with rhymes. Additionally, exercises focusing on building skills in visual discrimination of letter and word forms were presented.

Chapter 4

MOVING INTO READING

*P*rior to entering school most children will have had a myriad of experiences that will impinge on their learning to read. These children are already bona fide learning machines eager for challenges and poised to grow. They speak thousands of different words that are extremely close in pronunciation. They do not confuse words they hear that exhibit only the smallest phonemic differences. This achievement in acquiring language and concepts is of paramount importance in children's learning to read.

This points up a dilemma for educators. It is difficult to convince critics that both *learning* to read and *teaching* reading are difficult and frustrating experiences. Part of the problem is that educators are willing to stipulate that (a) reading is "getting meaning," (b) would-be readers come to school with a wealth of language meanings and concepts, and (c) beginning readers will not be asked to read materials that contain concepts beyond their grasp.

CONTRASTING LEARNING TO SPEAK AND LEARNING TO READ

If speaking were the only communication skill children had to learn, the process of schooling would be much easier. Learning to speak, for most children, is so easy, so rapid, so uncomplicated that it arouses awe among learning specialists. Debate on this phenomenon moves in circles:

"It's a miracle that any child learns to speak so fluently so rapidly."

"Wait! Acquiring speech is so universal it couldn't be a miracle!"

"Universal—yes, *that's* the miracle."

In acquiring speech, children immediately become immersed in a meaning-making process. They learn individual words—some of which function as sentences. Children are able to articulate practically all of the phonemes in their language, yet they are lacking in phonemic awareness. They are unaware of having uttered three phonemes in pronouncing *June* and nine phonemes in saying *September.* In speech, the whole word is much more than the sum of its parts (phonemes). Children might choose speechlessness if forced to deal extensively with phonemes as a prelude to acquiring speech. This is why children make rapid growth in learning speech.

In essence, children learned speech by listening to speakers speak. Next, they imitated or repeated what they heard and were constantly rewarded for every effort at speech. The essential difference between learning speech and learning to read is that children cannot learn to read solely by listening to readers read. This is not to imply that modeling of good reading is not important in teaching emergent readers essential reading skills. Adults' reading to children is one of the most important influences on children's progress in learning to read.

Learning to read is a most difficult part of the lengthy process of attaining literacy. Initial instruction must assure that children are:

- constantly expanding sight vocabulary, as words not recognized in a sentence interrupt the search for meaning.
- learning and applying the reading-writing code. Both writers and readers agree that visual symbols in print (A-B...Z) will represent speech sounds used in language.
- developing meaning vocabulary and concepts. Language is not static. It evolves. Word meanings are determined by the company they keep. Figures of speech may not mean what they say.

THE CASE FOR EXPANDING SIGHT VOCABULARY

Measuring sight vocabulary is the first meaningful test of reading achievement. Expansion of sight vocabulary is the skill that best illustrates the developmental nature of reading. Whenever children are making adequate progress in reading, their stock of sight words is increasing. This may have led to the question, "Can children learn to read through visual discrimination alone?"

Decades ago, Smith (1973) posed a question that addressed the essence of the great debate on reading instruction:

> We can both recognize and recall many thousands of words in our spoken language vocabulary, and recognize many thousands of different faces and animals and plants and objects in our visual world. Why should this fantastic memorizing capacity suddenly run out in the cast of reading? (p. 75)

The question Smith raises seems to invite the conclusion that visual memory of word configurations should be sufficient for learning to read. However, pedagogical experience has rendered the verdict that humans' fantastic memorizing capacity cannot be relied on to produce adequate readers. This is so because all printed words must be constructed (spelled) using a pool of only 26 visual (letter) symbols. Obviously, these few symbols must be used over and over in constructing all material printed in English. Many visual word forms begin to look very much alike because they *are* very much alike.

THE BLUE-COLLAR WORKING WORDS OF ENGLISH

There is a structural feature of English that impacts very early on learning to read is that a hundred-plus high-frequency words are used over and over in English speech and writing. These have been called "service words," "glue words," or "working words" because they literally hold the language together (see Table 4–1).

TABLE 4–1 *Introductory List of High-Frequency Working Words*

a	each	it	of	take	yes
about	enough	it's	off	talk	yet
again	even	I've	once	tall	you
all	ever		one	that	your
almost	every		only	the	
am			our	their	
an				them	
and		just		there	
any				they	
are	far			this	
as	fast		play	to	
ask	find		pretty	too	
at	first	keep	pull	two	
	four	kind	put		
	friend	knew			
		know			
be				up	
been			quiet	upon	
big	get			us	
both	give	let		use	
boy	go	live		usual	
bring	gone	look			
buy	great	love	ran		
			read		
			real		
			right	very	
			run		
can	had	made			
come	has	make			
could	have	me			
	head	most		want	
	help	move		was	
	her		said	wash	
	here		same	we	
	high		saw	went	
did	his		say	were	
do	hold	never	see	what	
does		new	she	when	
done		no	should	where	
don't		not	so	who	
down		now	some	why	
	I		soon	will	
	idea		stop	won	
	if		sure	would	
	I'm			write	
	in				
	is				

To illustrate this point, the brief preceding paragraph on page 42 contains 54 words, 26 of which are the working words under discussion. They are listed here in the order of their appearance: *there, is, a, of, that, very, on, to, read, is, that, a, high, are, used, and, in, and, these, have, been, or, they, hold, the, see.*

These words, standing alone, have little personality or warmth. However, what they do have to recommend them is that they are in charge. They are also equal opportunity words, which are essential to both great writers and beginning readers.

Shakespeare, using the blue-collar words in his 16-word classics, wrote:

The evil that men do lives after them.

The good is oft(en) interred with their bones.

(*the, that, do, after, them, the, good, is, with, their*)

The French poet Rostand, on a different subject, arranged for Cyrano de Bergerac to address Roxane:

I never think of you

but some new virtue is born in me.

This poetry of love succeeds despite being composed primarily of working words (*virtue* and *born* being exceptions).

The previous sentences are quoted to illustrate that noted writers and beginning readers have the same challenge—getting comfortable with the working words. They will be found in every sentence the beginning reader meets.

CHILDREN AS READERS

Certain assets available to the school must not be squandered. Some of these are imbedded in would-be readers themselves:

- Beginning readers are aware of the high value their parents, the school, and society places on learning to read.
- Reading is a mystery that children want to solve. They want to learn to read.
- Children at this stage of development are highly egocentric.

The school should harness the child's ego to the task of learning to read. Beginning reading activities must be failure proof. One way to structure an early activity might be to have class members learn the same four-word sight vocabulary. Then, working together, they build sentences using only these words. A word may be used more than once in a sentence. As the teacher writes the words on the board she points out that they are not arranged in sentence form. Children then dictate as many sentences as they can make. Predictable results will include:

| can | read | I | John[1] |

---

[1]Name choice optional. Can be a stand-in for each name in the class, a best friend, and so on.

Can I read?

I can read.

John, I can read.

I can read, can John?

John can read.

I can read, John can read.

To avoid being left behind, all children must learn to accept help from two friends of readers: punctuation symbols and sentence integrity. Both aids have pledged to follow the rules of speech. Punctuation symbols signal the nuances of how the message is to be interpreted. The sentence always fulfills its promise—to be a meaning-making unit of language. Thus, if the meaning of a sentence is hazy or fractured the reader should consider—"I may have missed something—Reread!"

Let children double their sight vocabulary by adding three more working words—*a, said, who,* and a larger word, *sentence.* They can now more than double their sentence production. (Previously listed sentences are not repeated.)

can	read	I	John
a	said	who	sentence

1. Who can read? 2. Who can read a sentence? 3. I can! 4. I can read a sentence. 5. Who said, "I can read a sentence"? 6. John said, "I can read a sentence." 7. John can read a sentence? 8. "I can," said John. 9. Who can read John a sentence? 10. "I can," I said. 11. I can read John a sentence. 12. John said, "Read a sentence."

Sentences are numbered to facilitate mini assignments (i.e., "Please read sentence 5" or "the last word in sentence 2"). These or similar tasks help establish that children recognize words in different settings and reward good listening habits. Children also enjoy and profit from the individual work of building sentences using their sight words. Single words are printed on cards can read I said who that the child then arranges into various sentences. Those ready for the task can copy their sentences on sentence strips. These can be taped to the *sentence board,* the child's desk, or other places of honor.

With the learning of four more working words (*will, you, yes, this*) the children will have amassed a sight vocabulary of a dozen words. This four-word addition will again double sentence-building possibilities. No previously listed sentences are repeated and each new sentence contains one or more of the four words just added.

can	read	I	John
a	said	who	sentence
this	you	yes	will

1. Can you read? 2. Yes, I can read. 3. Who will read this? 4. Can you read this sentence? 5. Yes, I can. 6. Who said, "Yes, I can"? 7. John said, "Yes I can." 8. "John,

will you read this?" 9. "Yes, I will." 10. "I will read this sentence." 11. Who will read John this sentence? 12. I will read John this sentence. 13. John said, "You will?" 14. I said, "Yes, John, I will."

Learning the first dozen sight words can produce an astounding amount of text available for reading. But eventually adding more dozens of sight words will demand much more effort and produce less growth in reading, because the visual patterns of words being learned will have too much in common with words already learned (*time, tune, tone, team, town, turn, term*).

To avoid frustration and failure in learning to read, children need insight into how print works. What is the code that writers use to represent the language or message they put into print? Then what do readers do to translate print back into the language the writer intended? None of this could happen without an alphabetic system of writing and a long-standing agreement between the writer and reader.

THE KEY TO LITERACY: INDEPENDENT READERS

Upon entering school, children know the meanings embedded in all of the material they will be expected to read in grades 1 and 2. Yet they are unable to read a simple sentence in a book that contains no more than 15 different words. If one should eavesdrop in first-grade reading classes, he will never hear children ask, "What do these words mean?" They already know. Their question is, "What are these words?" Their question expresses their immediate dilemma. However, to be relevant to both learners and their schools the question must be, "How do I solve the identity of these (and other) words?"

In real-life situations, children learning to read have to make significant progress in reading when no teacher, tutor, or parent is available. The school must produce readers who can "read on their own." Children become independent readers when they can solve the identity of printed words that they do not recognize.

Thomas Paine, a self-educated man of learning, recognized this when he wrote:

Every man of learning
eventually becomes his own teacher.

We have no way of ascertaining how much accomplished readers have actually achieved entirely on their own. However, the mastery of print is the key to literacy and accumulated knowledge. Print is a code wherein visual signs (letters) represent speech sounds. Writers spell out a message, while readers decode it. Thus, the perfect synergy develops between those with knowledge and those seeking it. However, first comes learning and applying the alphabetic code.

Prior to entering school, many children have had some experience with letters of the alphabet, with alphabet books or blocks, and alphabet songs. Unfortunately, whatever experiences they have had will not prepare them for their next experience with the alphabet. Now they must crack the alphabetic code and learn the secrets of letter-sound relationships. They are confronted with a task that is totally foreign to any of their preschool experiences. Now they must learn to associate 26 visual symbols (letters) with the 44 speech sounds they have learned to string into words and sentences when speaking.

Actually, cracking the code can be considerably less traumatic than the preceding paragraph implies. To illustrate one approach for teaching letter-sound relationships, the word *top,* a word in the children's speaking-listening vocabulary, will be used. The children have acquired several meanings for *top,* including "a toy that spins," and "Clean off the top of your desk." Children will now meet the printed word and learn several concepts.

1. *Top* consists of three visual cues (letters).
2. Each letter represents a different speech sound.
3. When blended, these three sounds result in the pronunciation of the word *top.*
4. The sounds must be blended from left to right.
5. The sounds blended must not result in a *three-syllable word.* Thus, *top* cannot be sounded as *tee-oh-pe* or as the softer syllables *tuh-ah-puh.*

What then is the sound of /t/? It is the first sound one makes when pronouncing the word *top.* Say this to children and they may hear you, but it is likely to be processed as meaningless jargon.

How might they learn the sound of /t/? A chalkboard presentation to young learners might proceed as follows.

1. Print the word *top* on the board. Invite children to join in reading (saying) the word. Explain that the letter *t* tells us what the first sound will be when we say *top.* Add other words that begin with *t.* Point to and pronounce each word with the children, emphasizing or prolonging the /t/ sound.

```
top
ten
tub
take
```

Ask children to supply other words that begin with the /t/ sound (t*ape,* t*wo,* t*est,* t*urn,* t*ax,* t*ruck,* t*ell,* t*old,* t*ime*).
2. Onset in search of a rime.

Onset = the consonant(s) that precede(s) the vowel(s) in syllables (including one-syllable words)

Rime = everything but the onset in syllables (including one-syllable words)

Example: top t = *onset;* op = *rime*

To help children distinguish the sound of the letter *t* in words, make a list of familiar words that begin with the sound of /t/. Pronounce, and have children repeat, each word in your list (see Column A).

Teacher: "I will start to say the first sound in *tag.* Before I finish, you say the rest of the word." (Column B) "Then we will repeat the word together." Follow the same procedure for each word in your list. Then reverse the procedure: children pronounce the onset /t/; the teacher adds the rime.

A	B
tag	_ag
tent	_ent
time	_ime
toast	_oast
took	_ook

3. *Children bring t to the party.*
   This activity allows children to think, subvocalize, and mentally add the /t/ sound in front of words to form different words. Explain that you will pronounce a word, and children are to add the /t/ sound in front of that word. Then they pronounce the word they have created.

   Examples: If I say the word *able*

When you add the /t/ sound, you say	*table*
If I say *all,* you would say	*tall*
If I say *rain,* you would say	*train*

   Print and pronounce the first word in Column A. Children add the /t/ sound and pronounce "their word" (Column B). Continue through all words in Column A.

A	B
each	*teach*
wig	*twig*
ask	*task*
old	*told*
ape	*tape*

Other *t* words ___in, ___rust, ___oil, ___rip, ___an, ___ray, ___race, ___win

Other initial consonants can be added to words to form new words.

Examples:

b: ___all, ___rain, ___ox, ___and, ___rag, ___at, ___us

s: ___eat, ___ink, ___top, ___cat, ___and, ___he, ___hop

m: ___any, ___eat, ___ask, ___end, ___ink, ___old, ___an

p: ___in, ___aid, ___ill, ___rice, ___it, ___each, ___art

CONSONANT CONSISTENCY

Point out to children that there is a bonus each time they learn a letter-sound relationship. The sound represented by /t/ in *top* will be the same sound when it is met in thousands of other English words. This is true regardless of where *t* occurs in words. The *t* in *time, took, tune, hunt, cat, west, hunter, catcher,* and *tomato* represents the same sound as heard in *top.* The letter *m* appears frequently in words and is extremely loyal to its assigned sound, regardless of its location in words: *mom, mama, minimum, my, mime, mummy, moment, milkman, momentum.*

Developing independence in reading progresses as instruction deals with letter-sounds in final and medial positions. The final letter in *top* represents the same sound in *pen, pill, partnership, snap, paper, pop, pup.* Other consonants are highly consistent in the sound they represent. The virtue of this consistency is that any instructional procedure will be equally effective in dealing with these letters.

Irregular spellings of words are troublesome to readers. Fortunately the *initial* letter-sound in the vast majority of these words represents its "regular" sound.[2] In addition, context is a valuable clue for the beginning reader.

CONTEXT AND WORD MEANINGS

Context clues are the aids to comprehension the reader gets from the text itself. Authors may help by including a description-definition of a word that might be new to the reader.

They were now traveling through _____ country. It was very hot, there was sand underfoot, and the wind blew sand in their eyes. There were no streams—no water whatsoever—and no shade trees. The _____ extended as far as the eye could see.

Other context clues include comparison, contrast, and the use of synonyms and antonyms.

At this point, the stream flowed very _____ [rapidly]. The water splashed over the rocks and sent up white spray as it moved swiftly through the pass.

Solving the identity of an unknown word is facilitated by understanding the meaning of the sentence in which the word occurs as well as by understanding what has occurred in previously read sentences and sentences that follow—assuming, of course, that the child is reading for meaning.

Beginning readers are not ready to profit fully from context clues. They have no trouble solving the meaning of words such as *set, air, pin, can,* or *top.* However, they will soon have to contend with well over a hundred meanings associated with these same words. They will encounter concepts such as *set* a bone, a table, a record, a clock, a fire, a good or bad example. One can lose a set in tennis or from a favorite ring.

---

[2]See Table 6–1, page 115. Exceptions include initial *wr, wh, kn,* and a limited number of creative spellings such as *of, eye, one, once, who, eight, do, cough, sew.*

Concepts and word meanings develop as a result of language experiences. Extensive reading accounts for significant growth in meaning vocabulary. Again, beginning readers profit least from this activity since they are not yet equipped for extensive reading. However, they live in a language environment that includes classroom, playground, bus, neighborhood, home, television, and parents reading at home.

All subjects in the school curriculum have special terms and concepts. These are taught, retaught, assigned, and tested. There is also a language of reading. It may be alive in the classroom but it rarely attains the status of being part of the curriculum. Beginning readers need to be familiar with a number of terms. The words *sentence* and *punctuation* were previously mentioned because of their importance in helping children arrive at the meaning of the sentences they were reading. Other words beginners should understand include *syllable, digraph, accent, prefix, root words,* and *compounds,* with *syllable* being the most elusive. *A* and *I* are letters of the alphabet; they are also words. They qualify as syllables based on their status as one-syllable words.

ADDRESSING CHILDREN LEFT BEHIND

The discussion of this problem has been couched in terms that prohibit its solution. It focuses almost exclusively on learning to read. The school has been assigned responsibility for teaching reading. Thus, it must be responsible for children left behind in developing reading ability. Is there faulty logic here? It is ironic that the emphasis on leaving no child behind comes so late in the lives of the children under discussion that neither a slogan nor an edict can affect getting the job done.

The school, by nature of its charter, is the only institution in our society that must wait from birth to kindergarten before it touches the lives of children. If the golden years of childhood are severely tarnished by poverty and a myriad of associated ills, the left behind syndrome becomes well established—long before children reach the school.

The nation must rethink its priorities. If it takes little cognizance of children being left behind prior to school, it is either naïve or cynical to pretend the school can compensate for the deficiencies accumulated by the time some children enter school.

SUMMARY

In this chapter three essential facets of reading instruction are discussed relative to how they impinge on beginning readers: developing sight vocabulary; solving the writer-reader code; and expanding meaning vocabulary.

Beginning readers will be moving into reading at higher and higher levels. They are on the launching pad in their quest for literacy. Some will be lost on launch, others will meet expectations, and some few will achieve far beyond expectations, making contributions to society that will benefit all of us. Sight vocabularies will grow. Dependence on applying letter-sound relationships will diminish and when utilized will be less disruptive to the reading process. Society, the school, and reading tests will demand more extensive mastery of word meanings, concepts, and textual cues. The definition of reading will shed any ambiguity it might have had—reading is getting meaning even though words strike different poses in different settings.

Chapter 5

CONSONANT LETTER-SOUND RELATIONSHIPS

We have so far dealt with skills that are prerequisites for learning letter-sound relationships. The two major skills are the ability to discriminate among letter forms and the ability to differentiate auditorily among speech sounds as heard in words. This chapter will focus on teaching that combines these skills and leads children to associate a particular sound with a specific letter or combination of letters.

A WORD ABOUT SEQUENCE

The phonics program consists of teaching many specific skills. In any systematic program, this myriad of skills would have to be arranged into some teaching sequence. There are some options in regard to sequence that undoubtedly are of little educational consequence (such as whether to teach the sound of *t* before *b*, or *m* before *n*). However, the question of whether to teach consonant or vowel letter-sounds first is worthy of consideration.

Rationale for Teaching Consonant Sounds First

The majority of words children meet in beginning reading are words that begin with consonants. For instance, 175 (or approximately 80%) of the 220 words on the Dolch Basic Sight Word Test begin with consonants. The Dale List of 769 Easy Words contains an even higher proportion (87%) of words beginning with consonants.

It is good learning theory to have children start phonic analysis with the beginnings of words, working their way through the words from left to right. This reinforces the practice of reading from left to right and focuses children's attention on the first part of the word. This is essential for facile reading and an absolute prerequisite if children are to solve the word by sounding.

Consonants tend to be much more consistent than vowels in the sounds they represent. For instance, a number of consonants (*j, k, l, m, n, p, b, h, r, v, w*) represent only one sound. Certain other consonants that have two sounds present no problem in beginning reading instruction because one of the two basic sounds can be left until the child has had considerable practice in reading.

If a child uses skills in combination, sounding the initial consonant letter and using context-meaning clues will frequently be all the analysis that is needed. Assume each blank line in the following examples represents an unknown word.

1. _____ (This could represent any of 600,000 words in English.)
2. f _____ (Here, more than 98% of all words are eliminated. The unknown word must begin with the sound associated with the letter f.)

It is probable that the reader will arrive at the unknown word(s) in the following sentences despite the very limited context that is provided.

3. "You will have to pay the f _____ now," said the judge.
4. Without a doubt, pumpkin is my f _____ pie.
5. During J _____ it is much colder than it is in J _____ and J _____.

The sequence of teachings suggested in this chapter follows.

1. Initial consonant letter-sounds
2. Initial consonant blends or clusters (bl, st, etc.)
3. Initial consonant digraphs (ch, wh, sh, th, etc.)
4. Final consonants, blends, and digraphs
5. Consonant irregularities

Listing this sequence does not imply that all the possible steps under 1 must be completed before introducing any of the teachings in 2, 3, 4, or 5. The procedures that follow illustrate some of the many approaches that can be used in teaching letter-sound relationships.

INITIAL CONSONANT LETTER-SOUNDS

One widely used technique for teaching initial letter-sounds is the use of children's names.

1. Write the names of several children in the class (or other common first names) that begin with the same letter (Bill, Beth, Ben, Brad) on the chalkboard.
2. Pronounce each name; then have the class pronounce each name.
3. Call attention to the fact that each name begins with the same letter, and that this letter (B) represents the same sound in each word.
4. Use other series of names for other letter-sounds.

Jason	Denise	Mary	Susan
Josh	Daniel	Matthew	Sam
Jill	Devon	Mike	Seth
Jamie	David	Maggie	Sarah

Other techniques for teaching initial letter-sounds follow.

1. Chalkboard Drill

For purposes of illustration, we will give the steps for teaching the sound of the consonant *m* in detail. All other consonant sounds can be taught in the same manner.

  a. Print the letter *m* (capital and lowercase) on the chalkboard. Indicate that for the next few minutes the group will study the sound of the letter *m* as it is heard in words. Write on the board a column of previously studied words, all of which begin with the letter *m*. Any words the children have met (as sight words) in experience charts or other materials may be used—words such as *me, must, moon,* and *mind*. Also, familiar names and names of children in the class that call for capital letters may be used.

```
M          m
Mary       my
Mike       most
           man
           much
           milk
```

  b. Ask the children to look at the words carefully and name the letter that begins each word. Indicate that a big *M* or capital letter is used in names.
  c. As you pronounce the words, ask the children to listen to the sound heard at the beginning of each word. The initial sound should be emphasized, but not distorted.
  d. Invite children to read the words in unison, listening carefully to the sound of *m* as they say the words.
  e. Ask children to supply other words that begin with the sound /m/.

2. Match a Pair

This game is an adaptation of Concentration; it involves the use of pictures and two or more children as participants (individual or team play).

Select pairs of pictures so that two picture-naming words begin with the same letter-sound: h*orse*—*hand;* be*ll*—*boat;* ta*ble*—*tub;* fi*sh*—*fox;* and de*sk*—*duck*. Shuffle the cards and lay them face down on the table.

The first player turns up two cards, hoping to match a pair of initial letter-sounds. If the player is successful, she picks up both cards. If she does not match initial letter-sounds, both cards are again turned face down. Other players continue taking turns. Each player attempts to note and remember the location of pictures that have been turned up but not matched.

The winner is the player or team with the most pictures at the end of the game.

3. Building a Picture Dictionary

Use a supply of pictures from workbooks, magazines, and catalogues. Work with one letter at a time: *B—b,* for example.

After teaching the initial sound of *B—b* in words, have the children gather pictures whose naming words begin with that letter-sound. Children may work individually or in small groups.

Prepare a page (or several pages) for each letter-sound. Print a capital and lowercase letter at the top of the page and fill the page with pictures whose naming words begin with that letter-sound.

4. Print and Sound

Compile columns of easy words that begin with the letter-sounds to be taught or reviewed. Delete the initial letter of each word, and provide space for students to write the letter.

As they print the initial letter, the children pronounce the word they have formed. (Material may be presented on the chalkboard, with transparencies, or as duplicated exercises.) Here are several examples.

a. *Teacher:* "In each blank space, add the letter above the column of words. Pronounce each word."

t	*s*	*c*	*l*
____ ag	____ ad	____ ap	____ og
____ ub	____ ix	____ ot	____ ap
____ en	____ un	____ up	____ ed
____ op	____ it	____ an	____ eg
____ ip	____ ob	____ ub	____ et

b. *Teacher:* "In each blank space, write one of the letters *h, w,* or *g.* Be sure the letter you choose makes a word. Pronounce the word."

____ im	____ ot	____ ip	____ ub
____ et	____ un	____ ad	____ id
____ um	____ at	____ ig	____ ug
____ eb	____ en	____ ap	____ em

c. *Teacher:* "In each blank space, add any letter that will make a word."

____ ug	____ og	____ eg	____ at
____ ox	____ un	____ it	____ op
____ ad	____ ig	____ ub	____ in
____ en	____ an	____ ot	____ us

Mental Substitution

Day by day, in the early stages of reading instruction, the child is learning both sight words and the sounds of initial consonants. Knowledge thus gained can be applied in arriving at the pronunciation of other words not known as sight words. Assume the child knows the words *king* and *ring* and meets the unknown word *sing*. He should be able to combine the /s/ sound, which he knows in words like *sat, some,* and *say,* with the sound of *ing* found in *king* and *ring.* This involves a process of "thinking the sounds." To illustrate, let us assume the following:

1. A child has learned the italicized words in Table 5–1.
2. He has learned the sounds of the initial consonants as heard in the italicized words.
3. He has not met or learned any of the other 34 words in Table 5–1.
4. By using his knowledge, plus some guidance from the teacher, he should be able to sound out all the words in Table 5–1.

TABLE 5–1 *Identifying Words Using Mental Substitution*

bat	can	fit	had	map	pet	run	say
cat	ban	bit	bad	cap	bet	bun	bay
fat	fan	hit	fad	rap	met	fun	hay
hat	man	pit	mad	sap	set	sun	may
mat	pan	sit	pad				pay
pat	ran		sad				ray
rat							

By using the process of thinking the sound of any known consonant and blending this sound with the phonogram that concludes a known sight word, the child should be able to pronounce the new word.

Other techniques for teaching mental substitution follow.

1. Place a known word on the board. Have the children observe closely as you erase the initial *b* and substitute a different known consonant.

    bat   _____ at   cat

    Follow the same procedure, substituting other consonants to make easy words, such as f*at,* h*at,* m*at,* and r*at.*

    For convenience in building mental substitution exercises, Table 5–2 provides a series of word families. In each, the words end in a common phonogram (*et, ick, ack, ay, ot, an, ill, im, ug, ad*). Not all the words in the table need to be used in beginning reading, and those beginning with blends should not be used in substitution exercises until the sounds of the blends have been taught.

2. *Teacher:* "Change the first letter and make a naming word for 'something living.' "

    Example:

    dish _____ ish   fish

log	_____ og	hat	_____ at	half	_____ alf
coat	_____ oat	purse	_____ urse	nice	_____ ice
box	_____ ox	mitten	_____ itten	grow	_____ row
house	_____ ouse	rug	_____ ug	pull	_____ ull

3. *Teacher:* "On the line following each word, write a new word by changing the first letter to the next letter in the alphabet: Then pronounce the new word and use it in a sentence."

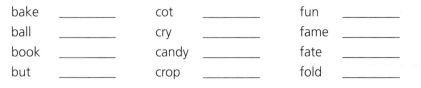

bake	_____	cot	_____	fun	_____
ball	_____	cry	_____	fame	_____
book	_____	candy	_____	fate	_____
but	_____	crop	_____	fold	_____

TABLE 5–2 *Words for Teaching Substitution of Initial Consonant Sounds (Words with initial consonant blends are in parentheses.)*

back	bake	day	cap	bug	bank	cot	Dick
Jack	cake	hay	gap	dug	rank	dot	kick
lack	fake	lay	lap	hug	sank	got	lick
pack	lake	may	map	jug	tank	hot	nick
rack	make	pay	nap	mug	(blank)	lot	pick
sack	rake	ray	rap	rug	(crank)	not	sick
tack	sake	say	tap	tug	(drank)	pot	(brick)
(black)	take	way	(clap)	(drug)	(flank)	(blot)	(click)
(crack)	wake	(clay)	(flap)	(plug)	(frank)	(plot)	(slick)
(slack)	(brake)	(play)	(slap)	(slug)	(plank)	(shot)	(stick)
(stack)	(flake)	(stay)	(snap)	(smug)	(prank)	(spot)	(thick)
(track)	(snake)	(tray)	(trap)	(snug)	(spank)	(trot)	(trick)
bag	bail	gain	bat	bump	can	came	Bill
gag	fail	lain	cat	dump	Dan	dame	fill
lag	hail	main	fat	hump	fan	fame	hill
nag	mail	pain	hat	jump	man	game	kill
rag	nail	rain	mat	lump	pan	lame	mill
sag	pail	vain	pat	pump	ran	name	pill
tag	rail	(brain)	rat	(plump)	tan	same	will
wag	sail	(drain)	sat	(slump)	van	tame	(drill)
(brag)	tail	(grain)	(brat)	(stump)	(bran)	(blame)	(skill)
(drag)	(frail)	(plain)	(flat)	(trump)	(clan)	(flame)	(spill)
(flag)	(trail)	(train)	(scat)		(plan)	(frame)	(still)
(snag)	(snail)						
best	bet	bunk	bell	bit	dim	dear	bad
lest	get	dunk	fell	fit	him	fear	dad
nest	jet	hunk	sell	hit	Jim	hear	fad
pest	let	junk	tell	pit	rim	near	had
rest	met	sunk	well	sit	Tim	rear	lad
test	net	(drunk)	yell	wit	(brim)	tear	mad
vest	pet	(flunk)	(smell)	(flit)	(grim)	year	pad
zest	set	(skunk)	(spell)	(grit)	(slim)	(clear)	sad
(blest)	wet	(spunk)	(swell)	(slit)	(swim)	(smear)	(glad)
(crest)	(fret)	(trunk)		(split)	(trim)	(spear)	

57

gold	_____	lad	_____	met	_____
got	_____	lake	_____	moon	_____
gate	_____	let	_____	mine	_____
gum	_____	line	_____	meat	_____
		lap	_____	mice	_____

Difficulty level can be increased by mixing the words instead of presenting a series of four words

boat	_____	map	_____	sail	_____
cash	_____	run	_____	rat	_____
fang	_____	sight	_____	bold	_____
ray	_____	bat	_____	sack	_____
kit	_____	kick	_____	ring	_____
lay	_____	vest	_____	kid	_____

Context Plus Minimal Phonic Cue

The following exercise illustrates that, in many situations, the context plus the phonic cue provided by the initial letter of an unknown word will provide enough clues to solve the unknown word. The blank space in each sentence under A could be replaced with several different words. The same blank space in the corresponding sentence under B provides the initial consonant letter of the word. Have children note that when they heed this phonic cue, they can eliminate many of the previously acceptable choices.

Directions: Read the sentences under A. Have children provide a number of words that could fit in each blank. Then read the sentences under B and have the children note their general agreement on choices.

A

1. The _____ would not start.
2. "She is my _____," said Billy.
3. Billy asked, "How much _____ do we have?"
4. Which _____ of the year is your favorite?
5. What word _____ in the blank space?

B

1. The c _____ would not start.
2. "She is my s _____," said Billy.
3. Billy asked, "How much m _____ do we have?"
4. Which t _____ of the year is your favorite?
5. What word f _____ in the blank space?

Oral Exercise

Directions: Have a volunteer read one of the following incomplete sentences, adding any word that will logically conclude the sentence. Other students then volunteer other words that fit. Stress that no word can fit unless it begins with the sound represented by the letter shown.

Written Exercise

Directions: Children write one (or more) words that begin with the letter shown.

1. Can you see the p _____?
2. Is this your b _____?
3. This is a t _____.
4. Here is the c _____.
5. The girls felt very s _____.

CONTEXT CLUES AND PHONIC SKILLS: WORKING TOGETHER

Under less than optimal teaching practices, phonics instruction can be so far removed from reading that it inhibits learning to read. All phonics instruction, however, need not focus exclusively on letter-sound relationships. Reading instruction can be made more effective if the learning task involves both reading (context) and a phonics task whose completion depends on the reading task.

In this chapter, as well as in following chapters, phonics instruction is embedded in a "Fun with Language" approach. The learner is asked to read in order to discover what phonics task he is being asked to perform. The difficulty levels of these exercises range from one-word clues to phrases and sentences. These materials can be adapted to almost any phonic teaching: initial, medial, and final consonants; blends, digraphs, and vowel patterns. In all of these exercises, the teacher reads the directions and any sample items with the student.

USING CONTEXT

Teacher: "Read the clue. What do they do? Write the correct word in the space."

Clue			Clue		
dogs	_____	(bark, dark)	cows	_____	(moo, boo)
birds	_____	(sly, fly)	bells	_____	(wing, ring)
boats	_____	(hail, sail)	fires	_____	(turn, burn)
horses	_____	(run, fun)	kings	_____	(mule, rule)
towels	_____	(cry, dry)	frogs	_____	(hop, mop)

Teacher: "Read the clue. Complete the word that fits the clue. Use either *c* or *t* to make a word that fits the clue."

Example:

pretty	____ ute	use *c* to spell *cute*
story	____ ale	use *t* to spell *tale*

	Clue			*Clue*	
1.	money	____ ash	**6.**	speaking	____ alk
2.	bath	____ ub	**7.**	knives	____ ut
3.	brush	____ eeth	**8.**	Christmas	____ ard
4.	bird	____ age	**9.**	gentle	____ ame
5.	spins	____ op	**10.**	penny	____ ent

Teacher: "Write either *p* or *n* in each blank space to make a word that fits the clue."

	Clue			*Clue*	
1.	fruit	____ ear	**6.**	loud	____ oise
2.	bird	____ est	**7.**	medicine	____ ill
3.	fence	____ ost	**8.**	pecan kernel	____ ut
4.	two	____ air	**9.**	sharp	____ eedle
5.	close	____ ear	**10.**	writes	____ en

Teacher: "Read the clue. Add the first letter to make a word that fits the clue."

Example:
you can read it ____ ook (b)

	Clue			*Clue*	
1.	not small	____ ig	**6.**	season before winter	____ all
2.	lives on a farm	____ ig	**7.**	not short	____ all
3.	false hair	____ ig	**8.**	round and bounces	____ all
4.	a dance step	____ ig	**9.**	from floor to ceiling	____ all
5.	make a hole in the ground	____ ig	**10.**	shopping center	____ all

Teacher: "Write the letter that spells the word that fits the clue. Use *p, b,* or *d.*"

	Clue			*Clue*	
1.	we read it	____ ook	**6.**	goes around waist	____ elt
2.	please open the	____ oor	**7.**	we sleep on it	____ ed
3.	lives on a farm	____ ig	**8.**	worth 10 cents	____ ime
4.	goes on the water	____ oat	**9.**	place where we play	____ ark
5.	a dog is a	____ et	**10.**	at night it is	____ ark

Teacher: "Change the first letter in each italicized word so that the new word names something living."

Examples:

I can change *big* to _____ ig. (*pig*)

I can change *see* to _____ ee. (*bee*)

I can change *hat* to _____ at.

                 dish to _____ ish.

                 pen to _____ en.

                 toy to _____ oy.

If a child or group has difficulty with a particular consonant letter sound, develop exercises that focus on this letter. The exercise that follows illustrates *c* and *f*.

Teacher: "Read the clue. Write the letter that spells the word that fits the clue."

Set 1		Set 2	
Clue		*Clue*	
1. wear on head	_____ ap	**1.** not slow	_____ ast
2. catches mice	_____ at	**2.** lives in water	_____ ish
3. not hot	_____ old	**3.** more than four	_____ ive
4. grows on farm	_____ orn	**4.** after summer	_____ all
5. baby cow	_____ alf	**5.** less than five	_____ our
6. ice cream	_____ one	**6.** good to eat	_____ ood
7. a baby bear	_____ ub	**7.** a tree	_____ ir

FUN WITH LANGUAGE

1. Fun with D, F, S, and G Words

Teacher: "Read the clues. Be careful; they're tricky. Complete the word that fits the clue. Use one of the consonant letters *d, f, s,* or *g* to spell the word that fits the clue."

Example:

Clue

not much money	_____ ime	*D* is the only letter that fits the clue; a dime is not much money.
front of head	_____ ace	Choose *f;* it makes sense.
four legs and butts	_____ oat	*G* makes goat, which has four legs. Have you ever heard of a goat butting someone?

Clue			*Clue*			
1. not back, not front	____ ide	**6.**	Don't ____ the bears.	____ eed	
2. 1492 . . .1776 . . .1976	____ ates	**7.**	always number one	____ irst	
3. hole-in-one	____ olf	**8.**	not here now	____ one	
4. damp minus *p*	____ am	**9.**	what I owe you	____ ebt	
5. goes in shoes	____ eet	**10.**	like the others	____ ame	

2. The 3-C Sentences!

In the sentences below:

A. Candy is a girl's name. (Candy starts with a capital letter!)
B. She has a candy cane.
C. The three c's get all mixed up, but when you read for meaning it's easy.

Teacher: "Fill in each blank space with one of these words: *Candy, candy,* or *cane.*"

Problem: _____ has a _____ _____.

Solved: Candy has a candy cane.

1. Does _____ have a _____ _____?
2. Yes, the _____ _____ belongs to _____.
3. Will _____ eat her _____ _____?
4. _____ may eat the _____ _____.
5. Then _____ will not have a _____ _____.
6. This ends the story of _____ and her _____ _____.

3. B(ware)—B(ready)—B(sharp)

Teacher: "Every blank space in the following sentences can be filled with the following *b* words: *book, boy,* or *bus.* As you read each sentence write the correct word in each blank space."

1. The _____ has a _____.
2. The _____ took the _____ on a _____.
3. The _____ left the _____ on the _____.
4. The _____ driver found the _____.
5. He gave the _____ to the _____.
6. Now the _____ has the _____.
7. Will the _____ read the _____?
8. The _____ read the _____, but not on the _____!

4. Double D Words

Teacher: "The word *dog* will fit in one space in each sentence below. One other word that also begins with *d* will fit in each of the other spaces. Complete the sentences."

1. _____ the _____ with the towel.

2. The towel will _____ the _____.

3. The _____ can _____ off in the sun.

4. Will the sun _____ the _____?

5. Keep the _____ _____ in winter.

5. More Double D Words

Teacher: "The word *dog* will fit in one blank space in each sentence below. Fill the other space with a word that begins with *d.*"

Example:

_____ said, "Where is the _____?"
    (Dad)   said, "Where is the   (dog)?"

1. The d _____ sat by the d _____.

2. The artist said, "I will d _____ a d _____.

3. The d _____ will d _____ the water.

4. D _____ the d _____ d _____ a hole in the yard?

5. Yes, the d _____ d _____ d _____ a hole in the yard!

Teacher: "Need a little help? These words fit the spaces: *dog, did, dig, drink, draw,* and *door.*"

6. Fun with Triple D Words

Teacher: "Each sentence has three missing words. Each missing word begins with the letter *d.* The words *dig, did,* and *dad* fit in each sentence. Where does each word fit?"

Example:

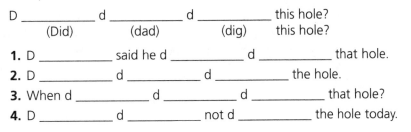

D _____ d _____ d _____ this hole?
  (Did)   (dad)   (dig)   this hole?

1. D _____ said he d _____ d _____ that hole.

2. D _____ d _____ d _____ the hole.

3. When d _____ d _____ d _____ that hole?

4. D _____ d _____ not d _____ the hole today.

INITIAL CONSONANT BLENDS

Consonant blends consist of two or more letters that are blended when pronouncing a word. If a child attempts to sound separately each of the consonants in a blend, distortion and confusion will result. These sounds must be blended to arrive at the correct pronunciation. Children already know these speech sounds; they must learn to recognize their printed equivalents. For example, students know the sound of /s/, as heard in *see, sit, some,* and *say,* and the sound of /t/, as heard in *tell, to, talk,* and *top.* The next short step, from the known to the unknown, would be teaching the blend sound /st/, as heard in *stop, still, stand,* and the like.

Two- and three-letter consonant blends may be divided into three major groups on the basis of a common letter:

- Those in which *r* is the concluding letter (Column A)
- Those in which *l* is the concluding letter (Column B)
- Those that begin with the letter *s* (Column C)

A		B		C
br	scr	bl	spl	sc
cr	spr	cl		sk
dr	str	fl		sm
fr	thr	gl		sn
gr		pl		sp
pr		sl		st
tr				sw

The blends are listed alphabetically, but they may be taught in any order. The two-letter blends are easier to learn and occur more frequently in words met in beginning reading than do the three-letter blends; therefore, it is better to teach the two-letter blends first. See Table 5–3 for words that can be used in teaching consonant blends.

There are several ways to teach children how to master these blend sounds. Regardless of what approach you use, the objectives in teaching blends are to have children (a) see the letter combination involved; (b) realize that in every case the letters combine into a blend sound; and (c) discriminate between the blend sound and the sound of individual letters, as for example, in *pay, lay,* and *play.*

Procedures for teaching initial blends closely parallel those for teaching initial consonant sounds. To illustrate, we will look at the steps in teaching the sound represented by *st* in detail. All other consonant blends may be taught in the same manner.

CHALKBOARD ACTIVITIES

Place a few *st* words on the board, such as *stop, still, star, stand,* and *stick.* Direct children's attention to the *st* beginning. As each word is pronounced, ask the students to listen to the /st/ sound in the initial position. Then invite the children to give other words that begin with the blended sounds /st/ (*stone, step, stood, stir*).

TABLE 5–3 *Words for Teaching Initial Consonant Blends*

br	cr	dr	fr	gr	pr	tr
brother	cry	dress	friend	grade	pretty	tree
bring	cross	drink	from	great	present	train
brought	crop	draw	front	ground	president	trip
brown	creek	dry	Friday	green	program	truly
brake	crowd	drive	fruit	grandmother	print	trick
bread	cream	drop	fright	grass	produce	truck
bright	crack	dream	free	grandfather	prize	trade
bridge	crawl	drove	fresh	group	promise	trap
break	crib	drum	frog	grew	proud	track
brave	cried	drew	freeze	gray	product	true
brush	crumb	drill	frozen	grain	prepare	trail
branch	crown	drag	friendly	grab	protect	treat
brick	crow	drank	fry	grape	press	trim
broom	crook	drug	frost	grand	price	tramp

bl	cl	fl	pl	sl	sp	st
black	close	flower	play	sleep	spell	start
blue	clean	fly	place	sled	spend	stay
blow	class	floor	please	slid	spot	story
block	clothes	flag	plant	slate	speak	stop
bloom	climb	flew	plan	slip	spent	store
blew	club	flood	plane	slowly	sport	study
blanket	cloth	float	plenty	slave	speed	still
blood	cloud	flat	plain	slow	spoke	state
blackboard	clear	flour	plate	slipper	spirit	stand
blossom	clay		pleasant	slept	speech	stick
blind	clothing	gl	plow	sleet	spoon	stocking
blame	clock	glad	player	sleepy	spear	step
blizzard	climate	glass	plantation	slim	space	star
blaze	clown	glove	playmate	slick	spin	stood

sc	sk	sm	sn	sw	tw
school	skate	small	snow	swim	twelve
scare	skin	smoke	snake	sweet	twist
scold	sky	smell	snowball	swing	twenty
scout	ski	smile	snail	sweater	twice
scream	skip	smart	snap	swan	twin
schoolhouse	skirt	smooth	snug	sweep	twig
score	skunk	smack	sneeze	swell	twinkle

AUDITORY-VISUAL ASSOCIATION

1. Key Words (Two-letter Blends)

  a. Duplicate a series of key words that emphasize the common letter in a number of consonant blends, such as *r, l,* and *s.* Provide each child with a copy.

  b. Lead children in seeing and saying the blends and the key words in each column: /br/ as in *bring,* /cr/ as in *cry,* /dr/ as in *drum.*

See the r		See the l		Begins with s	
br	*bring*	bl	*blue*	sc	*school*
cr	*cry*	cl	*clean*	sk	*sky*
dr	*drum*	fl	*fly*	sm	*small*
fr	*from*	gl	*glad*	sn	*snow*
gr	*green*	pl	*play*	sp	*spot*
pr	*pretty*	sl	*slow*	st	*stop*
tr	*tree*			sw	*swim*

2. Hearing Blends in Words (Identifying Blends Heard)

  a. Prepare columns showing three different blends.

  b. Pronounce a word that begins with one of the blends shown: *"blue," "stand," "train,"* and so on.

  c. Children underline the blend that is heard at the beginning of the stimulus word.

blue	stand	train	play	smoke
br	st	gl	pr	sn
pl	sl	tr	bl	sm
bl	sm	sk	pl	sp

3. Word Recognition (Auditory-to-Visual Patterns)

  a. Duplicate a number of three-word series as shown.

  b. Pronounce one word from each series. (The stimulus word is italicized here, but would not be on hand-out material supplied to children.)

  c. Children underline the word pronounced.

1	2	3	4	5
black	stay	smell	skin	*flew*
back	gay	*spell*	sing	few
brick	*gray*	sell	swing	true

6	7	8	9	10
snail	sin	dumb	grain	bake
scale	sink	*drum*	*rain*	*brake*
sail	*skin*	from	gain	rake

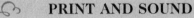

PRINT AND SOUND

1. Add a Blend

Here the student writes the two letters that represent the initial blended sounds.

Teacher: "Write the letters that are shown above the blank spaces. Then pronounce the words you have made."

br	*sp*	*cl*	*sw*
_____ ain	_____ eak	_____ ean	_____ im
_____ ake	_____ oon	_____ oth	_____ eet
_____ an	_____ ace	_____ ay	_____ ay
_____ own	_____ in	_____ imb	_____ ell
_____ ush	_____ ell	_____ ock	_____ ing

2. Change a Blend

Use word endings that will make different words when different blends are added.

Teacher: "In each blank space write the blend shown on the left. Then pronounce each word."

(br) _____ own	(sp) _____ ill	(sk) _____ ate
(cr) _____ own	(st) _____ ill	(pl) _____ ate
(dr) _____ own	(sk) _____ ill	(st) _____ ate
(fr) _____ own	(dr) _____ ill	(cr) _____ ate
	(gr) _____ ill	(sl) _____ ate

USING CONTEXT

Teacher: "Read the clue. Write a two-letter blend to make a word that goes with the clue."

Examples:

snake _____ awls

(a snake *cr*awls, so use *cr*)

fruit _____ and

(you can buy fruit at the fruit *st*and)

Note: All tasks in Set 1 begin with the same blend found in the clue. In Set 2 they are all different.

Set 1			Set 2		
Clue			Clue		
fresh	_____	uit	snow	_____	ake
tree	_____	unk	broom	_____	eeps
train	_____	ack	scare	_____	ow
brown	_____	ead	draw	_____	idge
sleds	_____	ide	glue	_____	icks
travel	_____	ip	tree	_____	ump

Teacher: "Read the clue. Complete the word that fits the clue. Use one of the blends *st, sp,* or *sn* to make a word that fits the clue."

Examples:

a place to buy	_____ ore	use *st* to spell *store*
football, tennis	_____ orts	use *sp* to spell *sports*

Clue			Clue		
1. hard metal	_____	eel	6. to say something	_____	eak
2. slow as a	_____	ail	7. shines at night	_____	ar
3. tops do this	_____	in	8. sleep noise	_____	ore
4. eat with this	_____	oon	9. bees can	_____	ing
5. to begin	_____	art	10. as white as	_____	ow

Teacher: "Write one of the blends *sl, sw,* or *sk* in the blank spaces to make a word that fits the clue."

Clue			Clue		
1. using a broom	_____	eep	6. above the earth	_____	y
2. women wear	_____	irts	7. moves on snow	_____	ed
3. not fast	_____	ow	8. a beautiful fowl	_____	an
4. very clever	_____	y	9. arm goes in	_____	eeve
5. a bunch of bees	_____ arm		10. smells bad	_____	unk

Teacher: "Write the blend that spells the word that fits the clue."

Examples:

pleased and happy _____ ad (gl)   train runs on it   _____ ack (tr)

```
                    ┌─────────────────────────────┐
                    │          Clue Box           │
                    │  sl    tr    bl    cl    sp  │
                    └─────────────────────────────┘
```

1. nearby	_____ ose	**6.** to go up the hill	_____ imb
2. close your eyes and	_____ eep	**7.** runs on track	_____ ain
3. what a top does	_____ in	**8.** to say something	_____ eak
4. cannot see	_____ ind	**9.** a pretty color	_____ ue
5. used to catch lobsters	_____ ap	**10.** not very fast	_____ ow

Teacher: "Read the clue. Write the word that fits the clue."

Example:

can write on this _____ (skate, *slate*)

Clue

1. food is placed on this	_____	(state, plate)
2. not big or large	_____	(small, star)
3. this jumps in the pond	_____	(frog, drop)
4. not very far away	_____	(slow, close)
5. what we do with a broom	_____	(sweep, speak)

Teacher: "How many *st*udents can *st*and on a *st*ump? Each of the following sentences has two missing words. The words *stand* and *stump* will fit in each sentence. Where does each word fit?"

Example:

Can you _____ on a _____?

Teacher: "This is easy; the context forces you to write: Can you *stand* on a *stump*? Finish the following sentences."

1. You can _____ on a _____.

2. A _____ can _____ in the woods.

3. A _____ can _____ a long time.

4. We can both _____ on this large _____.

5. Can this _____ _____ for 50 years?

Teacher: "Since you are well *gr*ounded in reading, it will be easy to *pl*ow through this exercise. Just *pl*ant a few words in the blank spaces. Each sentence has two missing words. Two of the words *plow, plant,* or *ground* will fit in each sentence. Which two words fit where?"

Example:

After you _____ you can _____ crops.

Teacher: "When you use the context of the sentence, you will probably make it read: After you *plow,* you can *plant* crops. Complete each of the following sentences using *plow, plant,* or *ground.*"

   1. You must _____ the _____ in the spring.
   2. Then you _____ seeds in the _____.
   3. You must _____ before you _____.
   4. Remember, _____ seeds after you _____.
   5. Always prepare the _____ before you _____.

Teacher: "One of the letter clusters in the clue box will complete *all* the words in one sentence. Study each sentence and fill in the blanks."

> **Clue Box**
>
> gr   cl   tr   st   dr

Example:

They _____ ew many kinds of _____ ain on the farm. (gr)

   1. The _____ own will, _____ ean the _____ othes.
   2. He _____ ood ready to _____ art telling the _____ ory.
   3. She did not _____ op the _____ um during the _____ ill.
   4. It was a _____ eat to _____ amp along the _____ ail.
   5. She _____ ove to town to buy a _____ ess.

Teacher: "John makes many speeches. The sentences that follow are all about John and his speeches. All blanks in these sentences are filled by one of these words:

   speak   spoke   spoken   speaking   speaks   speaker

—Wait! The last word in the last sentence begins with a different blend."

   1. John was invited to sp _____.
   2. He is sp _____ now.
   3. He will sp _____ again tomorrow.
   4. He sp _____ twice this week.
   5. He has sp _____ many times this year.
   6. He is a very good sp _____.
   7. After he sp _____ he will eat a _____ eak!

INITIAL CONSONANT DIGRAPHS (*SH, WH, TH,* AND *CH*)

A digraph is a combination of two letters that represent one speech sound. The sound heard is not a blend of the two letters involved, but a completely new sound. A given digraph may have more than one pronunciation, but the letter combination results in a single sound in each case (*ch* = /k/ in *chorus;* /sh/ in *chef;* /ch/ in *church*). Digraphs may be taught in a similar way to that used for teaching consonant sounds.

Steps in Brief

1. Place several stimulus words on the chalkboard: *shall, she, ship,* and *show.*
2. Ask the children to look at the words carefully and note how they are alike. Draw out the observation that all the words begin with *sh.* (Underline the digraph being taught: *sh, ch, th,* or *wh.*)
3. Ask the children to listen to the sound of /sh/ as they say the words together.
4. Invite children to supply other words that begin with the same sound as *shall, she, ship,* and *show.*

Note: The digraph *sh* usually has the sound heard in these stimulus words. Other common *sh* words are *shut, shop, shot, sheep, shape, shade, short, sheet, shoot, shoe, shell, shirt, shovel, shake, sharp,* and *shine.*

The digraph *wh* is usually pronounced as if spelled *hw:* when = hwen; white = hwite. The /wh/ sound may be taught as /sh/ was above, with *when, white, what,* and *which* as stimulus words. Other common *wh* words are *why, where, wheel, wheat, whisper, whether, whale,* and *whiskers.* Exceptions: When *o* follows *wh,* the *w* is silent, as in who = $h\overline{oo}$; whole = hōl; whom = $h\overline{oo}m$; whose = $h\overline{oo}z$. (Changing patterns of pronunciation have likely caused some dictionaries to recognize a second pronunciation: when = wĕn.)

The digraph *th* has two common sounds. There is the voiced /th/ sound as in *this, their, they, though, that, then, there, than,* and *them,* and the unvoiced *th* sound as in *thing, thin, thimble, thank, think, thick, third,* and *thumb.* (The concepts of voiced and unvoiced need not be taught in relation to reading.)

While the consonant digraph *ch* has three different sounds, the most common and the one met almost exclusively in beginning reading is that of /ch/ heard in *chair* or *chop.* Common words for use in teaching *ch* exercises include the following.

chair	chin	chose	charm	chalk
child	check	chop	chance	cheer
chicken	cheek	change	chimney	chief

Much later, children will meet the other sounds represented by *ch*. These need not be taught in beginning reading.

ch = k		*ch = sh*	
chorus	(kō rus)	chef	(shef)
character	(kar ak ter)	chassis	(shas ē)
chemist	(kem ist)	chauffeur	(sho fur)
choir	(kwir)	chic	(shēk)
chord	(kord)	chiffon	(shif on)
chrome	(krom)	chamois	(sham ē)

Blends in Sentence Context

Prepare a number of sentences in which a high percentage of the words begin with the digraphs *sh, ch, wh,* and *th*. These may be presented via the chalkboard, transparencies, or duplicated worksheets. After reading the material silently, children volunteer to read a sentence to the group.

1. Charles and Chip chatted in the church chapel.
2. Chester chose a chunk of cheese and some chips from the chest.
3. Shirley showed the shells to Sherman.
4. The shepherd sheltered the sheep in the shadow of the shed.
5. His white whiskers were whirled by the whistling wind.
6. Mr. White whispered when and where the whale would appear.
7. On Thursday, Thelma thought of thirty things to do.
8. Thad thought about a thorn in his thumb.

USING CONTEXT

Teacher: "Read the clue word. Following each clue, complete a word that has the opposite meaning. Use one of the digraphs *ch, th, sh,* or *wh* to do this."

Example:

pride _____ ame (write *sh* for *shame*)

Clue			*Clue*		
1. adult	_____ ild		**3.** open	_____ ut	
2. tall	_____ ort		**4.** fat	_____ in	

5. shout   _____ isper   **8.** freeze   _____ aw

6. dull   _____ arp   **9.** thin   _____ ick

7. retreat   _____ arge   **10.** warm   _____ illy

Teacher: "Read the clue. Build a word, using *ch, sh, th,* or *wh,* that fits the clue."

Example:

can dig with this _____ ovel (sh)

Clue

1. fits on foot   _____ oe

2. not very tall   _____ ort

3. round and rolls   _____ eel

4. speaking very softly   _____ isper

5. writes on blackboard   _____ alk

6. leader of the tribe   _____ ief

7. one on each hand   _____ umb

8. after first and second   _____ ird

9. we sit on this   _____ air

10. found on the beach   _____ ell

Teacher: "Each sentence shows two words containing blank spaces. One digraph—*ch, sh, th,* or *wh*—will fit the blanks in both words. Study each sentence and complete each word."

Example:

Don't let the (*ch*)icken eat the (*ch*)alk.

1. The _____ eep were resting in the _____ ade.

2. Who put the _____ alk mark on the _____ air?

3. _____ ich of the _____ eels is broken?

4. He bought a _____ irt in the _____ op.

5. She had a _____ imble on her _____ umb.

6. After a purchase, always _____ eck your _____ ange.

FUN WITH LANGUAGE

Teacher: "Each sentence below contains some incomplete words. A digraph—*ch, th, sh,* or *wh*—is missing in each word. Read the clue box carefully and then complete the sentences."

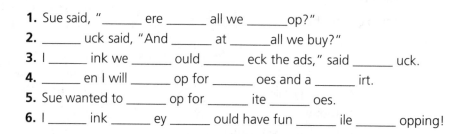

1. Sue said, "_____ ere _____ all we _____op?"

2. _____ uck said, "And _____ at _____all we buy?"

3. I _____ ink we _____ ould _____ eck the ads," said _____ uck.

4. _____ en I will _____ op for _____ oes and a _____ irt.

5. Sue wanted to _____ op for _____ ite _____ oes.

6. I _____ ink _____ ey _____ ould have fun _____ ile _____ opping!

THE *WH* ROUNDUP

Teacher: Tease out the meaning. In the following sentences, each unfinished word begins with *wh*. *Wh*ich word goes *wh*ere? All sentences are based on the clue box.

```
                          Clue Box
       "Sam lives in a white house on Whale Street."
```

Finish each word so that it makes sense in the sentence.

1. Wh_____ house on Wh_____ Street is Sam's house?

2. Sam lives on Wh_____ Street in a wh_____ house.

3. Sam, wh_____ house is wh_____, lives on Wh_____ Street.

4. Wh_____ house is the wh_____ house wh_____ Sam lives?

5. Wh_____ on Wh_____ Street is Sam's wh_____ house?

6. Wh_____ did Sam move into the wh_____ house?

FINAL CONSONANTS, BLENDS, AND DIGRAPHS

Some of the procedures for teaching initial sounds can be adapted to teaching final sounds. The teaching objective remains the same: to help children visually recognize letter forms and associate these with the sounds they represent in words.

1. Chalkboard Drill

  a. Select the letter-sound to be taught.
  b. Place stimulus words on the board.
  c. Call children's attention to the final letter.
  d. Pronounce each word carefully, so that children hear the sound at the end of the word.
  e. Have children pronounce words and supply others that end with the sound.

```
   t
at

hat

cut

sit

not
```

2. Print and Sound

  a. Prepare columns of easy words, all of which end with a particular letter-sound.
  b. Omit the final letter.
  c. Children print the letter indicated and pronounce the word.

Add d	*Add* n	*Add* p	*Add* g	*Add* t
sa_____	gu_____	li_____	ho_____	ne_____
mu_____	wi_____	ca_____	pi_____	hu_____
ha_____	te_____	na_____	ta_____	co_____
ro_____	ru_____	cu_____	wi_____	hi_____

Variations:
Add *m, x,* or *b* to make a word. Pronounce each word.

bo_____	gu_____	ro_____	dru_____	fo_____
roo_____	mi_____	ha_____	gra_____	so_____
hi_____	tu_____	si_____	wa_____	ta_____

Change the last letter of words in the first column so that the new word names something living.

Example:

pin	pi _____	(g)	pig
plane	plan _____	(t)	plant

1. but	bu _____			**6.** map	ma _____
2. lamp	lam _____			**7.** dot	do _____
3. fog	fo _____			**8.** hem	he _____
4. call	cal _____			**9.** owe	ow _____
5. cap	ca _____			**10.** sharp	shar _____

USING CONTEXT

Teacher: "Finish each of the following sentences so that it makes sense. Put the letter *m* or *n* in each blank space. You must read carefully to know which letter fits into which blank."

Example:

Pa_____ had a talk with a ma_____.

Teacher: " 'Pan had a talk with a mam' makes no sense. The sentence 'Pam had a talk with a man' is correct. Remember that every blank has to be filled with *m* or *n*."

1. Sa_____ can count to te_____.
2. Ca_____ you see the me_____?
3. She gave hi_____ a stick of gu_____.
4. Please pass the ha_____.
5. Mo_____ put ja_____ on the bu_____.

The purpose of the following exercise is to provide practice in hearing the letter-sounds *p*, *d*, and *b* at the end of words.

Teacher: "Finish each sentence below so that it makes sense. Put *b*, *d*, or *p* in each blank space. You must read carefully to know which letter fits in each space."

Example:

A baby bear is a cu_____. (can't be cup or cud)

A baby bear is a cub.

Set 1
1. Turn on the lam _____.
2. They rode in a taxi ca _____.
3. He took a short na _____.
4. I like corn on the co _____.
5. A bee stung him on the han _____.

Set 2
1. Bo _____ plays in the ban _____.
2. The guide said, "Here is the ma _____."
3. The water in the tu _____ was col _____.
4. Di _____ he leave his ca _____ in the ca _____?
5. Mother said, "Gra _____ the pu _____."

The following are some stimulus words to use in board or seatwork exercises:

b	d	f	g	k (ck)	l (ll)	m
Bob	sad	if	dog	back	call	him
tub	fed	calf	big	rock	tell	room
club	send	muff	flag	black	hill	gum
grab	glad	stiff	rug	trick	pull	ham
rob	cold	puff	drug	duck	still	whom
rib	band	off	bag	pick	small	drum

n	p	r	s (s)	s (= z)	t
can	hop	for	bus	his	cat
win	cap	star	yes	as	met
men	stop	her	dress	ours	shut
thin	up	dear	us	is	hit
when	step	door	less	has	set
ran	skip	clear	likes	runs	sat
moon	map	car	miss	days	but

Consonant Digraphs *ch*, *sh*, and *th* at the End of Words

The sounds of the digraphs *ch*, *sh*, and *th* will have been taught already because they occur at the beginning of words. Procedures for teaching these sounds at the end of words may parallel those used for teaching initial sounds.

1. Place stimulus words on the board.
2. Have the children look at the letter combinations under discussion.
3. Pronounce each word carefully so children hear the sound at the end of the word.
4. Have the children pronounce the words.

```
Which
reach
such
pitch
```

Other stimulus words ending with *ch, sh,* or *th* are *March, church, peach, branch, ditch, search, teach, patch, bench; fish, cash, fresh, rush, crash, dish, flash, wish, push; both, bath, tenth, north, health, path, length, fifth,* and *cloth.*

USING CONTEXT

Teacher: "Read the clue word. Complete the word that follows, using one of the digraphs *ch, sh,* or *th.*"

Clue Word		Clue Word	
fruit	pea_____	vegetable	squa_____
two	bo_____	direction	nor_____
month	Mar_____	meal	lun_____
money	ca_____	insect	mo_____
lightning	fla_____	wreck	cra_____
trail	pa_____	worship	chur_____

Teacher: "Some language games are easier than they look! To complete the following sentences you must write one of the digraphs *ch, sh,* or *th* in each blank space. Reading the rest of the sentence makes it easy."

Example:

Eat fre_____ fi_____ for your heal_____.

Teacher: "The only way for the sentence to make sense is by using *ch, sh,* or *th* in the three blanks. Remember, either *ch, sh,* or *th* will fit in each blank."

1. "Are the fi_____ fre_____?" he asked.
2. Bo_____ nor_____ and sou_____ are directions.
3. A bran_____ fell from the pea_____ tree.
4. The parade will mar_____ down the pa_____.
5. Whi_____ clo_____ needs the pat_____?
6. We had fre_____ fi_____ for lun_____.
7. Mar_____ is the third mon_____.

Consonant Digraphs *nk, ng,* and *ck* at the End of Words

Teaching *nk, ng,* and *ck* involves associating these letter combinations at the end of words or syllables with the sounds they represent. These digraphs may be taught by instructing children that, for example, "The sound of /nk/ at the end of words is the sound we hear in these words."

bank	link	junk
rank	mink	sunk
sank	pink	drunk
tank	sink	shrunk

Other words to use in board or seatwork exercises include *ink, blink, drink, think; plank, drank, spank, frank; trunk, chunk,* and *bunk.*

"The sound of /ng/ at the end of words is the sound we hear in these words."

bang	king	gong	hung
gang	ring	bong	rung
hang	wing	strong	sprung
sang	sing	song	sung

"The letters *ck* have the sound of /k/. Listen to the sound at the end of these words."

back	pick	dock	luck
pack	kick	lock	duck
sack	sick	block	truck
crack	trick	sock	buck

Final Consonant Blends (*st, sk, ld, mp,* and *nd*)

Teaching procedures described throughout this chapter can be used or adapted to teach blended consonants occurring at the end of words (*st, sk, ld, mp,* and *nd*).

mu*st*	a*sk*	co*ld*	ju*mp*	fi*nd*
fa*st*	de*sk*	wi*ld*	ca*mp*	ba*nd*
re*st*	ma*sk*	fie*ld*	du*mp*	fou*nd*
mo*st*	du*sk*	chi*ld*	cha*mp*	be*nd*

CONSONANT IRREGULARITIES

Fortunately, sounds represented by consonant letters involve less variability than is found in vowel letter-sounds. Nevertheless, a number of consonants and consonant combinations result in pronunciation irregularities that must be taught. The majority of these fall into one of the following groupings.

- Consonants that have more than one sound (for example, *c* sounded as /k/ or /s/; *g* sounded as /g/ or /j/; and *s* sounded as /s/, /z/, /sh/, or /zh/)

- Consonants that are not sounded (know, light, wrap)
- Consonant combinations with unique pronunciations (ph = /f/; que = /k/)

The Two Sounds of c (/k/ and /s/)

The letter c represents no distinctive sound of its own. It is sounded as /k/ when followed by the vowels a, o, and u, and as /s/ when followed by i, e, or y. The hard (k) sound occurs most frequently and for this reason is usually taught first. Eight words on the Dolch List begin with the letter c, and in all of these the letter has its /k/ sound. Only four of the 58 words on the Dale List that begin with c have the /s/ sound. Chalkboard and duplicated seatwork exercises can provide drill as needed. Here are some examples.

c is sounded /k/ when followed by	a	o	u
	call	cold	cut
	cake	come	cup
	care	coat	cute
	cap	cook	cub

c is sounded /s/ when followed by	i	e	y
	city	cent	cymbal
	cinder	cement	cypress
	cider	mice	cynic
	citizen	voice	cylinder

Some words include both sounds of c: circle, cycle, and circus.
Teacher: "Say each word softly aloud, then on each blank space write s or k to show the sound of the letter c."

_____ cat	_____ comb	_____ ceiling	_____ color
_____ center	_____ citizen	_____ cuff	_____ cellar

The Two Sounds of g (/g/ and /j/)

1. The letter g has its regular (hard) sound when followed by a, u, and o.
2. The letter g is often sounded as /j/ when followed by i, e, and y. (Common exceptions: give, girl, get, geese, and gift.)

Dealing with the two sounds of g is not so much a matter of teaching but of simply acquainting children with this phenomenon. Only a few words are met in beginning reading in which g is sounded as /j/. After stating the two rules, children may practice hearing the two sounds.

Teacher: "Pronounce each word softly, then on each blank space write g or j to show the sound that g represents."

_____ George	_____ goat	_____ gem	_____ game
_____ gum	_____ giant	_____ gave	_____ gentle
_____ garden	_____ general	_____ gold	_____ gun

Sounds Represented by the Letter *s*

1. The letter *s* usually represents its regular sound as heard in *said, set, sing, soap,* and *sun.*
2. The letter *s* is sometimes sounded as /z/ when it is the final sound in the word: *is, his, has, ours, please, cheese,* and *noise.*
3. The letter *s* is sounded /sh/ in *sure* and *sugar.*
4. The letter *s* is sounded /zh/ in *measure* and *treasure.*

It is highly doubtful that the irregularities associated with the letter *s* have any significant impact on learning to read.

Consonants Not Sounded

A large number of English words contain one or more letters that are not sounded. In some instances, particularly when the initial letter is not sounded, it pays to learn the words as sight words. Instant word recognition and independent reading are enhanced by deliberately calling to children's attention the more frequently occurring instances of consonants that are not sounded. We can make the following generalizations.

1. In words containing double consonants, the first is sounded, the second is not.
2. In words beginning with *kn*, the *k* is usually not sounded.
3. The combination *gh* is usually not sounded when preceded by the vowel *i.*
4. In words beginning with *wr*, the *w* is usually not sounded.
5. In words ending with the syllable *-ten*, the *t* is often not sounded.
6. The digraph *ck* is pronounced *k.*
7. In words ending with *mb*, the *b* is usually not sounded.

It is doubtful that learning these rules in isolation or as a series of generalizations has virtue. Working with a series of stimulus words that follow one or more of the rules will help children gain insight into the pronunciation of words. Table 5–4 provides examples of words that follow each of these seven generalizations.

While a given generalization may be introduced in a particular grade, it will probably have to be reviewed in subsequent grades. For some children, simple review will not be adequate, and the generalization and applications will have to be retaught. By means of close observation or diagnosis, the teacher—at any grade level—discovers which children need help on a particular skill and can work individually with these children or devise seatwork exercises that provide practice in the areas in which deficiencies are noted. Words of appropriate difficulty can be selected for use in various types of teaching exercises. The difficulty level of the exercises can be further controlled by the task or tasks the children are called upon to perform.

TABLE 5–4 *Consonants Not Sounded*

Double Consonants	kn Words	gh Words	wr Words	-ten Ending	-ck Ending	-mb Ending
ladder	know	sigh	write	often	sack	comb
collect	knee	light	wring	soften	neck	thumb
fellow	knight	sight	wrote	listen	block	climb
message	knew	bright	wrap	hasten	kick	bomb
roller	knit	flight	wrath	fasten	duck	lamb
summer	knife	night	wrist	glisten	clock	plumb
dinner	knock	might	wrong	moisten	black	limb
yellow	kneel	slight	wren	brighten	trick	numb
happen	knob	blight	wreck	tighten	back	crumb
kitten	known	right	wreath	frighten	pick	dumb

The purpose of the following exercises is to explain the concept that some letters in words may not represent a sound. At this level, one need not explain in the language of linguistic science. The term *silent letters* is inaccurate, since no letters make sounds; however, to use this term with 6-year-olds is not poor pedagogy.

1. *Directions:* Place material on the chalkboard similar to the examples in the box. Pronounce each word. Call attention to the pair of like consonants and the fact that they represent one sound. Draw a slash through the second consonant in each pair to indicate that it is not sounded.

> ***summer dress letter bell***
> Two like consonants stand for one sound.
> letter summer dress bell

Put words on the chalkboard that illustrate this concept or duplicate material for seatwork. Have children cross out the letter that is not sounded.

dinner	kitten	tall
glass	cuff	barrel
ball	ladder	yellow
hidden	doll	fuzz
cross	grass	sudden
rabbit	happen	class

2. *Purpose:* To provide practice in sight recognition of words that contain one or more of the irregular spellings *kn, wr, igh, mb, ph* = /f/, and *gh* = /f/.

   Directions: Explain the irregularities of the letter combinations discussed. Have the children note that the words in each line contain the letter pattern shown on the left. Have them practice pronouncing each word and learn these words as sight words.

kn:	knew known knee knight knit knock know (the *k* is not sounded)
wr:	write wrong wreck wrote wring wrap wrist (the *w* is not sounded)
igh:	light night sight bright right fight might (*i* = ī; *gh* is not sounded)
mb:	comb lamb thumb climb crumb bomb (the final letter *b* is not sounded)
ph:	phone photo nephew phonics autograph phrase (*ph* represents the sound of /f/)
gh:	laugh cough rough enough tough laughter (final letters represent the sound of /f/)

3. *Directions:* Have the children read the following sentences softly aloud to themselves, then underline the letters *kn, wr, ph, gh,* and *mb* each time they appear in a word.
   1. The knight knew how to write, so he wrote a pamphlet.
   2. He took a right turn on the wrong light and had a wreck.
   3. The wreck was quite a sight in the bright moonlight.
   4. Phil hurt his knee and thumb taking photographs that night.
   5. If you know the alphabet and phonics, you can learn to read and write.

4. *Teacher:* "Pronounce all the words in each A column. Then strike out each silent consonant in the words in the A columns. The first one is done for you. In the space under B, write the dictionary pronunciation of each word." (This will be used later in conjunction with dictionary work.)

A	*B*	*A*	*B*
si̸g̸ht	sīt	kni̸g̸ht	nīt
hasten	_____	glisten	_____
knew	_____	comb	_____
rabbit	_____	right	_____
thick	_____	write	_____
climb	_____	black	_____

wrote	_____	funnel	_____
dollar	_____	known	_____
debt	_____	doubt	_____
knock	_____	truck	_____
soften	_____	often	_____
summer	_____	tunnel	_____
sigh	_____	thumb	_____

5. The following exercise illustrates that unsounded letters are useful in that they produce a different word that has the same pronunciation but a different meaning from the word to which the unsounded letter is added. This letter provides a visual clue to the meaning of the new word.

Teacher: "In column B, add a letter that is not sounded to each word in column A in order to produce a different word."

A	B	A	B
new	_____	night	_____
hole	_____	be	_____
our	_____	cent	_____
rap	_____	not	_____
nob	_____	plum	_____
in	_____	ring	_____

Qu and *Que* Combinations (/kw/ and /k/)

Qu. The letter *q* has no sound of its own and is always followed by *u*, which in this case does not function as a vowel. The combination *qu* is pronounced /kw/, as in *quick* = kwik and *quack* = kwak.

Other *qu* words that might be used in teaching exercises include *queen, quart, quiet, quit, Quaker, quake, quite, quarter, quail,* and *quarrel.*

Que. *Que* at the end of words has the sound of /k/; usually *que* is blended with the preceding syllable.

picturesque = pĭk chûr ĕsk	plaque = plăk
antique = ăn tēk	grotesque = grō tĕsk
burlesque = bûr lĕsk	clique = klēk
opaque = ō pāk	brusque = brŭsk
critique = krĭ tēk	technique = tĕk nēk

Note that the final syllable in *que* words is accented.

SUMMARY

In this chapter, we built on children's previously acquired skills of auditory-visual discrimination and dealt with teaching consonant letter-sound relationships. There is a good rationale for teaching consonants in initial position in words. You now have steps for teaching single letters, blends (clusters), and digraphs, and suggestions for helping children master certain consonant letter-sound irregularities.

In general, consonant letters are quite consistent in the sounds they represent. Letters that represent only one sound include *b, d, h, j, k, l, m, n, p, r, w,* and initial *y.* Consonants that combine include the following:

- *Consonant blends* (clusters), in which two or more letters blend so that sound elements of each letter are heard: *bl, bl*ack; *str, str*ing; *spl, spl*ash; and *gl, gl*ide.
- *Consonant digraphs,* in which two-letter combinations result in one speech sound that is not a blend of the letters involved: *sh*all; *wh*ite; *th*is (voiced */th/*); *th*ink (unvoiced */th/*); *ch*air; *ch*orus (ch = */k/*); and *ch*ef (ch = */sh/*).

Some consonants and consonant combinations have irregular spellings.

Unsounded Consonants in Specific Combinations

1. The *k* is not sounded in *kn* (k̸new, k̸nee)
2. Double consonants—only one is sounded (summ̸er)
3. When the vowel *i* precedes *gh,* the latter is not sounded (lig̸h̸t)
4. The *w* is not sounded in *wr* at the beginning of words (w̸riting)
5. When a word ends with the syllable *-ten,* the *t* is often not sounded (of̸ten, fas̸ten)
6. The *ck* combination is pronounced */k/* (sa̸ck, clo̸ck)
7. The *b* is not sounded in *mb* at the end of words (comb̸, lamb̸)

There are two sounds for the consonant *c.*

1. c = */k/* in *cake, corn,* and *curl*
2. c = */s/* when followed by *i, e,* or *y* (*city, cent, cycle*)

There are two sounds for the consonant *g.*

1. regular sound in *go, game,* and *gum*
2. g = */j/* when followed by *e* or *i* (*gem, giant*)

Other irregularities include the following.

1. ph = */f/* (*photo = foto; graph = graf*)
2. qu = */kw/* (*quack = kwack*). The letter *q* has no sound of its own. In English spellings, *q* is always followed by the letter *u.*
3. The letter *s* may be sounded in a number of ways.
    a. s = */s/* (most common) (*sell, soft, said*)
    b. s = */z/* (*his = hiz; runs = runz*)
    c. s = */sh/* (*sugar*)
    d. s = */zh/* (*treasure*)

Chapter 6

VOWEL LETTER-SOUND RELATIONSHIPS

*T*eaching the vowel letter-sound relationships is undoubtedly the most difficult and confusing part of an entire phonics program. This stems from two factors:

1. The variability of the sounds that vowels represent.
2. The tendency to overteach certain vowel letter-sound relationships, which can be confusing rather than helpful.

We have discussed the variability of vowel letter-sounds in Chapter 1. In essence, all the rules or generalizations that have been advanced to cover vowel letter-sounds turn out to have numerous exceptions. Nevertheless, to be successful in the decoding process, children must develop insights relative to the relationship between visual letter patterns and the sounds these patterns *usually* represent. The apparent variability in spelling and sounds should point up the fact that a number of high-frequency words should be learned as sight words. A list of these sight words is provided in Table 6–1 at the end of this chapter.

PHONICS INSTRUCTION AS OVERKILL

The second problem in teaching vowel letter-sound relationships stems from the fact that teachers and schools sometimes forget the limited purpose of phonics instruction in the learning-to-read process (see Figure 6–1). Two issues emerge. Do we teach some "phonics" that has relatively little impact on learning to read? Do we overteach some facets of letter-sound relationships that are more appropriate for producing junior linguists rather than beginning readers?

When our goal is simply teaching children to read, some minute differences in letter-sounds need not be dealt with at all. Certain other differences can be pointed

FIGURE 6–1   The cartoonist Malcolm Hancock suggests that phonics can be overtaught as he shows an artistic disdain for vowels

out without forcing children to spend time discriminating these sounds in lists of words. What we sometimes forget in dealing with native speakers of English is that children can pronounce and thus differentiate among words that contain different sound values for a given vowel, such as *a* in *almost, loyal, path, idea,* and *father.* Furthermore, when children are reading for meaning, the problem diminishes in importance.

SEQUENCE IN TEACHING VOWEL LETTER-SOUNDS

There are certain factors relating to the sequence of teaching skills that have served as the basis for lengthy debate. Many of these may be of little importance to children learning to read; which vowel letter-sound to teach first, whether to teach short or long sounds first, or whether to teach these two sounds concomitantly are probably not crucial issues. In fact, a quite reasonable rationale could be made for opposite views pertaining to most matters of sequence.

In advocating the teaching of short vowel sounds first, it can be pointed out that a majority of the words children meet in beginning reading contain short vowel sounds. Many of these words are single-vowel-in-medial-position words. The phonic generalization for this situation—one vowel in medial position usually has its short sound—applies in a large percentage of words met in beginning reading.

Advocacy of teaching long vowel sounds first rests on the fact that the vowel name is the long sound of the vowel (*a, e, i, o, u*). It is frequently suggested that this fact makes it easy to teach the letter-sound association.

SHORT VOWEL SOUNDS

The generalizations that cover short vowel sounds deal primarily with initial single vowels and single vowels in medial position in words. Both of these vowel situations can be covered by the statement, "A single vowel that does not conclude a word usually has its short sound"; for example, *am, an, and, ant, as, ask, at,* and *act.*

The vast majority of words covered have a vowel in medial position, however, and as a result, the following generalization is used more frequently: "A single vowel in medial position usually has its short sound," as we see when we add an initial consonant to the words for the first generalization: *ham, can, hand, pant, gas, task, bat,* and *fact.*

We will illustrate methods for teaching the short vowel sound in medial position. To avoid repetition, we will use a teaching procedure to illustrate only one vowel sound; however, any of the approaches described can be used to teach each of the other vowel letter-sounds that fit the generalization. You will also find brief word lists for teaching each of the vowel letter-sounds.

For the short sound of *a* (ă), explain to children that they have learned a number of the sounds consonants represent in words and that they will now practice hearing one of the sounds represented by the vowel *a.*

Teacher: "When we say the name of the vowel letter, we hear what is called the vowel's long sound."

"Today we are going to listen carefully and learn to hear another sound for the vowel *a*—its short sound. I am going to put some words on the board. We have studied these words before. Each of the words has the letter *a* in it. Listen to the sound the *a* has in each word."

Begin by writing these words on the chalkboard: *man, had, back, ran, cap, tag.*

1. Pronounce each word, moving your hand from left to right through the word.
2. Emphasize the sound /ă/ in each word, but do not distort the sound.
3. Have the children say the words in unison, asking them to listen for the sound /ă/.
4. Stress that the sound heard is called the short sound of *a.* Have the children note how this sound differs from the letter name.
5. Ask students how many vowels they see in each word and where the vowel is located (middle of the word).

6. Have children state what sound is heard when there is one vowel in the middle of a word.[1]
7. Have children state in their own words the rule that covers this vowel situation.

Using this approach, the following generalization will evolve: "One vowel in the middle of the word usually has its short sound." It is probably not essential that each child be able to recite all the generalizations in this chapter. At this point, it might be profitable to cite other familiar words that follow the generalizations under discussion, even though all the stimulus words are not yet known as sight words.

Using Word Families

Some teachers find that certain children can do better in fixing the short sound of a given vowel if they see and pronounce a series of words that contain larger identical units than the vowel alone: the words *big, ship, tin,* and *hill* have an identical unit—*i*. The words *big, pig, dig,* and *fig,* and *hill, fill, bill,* and *pill,* and *sit, fit, bit,* and *kit* have rhyming units composed of several letters that have precisely the same phonic value in each word. Word families can be used both for teaching common phonic elements and for rapid recognition as sight words.

To teach the phonogram *ad,* you might begin with these words: *dad, had, sad, mad, bad,* and *lad.* Use the seven steps previously outlined to teach this and other identical phonogram words.

1. Pronounce each word; have children pronounce the words.
2. Stress the vowel sound heard and the visual pattern: one vowel, medial position.

Sample words follow for the vowels *e, i, o,* and *u.* The first column under each vowel includes words with mixed initial and final consonants; the second column presents the same final phonogram (letter-pattern) in each word.

e		*i*		*o*		*u*	
red	jet	big	hit	hop	cot	bus	bug
let	pet	tin	bit	job	not	run	rug
bell	let	hill	sit	stop	hot	cup	hug
send	bet	did	pit	log	pot	jump	jug
men	met	pig	fit	box	got	cut	mug
step	set	lift	lit	rock	lot	must	tug

---

[1]Strictly speaking, the vowel in words such as *back, bank,* and *trap* is not in the middle of the word. Children are usually not confused by this statement, but you can modify the generalization if you wish.

USING CONTEXT

Teacher: "Read the clue. Use one of the vowel letters *a, e,* or *o* to spell the word that fits the clue."

Example:

Clue

spider	w_____b	use *e* to spell *web*
angry	m_____d	use *a* to spell *mad*
horses	tr_____t	use *o* to spell *trot*

	Clue			*Clue*	
1.	fishing	n_____t	**6.**	soda	p_____p
2.	chicken	h_____n	**7.**	number	t_____n
3.	steal	r_____b	**8.**	floor	l_____mp
4.	bird's	n_____st	**9.**	cry	s_____b
5.	paper	b_____g	**10.**	lion's	d_____n

Teacher: "Use one of the vowel letters *i, u,* or *e* to spell the word."

	Clue			*Clue*	
1.	chewy	g_____m	**6.**	fish	sw_____m
2.	color	r_____d	**7.**	scissors	c_____t
3.	tops	sp_____n	**8.**	rings	b_____ll
4.	plane	j_____t	**9.**	fruit	pl_____m
5.	ruler	k_____ng	**10.**	large	b_____g

Teacher: "Read the clue. Write the vowel that completes the word that fits the clue."

Example:

you sleep on this   b_____d (e)

	Clue			*Clue*	
1.	it's large	b_____g	**5.**	can ring it	b_____ll
2.	paper sack	b_____g	**6.**	can throw it	b_____ll
3.	an insect	b_____g	**7.**	lives on a farm	b_____ll
4.	to keep asking for	b_____g	**8.**	ra boy's name	B_____ll

Teacher: "Read the clue. Write the word that fits the clue."

Example:

The pig is in the _____.   (pin, pen)

Clue

Do you like corn on the _____?   (cab, cob)

John said, "I can read the _____."   (mop, map)

The cat drank milk from the _____.   (cap, cup)

Cats and dogs are _____.   (pots, pets)

A baby bear is a _____.   (cab, cub)

Teacher: "Each sentence has two blanks. Either the word *pig* or *pen* will fit in each space. Study each sentence and write the correct words."

Example:

The (*pig*) is in the (*pen*).

1. Put the _____ in the _____.

2. Will the _____ hold the _____?

3. The _____ will hold the _____.

4. The _____ should be in the _____.

5. The _____ is for the _____.

6. Is the _____ in the _____?

7. The _____ belongs in the _____.

8. It is time to _____ up the _____.

Teacher: "Read each sentence. One of the words at the right fits in the blank space. The only difference in the words is the vowel letter. Write the correct word in the blank space."

Example:

The _____ was many years old.   click

                                                     clock

1. There was a _____ on the beach.   crab

                                                             crib

2. The _____ was full of coal.   trick

                                                         truck

3. John was able to _____ the word.   spell

                                                             spill

4. Spot is a _____ dog.   smell

                                                 small

5. _____ the letter in the mailbox.   Drop

                                                                Drip

---

FUN WITH LANGUAGE

Teacher: "Fill every blank space with a vowel. The context will help you pick the right vowel."

Clue: Suzy sings a lot.

Will she sing a song again if she has just sung that song?

1. Just ask Suzy and she will s_____ng any s_____ng.

2. Once she s_____ng a very pretty s_____ng.

3. Later, someone asked her to s_____ng that s_____ng again.

4. She said, "I just s_____ng that s_____ng."

5. I should not s_____ng a s_____ng that I have just s_____ng.

6. Was Suzy right not to s_____ng that s_____ng again?

7. Would you s_____ng a s_____ng you had just s_____ng?

8. If you have just s_____ng a s_____ng and you want to s_____ng it again, s_____ng it!

BUCKETS AND BLANK SPACES

Teacher: "Note that each word with a blank in it has the same three letters. To complete each word, you must add a vowel. Which vowel goes where? As you read the sentence, the context will indicate where to add *a, e, i,* and *u.*"

1. First, you f_____ll the bucket f_____ll of water.

2. Don't f_____ll while carrying a bucket f_____ll of water.

3. If you f_____ll, the bucket might not be f_____ll.

4. He f_____ll, then he had to f_____ll the bucket again.

5. Don't f_____ll if you want a f_____ll bucket.

Teacher: "In each of the following sentences, two words need a vowel. The context will help you decide which words fit. Write the vowel letter to complete each word."

Set 1

Use only the vowels *u, i,* and *e.*

1. Is the b_____g very b_____g?

2. S_____t the basket down and come s_____t by me.

3. Don't d_____g where we d_____g yesterday.

4. That t_____n cup cost t_____n cents.

5. She asked h_____m, "Can you h_____m this song?"

6. You write with a p_____n, not with a p_____n.

Set 2

Use only the vowels *a, o,* and *i.*

1. The c_____t was asleep on the c_____t.

2. "Watch out," said Joe, "the p_____t is very h_____t."

3. I want to s_____t where we s_____t yesterday.

4. Ask h_____m if he wants a h_____m sandwich.

5. Put the b_____g dish in the paper b_____g.

6. When the weather is h_____t you should wear a h_____t.

Minimal Contrast Vowels

Practice in associating vowel letter forms with the short sounds they represent can be presented in many ways. The examples start with contrasting two vowel sounds and gradually move through all vowels in medial position.

Contrasting two vowel sounds.   As soon as two vowel sounds have been introduced, the difference between them can be stressed.

1. Write pairs of words on the chalkboard.

bat—bet	mat—met	pat—pet	sat—set
man—men	tan—ten	bad—bed	lad—led

2. Pronounce these words, inviting children to listen to the difference in the vowel sounds heard in the middle of the words.
3. Have children pronounce the pairs of words, noting each vowel letter form and the sound it represents.

The short sounds of *e* and *i* often pose special difficulty because of either poor auditory discrimination or dialectical differences in pronunciation. The following pairs of words, identical except for the vowel *i* or *e,* can be used in both auditory and visual drill.

led—lid	big—beg	pig—peg	wit—wet
pin—pen	tin—ten	din—den	met—mitt
bed—bid	pep—pip	bet—bit	rid—red
lit—let	pit—pet	sit—set	hem—him

Various exercises using different modes of presentation can be built from pairs of words such as these.

u, i	*u, e*	*a, u*	*o, u*
bug—big	bug—beg	bag—bug	cot—cut
but—bit	but—bet	bat—but	hot—hut
hut—hit	nut—net	cat—cut	not—nut
dug—dig	hum—hem	cap—cup	hog—hug

e, o	*a, o*	*a, i*	*i, o*
get—got	cat—cot	lap—lip	hip—hop
let—lot	hat—hot	nap—nip	tip—top
net—not	pat—pot	rap—rip	Tim—Tom
pet—pot	rat—rot	tap—tip	hit—hot

Seeing and sounding drill.   After all short vowel letter-sounds have been introduced, exercise material can help children fix the visual-auditory relationship involved in the single-vowel-in-medial-position generalization. To use the following material, children should be told that the words in each line are exactly the same except for the vowel letter-sound.

1. "Listen for the difference (vowel sound) in each word."
2. "If the word is underlined, it is a nonsense word you haven't met—but you still can pronounce it."
3. "Read across each line of words."

a	*e*	*i*	*o*	*u*
bag	beg	big	bog	bug
→	→	→	→	
lad	led	lid	lod	lud
pat	pet	pit	pot	pud
dask	desk	disk	dosk	dusk
jag	jeg	jig	jog	jug
ham	hem	him	hom	hum
fan	fen	fin	fon	fun
Nat	net	nit	not	nut
lack	leck	lick	lock	luck
sap	sep	sip	sop	sup

BLEND AND SAY

Teacher: "Each word has a blank space. A vowel letter is shown above each blank space. Think of the sound of the vowel letter and say each word."

a	e	i	o	u
b____t	b____d	h____t	h____p	f____n
a	e	i	o	u
c____n	j____t	p____g	l____g	b____s
e	u	o	i	a
m____n	g____m	c____t	s____x	f____t
i	o	a	u	e
d____g	m____p	r____t	f____n	l____g

CHANGE THE VOWEL

Teacher: "Change the vowel and make a naming word for something living using the vowels *a, e, i, o,* or *u.*"

Examples:

cot—cat

pep—pup

dig	d____g	big	b____g
dock	d____ck	limb	l____mb
pit	p____t	crib	cr____b
cot	c____t	bell	b____ll
fix	f____x	peg	p____g

WRITE AND SAY

This material can be presented in many different ways, including the chalkboard and duplicated exercises.

Teacher: "Put the vowel *a* in each of the following blank spaces. Then pronounce the word."

t____p	b____d
n____p	d____d
l____p	h____d
m____p	m____d
c____p	s____d

Teacher: "Put the vowel *e* in each of the following blank spaces. Then pronounce the word."

m____n	l____t
p____n	n____t
d____n	p____t
h____n	j____t
t____n	b____t

Teacher: "Put the vowel *i* in each of the following blank spaces. Pronounce the word."

p____n	h____t
t____n	b____t
b____n	s____t
f____n	f____t
s____n	p____t

Teacher: "Put the vowel *u* in each of the following blank spaces. Pronounce the word."

r____g	r____n
j____g	s____n
h____g	f____n
t____g	g____n
d____g	b____n

Teacher: "Add a vowel to make a word. Only one vowel fits in each word."

Examples:

w____b (e)		*a, e, i, o, u*
f____sh (i)		

y____s	gl____d	k____ss
v____m	c____n	pl____n
sw____n	y____t	b____s
cl____b	s____ch	m____lk
r____ch	d____st	s____nt
k____g	d____t	n____st

Combining Teaching of Initial and Medial Vowel Sounds

Some teachers prefer to teach the short sound of initial and medial vowels simultaneously. The procedure can be much the same as for the medial-vowel situation;

however, the generalization that emerges will be stated differently. To illustrate this concept, place a number of stimulus words on the board.

a	*a*
am	ham
ask	task
at	bat
and	sand
as	gas
act	fact
an	pan

Words in the first column contain one initial vowel, and the short sound is heard. Words in the second column contain one medial vowel, and the short sound is heard. As children see and hear the letter-sound relationship, the generalization will emerge: "When the only vowel in a word does not come at the end of the word, it usually has its short sound."

LONG VOWEL (GLIDED) LETTER-SOUNDS

In teaching the long vowel letter-sounds, keep in mind that children differentiate these sounds when they process or use oral language. In the reading process, teaching the long vowel letter-sounds focuses primarily on having children recognize several visual patterns and associate these with the sounds they characteristically represent.

Using Visual Patterns as Cues to Sounding

Despite the large number of exceptions to any generalizations advanced to cover vowel letter-sounds, certain visual cues must be heeded. We will look at the following major patterns.

Two adjacent vowels (particularly m*ee*t, s*ea*t, c*oa*t, s*ai*l)
Medial vowel and final *e* (r*o*pe, c*a*pe, c*u*te, t*i*re)
Single vowel that concludes a word (g*o*, m*e*)
How *y* functions at the end of words (m*y*, ma*y*)

Two adjacent vowels are covered by this generalization: "When two vowels come together, the first one usually has its long sound and the second is not sounded."

Data from studies of a large sample of words met in elementary reading materials indicate that this generalization actually applies to less than half the words that meet the two-vowel criterion; however, the generalization held fairly consistently for the *ee*, *oa*, *ai*, and *ea* patterns. Studies revealed the percentage of instances in which the two-vowel rule applies: *ee*, 98%; *oa*, 97%; *ai*, 64%; *ea*, 66%; and all two-vowel situations combined, 48% (Clymer, 1963; Oaks, 1952).

In the following examples, teaching does not start with a statement of generalizations, but with material that emphasizes the visual patterns *oa, ee, ai, ea*. The patterns are linked to the sound heard in words and permit the children to discover the relationship and arrive at the generalization.

1. Place a column of *oa* words on the board: *boat, coat, load, road,* and *soak.*
2. Pronounce each word, emphasizing the long /ō/ sound.
3. Have children note the visual pattern of the two vowels.
4. Point out that in each word you hear the long sound of the first vowel and the second vowel is not sounded. This may be illustrated, as in the right-hand column.

boat	bōát
coat	cōát
load	lōád
road	rōád
soak	sōák

A similar procedure can be followed to introduce the patterns *ai, ea,* and *ee.*

ai		**ea**		**ee**	
chain	chāín	beat	bēát	feed	fēéd
mail	māíl	dream	drēám	seed	sēéd
wait	wāít	leaf	lēáf	keep	kēép
rain	rāín	teach	tēách	queen	quēén
paid	pāíd	seat	sēáct	steel	stēél

Teaching Short and Long Sounds Together

Some teachers prefer to present short and long sounds simultaneously. This procedure permits children to see both patterns (single and double vowel letters) and to contrast the sounds in familiar words. Material can be presented in two- or three-step fashion.

Teacher: "Today we want to practice hearing the difference between two sounds of the vowel letter *a.* In the first column, each word has one vowel letter. In the second column, each word has two vowels together."

ran	rain
pad	paid
bat	bait
lad	laid
pal	pail
mad	maid
pan	pain

1. Pronounce the words in the first column; then have the children read these words.
2. Have children note the following.
    a. Each word has one vowel.
    b. The vowel is in the middle of the word.
    c. The short sound /ă/ of the vowel is heard.
3. Repeat the procedure for the words in the second column, having children note the following.
    a. Each word contains the vowel pattern *ai*.
    b. They say and hear the letter a /ā/.
    c. They do not sound or hear the second vowel letter.

The three-step approach permits children to see the process of adding a second vowel. This produces a new word containing two vowels that represent the long vowel sound heard.

One Vowel	Add i	New Word	
ă	↓	ā	
ran	ra*i*n	rā*i̸*n	(second vowel not sounded)
pad	pa d	pāid	
bat	ba t	bāit	
lad	la d	lāid	
pal	pa l	pāil	
mad	ma d	māid	
pan	pa n	pāin	

These words can be used to teach the other two-vowel patterns, *ee*, *ea*, and *oa*.

ă	ē¢	ĕ	ēa̸	ŏ	ōa
bet	beet	set	seat	cot	coat
met	meet	men	mean	got	goat
fed	feed	bet	beat	rod	road
step	steep	bed	bead	Tod	toad
pep	peep	met	meat	cost	coast

USING CONTEXT

Teacher: "Read the clue. Complete the word that fits the clue. Use one of the vowel patterns *a—e*, *i—e*, or *o—e* to spell the word."

Example:

Clue

Opening in fence	g_____t_____	(*a—e* for *gate*)
A pretty flower	r_____s_____	(*o—e* for *rose*)

Clue		Clue	
ten cents	d_____m_____	sticky stuff	p_____st_____
a brief letter	n_____t_____	a two-wheeler	b_____k_____
a number	n_____n_____	a body of water	l_____k_____
glass in window	p_____n_____	a funny story	j_____k_____
where there's fire	sm_____k_____	go fly a	k_____t_____

Teacher: "Use one of the vowel patterns *ai, ee,* or *ea* to spell the word."

Clue		Clue	
used for thinking	br_____n	a lady ruler	qu_____n
falls from clouds	r_____n	when it hurts	p_____n
a vegetable	b_____t	path in woods	tr_____l
to cure the sick	h_____l	along the ocean	b_____ch
not very strong	w_____k	back of foot	h_____l

Teacher: "The two words *not* and *note* fit in the two blanks in each sentence. Study each sentence and fill in the blanks."

1. He did _____ see the _____.

2. The _____ was _____ seen.

3. Why did he _____ see the _____?

4. Was the _____ seen or _____?

5. No, the _____ was _____ seen.

Teacher: "One of the words *met* or *meet* will fit in each blank space. Complete each sentence."

Examples:

Did you _____meet_____ the new teacher?

Yes, we _____met_____ yesterday.

1. _____ me at the ball game.

2. They _____ last year at camp.

3. The boys _____ at the track _____.

4. She will _____ us at four o'clock.

5. He said, "_____ me where we _____ last time."

Teacher: "All of these sentences contain two blank spaces. Each word following a sentence will fit in one blank space. You decide which one."

Example:

When the _____rain_____ started, he _____ran_____ home.

ran
rain

1. They _____ at the _____ market.

met
meat

2. Some of the _____ were _____.

mean
men

3. Do not _____ it where you _____ it before.

hid
hide

4. The doctor said, "You _____ walk with a _____."

cane
can

5. She _____ some of the people _____.

mad
made

FUN WITH LANGUAGE

Teacher: "In each sentence, three words need a pair of vowels. Write *ee, ea,* or *oa* in each blank space."

1. T_____ch children to k_____p off the r_____d.
2. You don't f_____d m_____t to a g_____t.
3. We n_____d a r_____l rain to s_____k the ground.
4. It's hard to k_____p a c_____l mine cl_____n.
5. We n_____d some m_____t and a l_____f of bread.
6. I f_____l like having r_____st beef and pie with my m_____l.
7. It was m_____n to k_____p the g_____t tied up.

Teacher: "Each of the following sentences contains two words with missing vowels. The clue tells you which vowel patterns will fit. Read the sentence to learn where they fit."

Set 1

Clues to Use: ee, oa, *and* ea

1. M_____t me at the m_____t market.
2. He sat near the r_____d to r_____d his book.
3. The doctor said, "This will h_____l your injured h_____l."
4. She took a last p_____k at the high mountain p_____k.

Set 2

Clues to Use: ea, ai, *and* oa

1. If we s_____l to the island we may see the s_____l.
2. The guide said, "Put the b_____t in the b_____t."
3. The g_____t walked with a funny g_____t.
4. Is the r_____l made of r_____l walnut wood?

Two Vowels, One of Which Is Final *e*

The generalization for this C-V-C-V pattern is: "In words with two vowels, the second being final *e,* the first vowel usually has its long sound and the final *e* is not sounded." Clymer (1963) found that the pronunciation of 60% of the final-*e* words in his sample were governed by this generalization. Again, material can be presented so that children see the pattern, hear the long vowel sound, and arrive at the generalization.

1. Write on the board words that have a single vowel in medial position. Choose words to which a final *e* may be added to form a new word.
2. In an adjacent column, print these final-*e* words.
3. Have children pronounce these pairs of words, listening to the difference in the vowel sounds.

Stress the visual pattern vowel + *e,* and guide children in verbalizing the generalization: "In words with two vowels, the second being final *e,* the final *e* is not sounded and the first vowel usually has its long sound." You can use diacritical marks as shown in column C.

A	B	C
hat	hate	hāte̸
hid	hide	hīde̸
past	paste	pāste̸
pal	pale	pāle̸
cut	cute	cūte̸
plan	plane	plāne̸
rat	rate	rāte̸
pin	pine	pīne̸
strip	stripe	strīpe̸
rid	ride	rīde̸

FUN WITH LANGUAGE

Teacher: "In each sentence, two words need a vowel. The same vowel letter fits in both blanks. One word will have its short sound; the other will have the long sound. Write in the vowel that makes sense."

1. John said, "I would h_____te to lose my new h_____t."
2. Do n_____t forget to leave a n_____te.
3. I h_____pe the rabbit will not h_____p on the flowers.
4. His friend P_____te has a p_____t turtle.
5. A r_____t can run at a very fast r_____te.
6. Their job was to c_____t out some c_____te cartoons.
7. Under the p_____ne tree, he found a pretty p_____n.
8. If you h_____d there once, don't h_____de there again.

Teacher: "Every word with a blank space ends with a silent *e*. Each blank space needs a vowel. This vowel will have its long vowel sound. Complete all of the words so that each sentence makes sense."

1. D_____ve, M_____ke, and K_____te m_____de plans for a picnic.
2. M_____ke will b_____ke a c_____ke.
3. K_____te will t_____ke a l_____me-and-lemon drink.
4. D_____ve will t_____ke a pl_____te of r_____pe fruit.
5. Later, D_____ve and M_____ke met K_____te at the l_____ke.
6. She r_____de her b_____ke; she l_____kes to r_____de it.
7. They will w_____de in the l_____ke, then t_____ke a h_____ke.

Single Final Vowels

When the only vowel in a word comes at the end of the word, it usually has its long sound. There probably are enough high-frequency words covered by this generalization to justify calling it to children's attention.

1. Place on the board words that contain one vowel in final position.
2. Have the children pronounce each word, noting the vowel at the end of the word and the sound it represents.
3. Invite children to supply a generalization covering these words (one final vowel has the long sound).

we	no
be	go
me	so
she	
he	

Notable exceptions to this generalization include *do, to, who,* and *two.* In words that end with *y* and that contain no other vowel, the *y* functions as a vowel. In these words the *y* is sounded as long /ī/ (*my, by, try, fly, cry, dry, sky, shy*).

At the end of words, ay has the sound of long /ā/.   Children have learned that *y* functions as a vowel when it ends a word that has no other vowel letter. Here they learn that *y* following the vowel *a* fits a generalization learned previously: "When two vowels come together, the first usually has its long sound."

1. Place a few stimulus words on the board.
2. Lead the children in pronouncing these words.
3. Focus attention on the visual pattern *ay* and on the resulting sound of long /ā/.
4. Other words that fit this pattern: *play, hay, ray, pray, sway, jay, stray, gray, away,* and *tray.*

> say
> may
> day
> pay
> lay
> stay

Sound of y at the end of longer words.   When *y* concludes a word of two or more syllables, it has the long sound of /ē/ heard in hob*by,* win*dy,* fog*gy,* luc*ky,* jol*ly,* fun*ny,* hap*py,* mer*ry,* noi*sy,* and rus*ty.* Other words to use in teaching exercises are *badly, angry, plenty, honestly, closely, beauty, mainly, guilty, history, lively, nasty, January, partly, ready, seventy, rocky, penny, muddy, simply, sorry, jelly, nearly, costly,* and *sleepy.*

EXCEPTIONS TO VOWEL RULES PREVIOUSLY TAUGHT

There is no vowel rule or generalization that will apply in all situations. When exceptions to a given rule occur, they may be taught as sight words, or a new rule can be devised to cover the exception. It has been suggested that children not be burdened with rules that have limited applications. Different teachers will, of course, arrive at different conclusions as to which generalizations should be included in phonics instruction. Some exceptions to a given rule occur with such frequency as to merit calling children's attention to the exceptions.

For instance, one of the most useful phonic generalizations we have discussed states: "One vowel in medial position usually has its short sound." There are several series of words that meet the criterion of one vowel in medial position but in which the vowel has its long sound. For example, the vowel *o* followed by *ld* or *lt* usually has the long sound: *bold, mold, gold, sold, hold, told, fold, cold, colt, bolt, volt,* and *jolt*. Also, the vowel *i* followed by *nd, gh,* or *ld* frequently has the long sound: *find, blind, behind, mind, kind, light, fight, sight, right, wild, mild,* and *child*.

Two Adjacent Vowels

The generalization covering two adjacent vowels ("The first usually has its long sound; the second is not sounded") has some exceptions in the patterns *oa, ai, ee,* and *ea*. While children are learning the words that follow the rule, they should also understand that exceptions will occur, such as *been, again, against, aisle, said, bread, break, head, dead, heart, steak,* and *broad*. There are many more exceptions found among other two-vowel patterns, including the following.

ei	*ou*	*ie*	*au*	*ui, -ue, -ua*
their	could	chief	caught	build
weigh	enough	field	laugh	guide
eight	rough	friend	fault	quiet
neighbor	should	piece	haunt	guess
vein	would	quiet	taught	guest
freight	touch	view	daughter	guard
rein	double	believe	haul	usual

Medial Vowel Plus Final *e*

Since a number of frequently met words, particularly *o* + *e* words, do not follow the generalization that one vowel in medial position usually has its short sound, some teachers prefer to deal with this fact rather than ignore it. Teachers might point out several exceptions, noting that applying the generalization will not help in solving the words *come, done, none, move, have, were, there, one, some, gone, love, glove, give, sense, where,* and *lose*.

VOWEL SOUNDS AFFECTED BY *R*

A vowel (or vowels) followed by the letter *r* results in a blended sound that is neither the short nor the long sound of the vowel. This phonic fact—as it relates to learning to read—is probably not extremely important; however, calling children's attention to this role of the letter *r* is a justifiable procedure. Since children use and understand hundreds of words that include a vowel followed by *r*, this is not a particularly difficult fact to teach. More important, children will have mastered several such words as sight words, and these can serve as examples when the generalization is introduced. Following are some of the more common vowel -*r* words for use in board work or seatwork exercises.

-*ar*		-*er*	-*or*
car	yard	her	for
farm	park	person	corn
march	card	term	storm
part	far	serve	horn
star	smart	ever	short
dark	arm	certain	north
hard	bark	berth	horse
barn	tar	herd	corner
start	spark	under	form

The spelling *ir* is usually pronounced û*r* (bird = bûrd), except when followed by a final *e* (fire): *bird, dirt, firm, third, fir, thirst, girl, first, sir, shirt, birth,* and *stir.*

A FOLLOWED BY *L, LL, W,* AND *U*

The letter *a* has the sound /ô/ (aw) when it is followed by *l, ll, w,* or *u.* For example:

talk	all	wall	saw	claw	haul
walk	tall	fall	draw	straw	because
salt	small	call	lawn	drawn	fault
halt	hall	ball	drawn	jaw	Paul

THE *OO* SOUNDS

Explaining the sounds of *oo* is much more complicated than actually learning to arrive at the correct pronunciation of the frequently used words that contain this letter combination. Most words containing *oo* are pronounced in one of two ways:

With the sound heard in *boo* and *boot*
With the sound heard in *book* and *foot*

Native speakers of English do not confuse these sounds while speaking or listening. When reading for meaning, children will not confuse the medial sounds heard in the two words used in each of these sentences:

The boot is larger than the foot.
The food is very good.

Beginning readers may not consciously note that the sounds are different because they never substitute one for the other. Practice in hearing differences can be provided by having children tell which of the following pairs of words rhyme.

cool—pool	food—good	soon—moon
boot—foot	book—look	look—hook
hoot—foot	wood—good	boot—hoot

The markings o͞o and o͝o may help children note the differences between these sounds, as in these sentences.

The bo͞ot is larger than the fo͝ot.
The mo͞ose drank from the co͞ol po͞ol.
He to͝ok a lo͝ok at the bro͝ok.

In the final analysis, it is the context that helps children arrive at the correct pronunciation. For convenience in creating board or seatwork exercises, here are some o͞o and o͝o words:

o͞o				o͝o	
bo͞o	so͞on	mo͞on	bo͞ost	bo͝ok	fo͝ot
co͞ol	to͞ol	bro͞om	lo͞op	go͝od	to͝ok
fo͞od	bo͞ot	po͞ol	ho͞ot	sto͝od	lo͝ok
ro͞om	bo͞on	lo͞ose	mo͞ose	sho͝ok	cro͝ok
to͞oth	zo͞o	ro͞ot	pro͞of	wo͝od	ho͝ok

A few oo words are neither o͞o or o͝o, such as *blood* (blŭd), *door* (dōr), *flood* (flŭd), and *floor* (flōr). These should be taught as sight words.

DIPHTHONGS

A diphthong is two adjacent vowels, each of which contributes to the sound heard. The diphthongs discussed here are *ou, oi,* and *oy.* In pronouncing diphthongs, the two vowel sounds are blended, as in *house, oil,* and *boy.*

1. The diphthongs *oi* and *oy* have the same sound (boy = bo*i*; boil = bo*i*l).
2. Sometimes *ow* represents the diphthong sound of *ou.*

Diphthong Sounds

1. Place several words on the board that illustrate the diphthong sound *oy* (column A).
2. In column B, change the spelling to *oi,* and in column C, add a final consonant to form a known word.

A		B		C
boy	→	boi	→	boil
toy	→	toi	→	toil
joy	→	joi	→	join
coy	→	coi	→	coin

3. Pronounce the words across each line, emphasizing that the *oy* and *oi* spellings represent the same sounds.
4. Point out that each vowel contributes to the sound heard.
5. Have children note that these vowel patterns do not follow the generalization that the first vowel has its long sound, and the second is not sounded.

    Teaching that *ou* and *ow* represent the same sound may be done as follows.

1. Have children pronounce these pairs of words, noting that *ou* and *ow* represent the same sound.

owl	*foul*
crowd	*cloud*
fowl	*ground*

2. Place other *ou* and *ow* stimulus words on the board. In pronouncing the words in columns A and B, help children note that the letters *ou* and *ow* represent the same sound.

A	B
how	out
howl	foul
town	found
drown	ground
clown	round
crown	sound

Words to use in chalkboard or seatwork drill include the following:

cow	owl	mouse	mouth	boil	boy
how	gown	sound	proud	coin	toy
brown	howl	loud	shout	toil	oyster
tower	brow	couch	found	joint	joy
crown	town	south	count	soil	Troy
powder	fowl	ground	bound	moist	employ

ow as the Long Sound of *o*

In a number of English words, the *ow* combination has the sound of /ō/. You can use the following steps to teach the sound.

1. The letter combination *ow* has two sounds: the diphthong sound heard in *plow* and the /ō/ heard in *snow.*

A	B
cow	low
plow	snow
how	grow
owl	show
town	flow

2. Pronounce the words in column A, with the children listening to the sound of /ow/.
3. Pronounce pairs of words (*cow, low*) with the children listening to contrasting sounds.
4. Have the children pronounce the words.
5. Point out that as words are read in context, the proper sound becomes obvious because the children know these words.

HOMONYMS

Homonyms are words that have the same pronunciation but different spellings and meanings. These words involve both structural and phonic analysis skills. Some homonyms follow one of the generalizations we have already introduced; many do not. For example, the rule "When two vowels occur together, the first is long, and the second is not sounded" applies to both words in the following pairs: *meet, meat; see, sea;* and *week, weak.*

Sometimes the rule applies to one word in a pair, and the final -e rule applies to the other word: *road, rode; sail, sale;* and *pain, pane.*

Some pairs involve unsounded consonants: *rap, wrap; new, knew;* and *our, hour.*

Other examples of phonic irregularities are *wait, weight; wood, would; ate, eight;* and *piece, peace.* The following exercises may be used or adapted to help children recognize homonyms that have irregular spellings.

WORKING WITH HOMONYMS

1. Recognizing Homonyms

Directions: Explain the concept of homonyms: words that are pronounced the same but have different spellings and meanings. Have children pronounce the pairs of words at the left and answer the questions by writing *yes* or *no*.

	Same Spelling?	Same Sound?
there—their	_____	_____
ate—eight	_____	_____
two—to	_____	_____
would—wood	_____	_____
one—won	_____	_____
I—eye	_____	_____
some—sum	_____	_____
by—buy	_____	_____
our—hour	_____	_____
do—due	_____	_____

2. Matching Homonyms

Directions: Draw a line from the word in column A to the word in column B that is pronounced the same.

A	B	A	B
won	no	knot	blew
know	sew	blue	maid
so	one	made	not
pole	some	son	I
hour	eight	eye	sea
ate	our	pear	sun
sum	poll	see	pare

3. Match and Write Homonyms

Directions: Explain that each word in the clue box is pronounced like one of the words below the box. Children are to write the correct word on each blank space.

	Clue Box						
eight	one	weigh	sew	some	would	wait	hole

so _____   ate _____

won _____   sum _____

way _____   wood _____

whole _____ weight _____

These are some common homonyms to use in chalkboard or seatwork exercises.

beat—beet	maid—made	pair—pare
know—no	I—eye	mail—male
hear—here	hair—hare	steel—steal
there—their	by—buy	waist—waste
sun—son	fair—fare	one—won
whole—hole	dear—deer	some—sum
oh—owe	not—knot	tail—tale

USING CONTEXT

Teacher: "Two words follow each clue. These are homonyms: words pronounced the same but spelled differently. Read the clue and write the correct word in the blank space."

Example:

big price cut _____sale_____   sail   sale

Clue

1. the ears do it _____ here   hear
2. part of a window _____ pain   pane
3. seven days in a _____ week   weak
4. the eyes do it _____ sea   see
5. an odd-shaped fruit _____ pair   pear
6. fuel for a fireplace _____ wood   would
7. a vegetable _____ beat   beet
8. top of a mountain _____ peek   peak
9. back part of the foot _____ heal   heel
10. cars move on it _____ rode   road

Teacher: "One of the words *weak* or *week* will fit in each blank space. Study each sentence and fill in the blanks."

Example:

There are seven days in a _____. (week)

He felt very _____ after the fever. (weak)

1. John was sick last _____.

2. He feels _____ this _____.

3. John has felt _____ since last _____.

4. Next _____, John will not be _____.

5. How did John feel last _____?

Teacher: "Each sentence has an underlined word and a blank space. In the blank space, write a homonym for the underlined word."

Examples:

We can be at <u>our</u> house in an _____. (hour)

Who <u>knew</u> about the _____ plans? (new)

1. The team <u>won</u> only _____ game.

2. <u>Eight</u> of the boys _____ all of the chicken.

3. _____ house is over <u>there.</u>

4. <u>Would</u> you please bring in some _____.

5. You can _____ the ocean if you come over <u>here.</u>

Teacher: "Each of these sentences has two missing words. The words *our* and *hour* will fit in each sentence. Where does each word fit?"

Example:

There was a one _____ meeting at _____ house.

Teacher: "Using the context of the sentence you would write:

There was a one *hour* meeting at *our* house."

1. _____ game will start in one _____.

2. In about an _____ _____ game will start.

3. Will it take an _____ to play _____ game?

4. We can play _____ game in less than an _____.

Teacher: "The words *mail* and *male* are homonyms. Homonyms are words that are pronounced the same, but have different meanings. Each of these sentences has two missing words. The words *mail* and *male* will fit in each sentence. Where does each word fit?"

Example:

A _____ or a female may bring the _____.

Teacher: "Note that the context helps you get it right.

A *male* or a female may bring the *mail.*"

1. When a _____ delivers the _____ he is called a mailman.

2. A _____ delivering the _____ is not a "maleman."

3. _____ can be delivered by a _____ or a female.

4. Who is the _____ delivering the _____ today?

5. That _____ delivering the _____ is Charlie.

THE SCHWA SOUND

In a large number of words of more than one syllable, there is a diminished stress on one of the syllables. The sound of the vowel in these unstressed syllables undergoes a slight change, referred to as a "softening" of the vowel sound. This softened vowel sound is called the *schwa* sound, and it is represented by the symbol ə.

All of the vowels are represented by the schwa sound, as illustrated by each of the italicized vowels in these words.

bedlam	=	bed'ləm
beaten	=	be'tən
beautiful	=	bū' tə fəl
beckon	=	bek'ən

In other words, if vowels were interchanged in unstressed syllables, the spellings would change, but the sound heard would remain the same for the different vowels. For instance, read both of these sentences without stressing the second syllable in any word.

> **A.** Button, button, who has the button?
> **B.** Buttun, buttan, who has the butten?

If, in reading sentence B, you give each second syllable the same stress as it was given in the word directly above it, the sounds remain constant. Thus, teaching the schwa sound in the initial stages of reading would have little impact on one's ability to sound out words. Once the child begins to use a dictionary that utilizes the schwa symbol ə, however, these points should be explained.

SIGHT-WORD LIST

Table 6–1 is a list of words, most of which are met in primary reading, that illustrates irregular spellings. From the standpoint of spoken language, all words are phonetic; however, the spellings (visual patterns) of these words are such that the more common phonic generalizations learned in beginning reading will not apply.

TABLE 6–1 *Sight-Word List: Words with Irregular Spellings Resulting in Confusion Between Letters Seen and Sounds Heard*

above	could	ghost	love	quiet	together
across	couple	give			ton
again	cousin	gives	machine	ranger	tongue
against	cruel	gloves	many	ready	too
aisle	curve	gone	measure	really	touch
already		great	might	right	two
another	dead	guard	mild	rough	
answer	deaf	guess	million		use
anxious	debt	guest	mind	said	usual
any	desire	guide	minute	says	
	do		mischief	school	vein
bear	does	have	mother	science	very
beautiful	done	head	move	scissors	view
beauty	don't	heart	Mr.	sew	
because	double	heaven	Mrs.	shoe	was
been	doubt	heavy		should	wash
behind	dove	here	neighbor	sign	weather
believe	dozen	high	neither	snow	weight
bind			night	soften	were
both	early	idea	none	soldier	what
bough	earn	Indian		some	where
bread	eight	instead	ocean	someone	who
break	enough	isle	of	something	whom
bright	eye		office	sometime	whose
brought	eyes	key	often	son	wild
build		kind	oh	soul	wind
built	father	knee	once	special	wolf
bury	fence	knew	one	spread	woman
busy	field	knife	onion	square	women
buy	fight	know	only	steak	won
	find		other	straight	would
calf	folks	language	ought	sure	wrong
captain	four	laugh		sword	
caught	freight	laughed	patient		you
chief	friend	leather	piece	their	young
child	front	library	pretty	there	your
clothes		light	pull	they	
colt	garage	lion	purpose	though	
coming	get	live	push	thought	
cough	getting	lived	put	to	

Summary

There is considerable variability in the sounds of vowels and vowel combinations in English. This increases the difficulty of teaching or learning vowel sounds. The sequence in which vowel sounds are taught—that is, whether to teach long or short sounds first or which vowels to teach first—is probably not a significant issue. The teaching procedures in this chapter are meant to be illustrative rather than prescriptive.

Some generalizations covering vowel situations include the following:

- A single vowel in medial position in a word or syllable usually has its short sound (man, bed, fit).
- When two vowels are side by side in a word, the first usually has its long sound and the second is not sounded.
- When a word has two vowels, the second being final e, the first usually has its long sound and the final e is not sounded.
- *Ay* at the end of a word has the long sound of /ā/ (may, pay, play).
- When the only vowel in a word (or accented syllable) comes at the end of the word (or syllable), it usually has its long sound.
- When *y* concludes a word of two or more syllables, it has the long sound of /ē/ heard in *lucky* and *badly.*
- *Y* functions as a vowel when it concludes a word or syllable that has no other vowel:

my, sky, dy • ing, hy • phen

- or falls in the middle of a syllable that has no other vowel:

sym • bol, syn • o • nym, typ • ist

- A diphthong is two adjacent vowels, each of which contributes to the sound heard (house, oil, boy).
- The combination *ow* is sometimes pronounced as /ō/ (snow, show); the context provides the major clue to pronunciation.

Chapter 7

STRUCTURAL ANALYSIS SKILLS

*L*earning to read is a long-term, developmental process, and teaching a total word-analysis skills program is also developmental in nature. Previous chapters have presented data on letter-sound relationships; this chapter continues to deal with letter-sound relationships, but we will also stress other important word analysis skills that fit under the broad heading of structural analysis. To maintain normal growth in reading, children must learn to recognize and react to certain features of written language, including inflectional endings (-*s, -ed, -ing, -ly*), compound words, plural forms, prefixes and suffixes, syllabication, contractions, and accent within words.

As we have noted, when children meet a printed word that they do not instantly recognize, they have several options: sounding out the word, using context clues, or combining these two approaches.

Early in beginning reading, children add another option, that of recognizing a root word embedded among affixes. English orthography utilizes a number of structural changes that occur again and again in thousands of words. In learning to read, one must develop expertise in recognizing prefixes, suffixes, and inflectional endings.

To successfully master the structural variations that occur in English orthography, children must come to the reading task with certain skills and abilities. In essence, they must apply or transfer something they already know about letter-sounds and word forms to new situations. For example, assume that a child can recognize the word *ask* but has not yet met *asks, asked,* or *asking.* His prior experience and his ability to respond to *ask* should help him in decoding the inflected forms.

While the child still has the option of sounding out these new words, he also can use the established response to the word *ask.* If one is reading for meaning, this root clue plus the contextual demands of the passage will unlock the inflected forms that are used constantly in the child's oral language.

Different readers, however, will require a differing number of experiences and varied amounts of instruction to acquire the necessary insights. For some children, a prefix and suffix added to a known word tends to obscure what is known. In such cases, more trials are needed for transfer to take place. All children must have a certain amount of practice in recognizing the visual patterns of words that result from the addition of affixes.

One factor that aids both the learner and the teacher is that a great majority of affixes represent the same sound(s) in thousands of different words. Thus, the major objective in working with structural changes in words is to teach children to instantly recognize these visual patterns in written English.

INFLECTIONAL ENDINGS

The word endings -s and -ed represent variations in letter-sound relationships that probably have little impact on learning to read. The fact that final s represents the sound of /s/ in *asks* and /z/ in *dogs* is not a cause of confusion to beginners. Nor is the fact that -ed in *added, asked,* and *played* is pronounced as ed, t, and d, respectively. The rules that govern these differences are complicated and are much more important to linguists than to native speakers of English whose objective is to learn to read English. Children have never heard, said, or read, "The man work-ed hard" or "Where are my glove-s?"

Nonetheless, children will likely need some practice in visual recognition of inflected word forms because of the structural differences between these and known root words.

Adding -s, -ed, and -ing to Words

1. In the spaces provided, write the word on the left adding -s, -ed, and -ing.
2. Pronounce each word.

Word	-s	-ed	-ing
walk	_____	_____	_____
show	_____	_____	_____
look	_____	_____	_____
ask	_____	_____	_____
call	_____	_____	_____
answer	_____	_____	_____
load	_____	_____	_____
paint	_____	_____	_____

Adding -er, -est, and -ly to Words

1. Make new words by adding the endings -er, -est, and -ly to the root word on the left.
2. Pronounce each word.
3. How do these endings change the meaning of words?

Word	-er	-est	-ly
slow	_____	_____	_____
light	_____	_____	_____
warm	_____	_____	_____
soft	_____	_____	_____
bright	_____	_____	_____
calm	_____	_____	_____

Words ending with e.   Drop the final *e* before adding a suffix beginning with a vowel.

Word	+ed	+ing	+er	+est	+ous
bake	baked	baking	baker		
trade	traded	trading	trader		
pale	paled		paler	palest	
fame	famed				famous
late			later	latest	

Adding Suffixes Following *y*

Change *y* to *i* before adding a suffix beginning with a vowel.

Word	Common Endings Beginning with a Vowel			
	-ed	-er	-est	-ous
busy	busied	busier	busiest	
fury				furious
dry	dried	drier	driest	
muddy	muddied	muddier	muddiest	
happy		happier	happiest	
glory				glorious
carry	carried	carrier		

Exception: If the suffix begins with *i,* leave the *y: crying, drying, frying, flying, copying,* and *carrying.*

DOUBLING FINAL CONSONANTS

Explain to children the generalization, "Words that contain one vowel and end with a single consonant (*beg, stop, fan*) usually double that consonant before adding an ending beginning with a vowel," as in *begged, begging, beggar, stopped, stopping,* and *stopper.*

Teacher: "Look carefully at the words on lines 1, 2, and 3. Add the same endings to the other words."

Word	-ed	-ing	-er
1. log	logged	logging	logger
2. dim	dimmed	dimming	dimmer
3. stop	stopped	stopping	stopper
4. pop	_____	_____	_____
5. skip	_____	_____	_____
6. trot	_____	_____	_____
7. bat	_____	_____	_____
8. trap	_____	_____	_____
9. plan	_____	_____	_____
10. spot	_____	_____	_____

USING CONTEXT

Teacher: "Each of the following sentences has a blank space. Complete each sentence using one word in the clue box that will make the sentence correct."

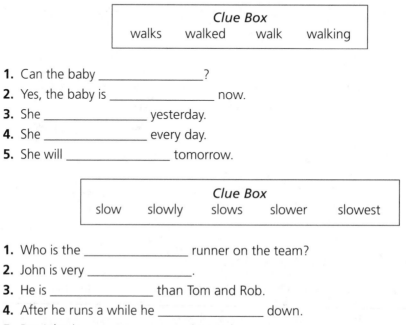

> **Clue Box**
> walks   walked   walk   walking

1. Can the baby _____?
2. Yes, the baby is _____ now.
3. She _____ yesterday.
4. She _____ every day.
5. She will _____ tomorrow.

> **Clue Box**
> slow   slowly   slows   slower   slowest

1. Who is the _____ runner on the team?
2. John is very _____.
3. He is _____ than Tom and Rob.
4. After he runs a while he _____ down.
5. But John is _____ improving.

Teacher: "In the following sentences, write the form of the word that makes the sentence correct."

fast   **1.** John is _____ than Bill, but Ted is the _____ runner on the team.

kind   **2.** The mayor is a _____ old gentleman.

cold   **3.** November is _____ than July.

short   **4.** If they took the _____ trail they should arrive _____.

long   **5.** What is the _____ word in the dictionary?

Teacher: "Each of these sentences is followed by three words. Two of these words will fit in the blank spaces. Read each sentence and fill in the blanks."

Example:

June is _____ but July is _____.   warm

June is ___warm___ but July is ___warmer___.   warmer

                                                                      warmest

1. John _____ , "Did anyone _____ for me?"   ask

                                                                      asking

                                                                      asked

2. She _____ yesterday and is also _____ today. paints

                                                                      painted

                                                                      painting

3. Speaking _____ , John said, "Cotton is _____ than linen."   softer

                                                                      softly

                                                                      softest

4. The car _____ at the _____ sign.   stop

                                                                      stopping

                                                                      stopped

5. It _____ yesterday and is _____ now.   rain

                                                                      rained

                                                                      raining

Teacher: "In each sentence there is a blank space with a root word below it. Add the proper ending to this word so that it will be correct in the sentence."

Example:

Mother is <u>bringing</u> cookies.
        (bring)

   1. The bird _____ its wings.
          (flap)

2. We are _____ to leave tomorrow.
                    (plan)

3. We saw a _____ in the woods.
                    (hunt)

4. A man who cuts down trees in a forest is called a _____.
                                                                    (log)

5. One who traps animals is called a _____.
                                                (trap)

6. The little dog was _____.
                            (bark)

7. Who is the best _____ on the baseball team?
                        (hit)

8. John is the _____ _____ on the team.
                    (fast)   (run)

9. Two boys were _____ in the sand.
                        (dig)

10. The _____ it rained the _____ we got.
            (hard)   (wet)

COMPOUND WORDS

Mastery of compound words is a developmental process. Children meet a few compounds in first grade and an increasing number thereafter. They need to know that some words are formed by combining two or more words. In most instances, children will be familiar with one or both words that make up a compound.

Recognition of compound words is achieved through every type of word-analysis skill: structural analysis, phonic analysis, and context examination. When teaching compound words, each of these aids should be employed. Learning sight words and structural phonic analysis actually go hand in hand. Keep these points in mind:

- Compound words are part of children's speaking and meaning vocabulary. When they meet compounds in reading, they will combine recognition and sounding techniques.
- The meaning of many compound words is derived from combining two words.
- The pronunciation of the compound word remains the same as for the two combining forms, except for accent or stress.
- Procedures for teaching compound words vary with the instructional level.

BUILDING COMPOUND WORDS

1. Oral Exercise

Purpose: To provide practice in using compound words.

Directions: Explain to children the concept of compound words: combining two or more words to make a different word.

Demonstrate on the chalkboard: some + thing = something

some + one = someone

some + time = sometime

Other words to use include *schoolhouse, barnyard, football, birdhouse, firefighter.*

Teacher: "I'll say a word and you add a word to it to make another word."

1. base _____ (ball)
2. sail _____ (boat)
3. door _____ (way, man, mat)
4. motor _____ (cycle, boat)
5. road _____ (way, side, block)
6. over _____ (head, board, shoe)
7. moon _____ (light, beam, glow)
8. air _____ (plane, port)
9. bath _____ (tub, house, room)
10. tooth _____ (brush, ache, paste)

2. Seeing Compound Words as Wholes and Breaking Them into Parts

Teacher: "Each of the words on the left is a compound word. Write the two words found in each compound word."

Example:

snowman	____snow____	____man____
1. waterfall	_____	_____
2. bluebird	_____	_____
3. policeman	_____	_____
4. notebook	_____	_____
5. himself	_____	_____
6. homework	_____	_____
7. anyone	_____	_____
8. seaside	_____	_____
9. turnpike	_____	_____
10. airplane	_____	_____

3. More Compound Words

Teacher: "Combine one word from the clue box with each word below the box to form compound words."

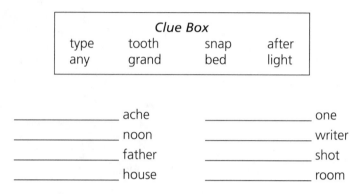

Clue Box			
type	tooth	snap	after
any	grand	bed	light

_____ ache   _____ one

_____ noon   _____ writer

_____ father   _____ shot

_____ house   _____ room

To provide practice in recognizing and writing compound words, illustrate how the same word can be used in a number of compound words.

Teacher: "Using the word in the first column, write three compound words."

Example:

air	plane	craft	port
	airplane	*aircraft*	*airport*
1. book	case	keeper	worm
	_____	_____	_____
2. door	way	man	mat
	_____	_____	_____
3. candle	light	maker	stick
	_____	_____	_____
4. moon	glow	beam	light
	_____	_____	_____
5. down	town	wind	stream
	_____	_____	_____
6. shoe	lace	horn	maker
	_____	_____	_____

Teacher: "Each line contains one compound word. Underline the compound word and write it on the blank space at the end of the line."

1. children	dancing	sometime	_____
2. someone	beaches	crawling	_____

3. alike	mousetrap	puzzle	_____
4. downpour	happily	permitted	_____
5. autumn	mistake	handbag	_____

4. Identifying Compound Words

Directions: Some of the following are compound words, and some are two words written together that do not make a word. Have the children underline the compound words.

beehive	ballback	ballpark
anyelse	everyone	everysome
roommate	roompost	signpost
aftermuch	afternoon	afterman
fireplace	photodog	overland
overleft	houseboat	housemake
nearby	overstill	lifeboat

5. Using Context

Directions: Have the children underline each compound word. Then have them draw a line between the two words in each compound (mail/box).

1. Everyone went to the football game that afternoon.
2. Josh is upstairs writing in his scrapbook with his ballpoint pen.
3. We ran halfway to the clubhouse without stopping.
4. Doug received a flashlight, a raincoat, and a sailboat for his birthday.
5. He read the newspaper headline, "Big fire at sawmill."
6. They saw the shipwreck from a hilltop near the lighthouse.

6. Sentence Completion

Directions: Develop a series of sentences in which a common compound will complete the sentence. Have children read the sentence and write the compound word. Material can be presented orally, or by means of the chalkboard, transparencies, or duplicated exercises. The first exercise is made easy by presenting the compound words in random order above the sentences. In the second exercise, the children provide the words.

| baseball | mailbox | bedroom |
| raincoat | football | seashore |

A.

1. Letters are mailed in a _____.
2. The room we sleep in is called a _____.
3. A bat is used in the game of _____.

   4. The girls gathered shells at the _____.

   5. A _____ field has goalposts at each end of the field.

   6. Mother said, "It's raining; be sure and wear your _____."

B.

   1. A player can hit a home run in the game of _____.

   2. The teacher wrote on the _____ with a piece of chalk.

   3. The airplane landed at the _____.

   4. The front window in a car is called the _____.

   5. The mailman puts mail in our _____.

7. Combining Words to Make Compounds

Directions: Have children add the correct word in sentences 1 and 2, then combine those two words in sentence 3.

Example:

   1. The opposite of work is _____. (play)
   1

   2. In the spring we plant seeds in the _____. (ground)
   2

   3. We go to the _____ at recess. (playground)
   1 & 2

   1. Let's take our sleds and play in the _____.
   1

   2. The pitcher threw the _____ over the plate.
   2

   3. We like to have _____ fights in the winter.
   1 & 2

   1. The house we live in is called our _____.
   1

   2. The opposite of play is _____.
   2

   3. Schoolwork we do at home is called _____.
   1 & 2

   1. A mailman delivers the _____.
   1

   2. He carries the mail in a _____.
   2

   3. The mailman carries the mail in a _____.
   1 & 2

Teacher: "Each sentence contains a blank space. Select a word from the clue box that will complete a compound word."

Examples:

Clue Box		
snap	house	grand

1. Mother read the letter from our _____ father.
2. The letter contained a _____ shot.
3. It showed our grandfather in front of a light _____.

Clue Box			
way	point	wreck	some
brush	house	teller	star

1. John lost his ball _____ pen.
2. The captain gave details about the ship _____.
3. The sign read, "Don't block the door _____."
4. Some of the golfers ate dinner at the club _____.
5. Susan found a _____ fish on the beach.
6. Grandfather was a great story _____.
7. _____ one will have to help the guide.
8. Clean the paint _____ when you finish painting.

WORKING WITH PLURALS

Forming plurals by adding *-s, -es,* or *-ies* results in structural changes in word forms that can be puzzling to children in their early reading experience. Exercises can help children instantly recognize the plurals of common root words.

Adding *-s* to Form Plurals

1. Illustrate the singular-plural concept at the chalkboard using any words to which the letter *-s* is added to form a plural (*book—books, hat—hats, chair—chairs*). Teach the concept that *plural* means "more than one."

2. Write the plural of each word on the blank space.

cup	_____	game	_____
rat	_____	bag	_____
fan	_____	kitten	_____
boat	_____	comb	_____
desk	_____	nail	_____
rabbit	_____	table	_____
king	_____	ship	_____
crop	_____	sled	_____

3. Prepare materials similar to the illustrations.
4. Read the sentences with the children.

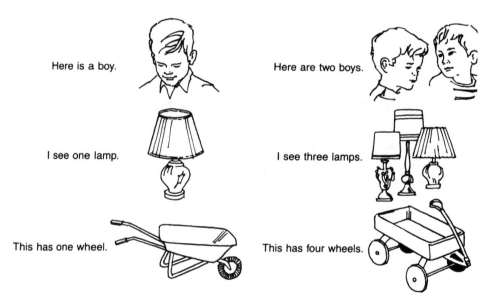

Here is a boy.   Here are two boys.

I see one lamp.   I see three lamps.

This has one wheel.   This has four wheels.

Plurals Formed by Adding *-es*

Teach the concept that words ending with *s, ss, ch, sh,* and *x* form plurals by the addition of *-es*. Use the chalkboard or duplicated handouts to present material similar to the following.

When do we add *-es* to show more than one?
When words end with

ss	ch	sh	x
dress	church	dish	box
dresses	*churches*	*dishes*	*boxes*

Teacher: "Write the plural for each word."

glass	_____	brush	_____
pass	_____	wish	_____
cross	_____	crash	_____
witch	_____	fox	_____
watch	_____	six	_____
inch	_____	tax	_____

Teacher: "Practice reading these words."

matches	sketches	speeches	benches	waxes
splashes	wishes	batches	ashes	fusses
beaches	kisses	gulches	hisses	birches
bosses	dashes	misses	lashes	gashes

Plurals of Words Ending with *y*

When a word ends with *y,* its plural is formed by changing the *y* to *i* and adding *-es.*

city—cit*ies*   lady—lad*ies*   fairy—fair*ies*

Teacher: "Write the plural for each of these words."

baby _____	party _____	cherry _____
puppy _____	body _____	buddy _____
army _____	fly _____	berry _____

RECOGNITION OF PLURALS

Teacher: "Each of the following words means that there is more than one. These plurals were formed by adding *-s, -es,* or (*y* =) *-ies.* Read these words as quickly as possible."

porches	foxes	cubs	lunches	watches	witches
girls	benches	guesses	coaches	inches	taxes
speeches	peaches	dresses	answers	matches	candies
funnies	factories	cookies	berries	pennies	armies
buses	glasses	frogs	boxes	brushes	dishes

Other Plural Forms

Some plurals involve vowel changes within the word: *foot—feet, man—men, goose—geese, mouse—mice, tooth—teeth,* and *woman—women.*

For words ending with *f*, change *f* to *v* and add *-es: wolf—wolves, shelf— shelves, calf—calves, loaf—loaves, thief—thieves,* and *leaf—leaves.*

Some singular and plural forms have the same spelling: *deer—deer, sheep— sheep,* and *moose—moose.*

For words ending with *o* following a consonant, add *-es: potato—potatoes, echo—echoes,* and *hero—heroes.*

USING CONTEXT

Teacher: "The words in column A each mean that there is only one. If the word under Clue means that there is more than one, write the plural of the word in column A on the blank space."

Example:

goose	these	___geese___
A	*Clue*	
lady	one	_____
church	many	_____
city	some	_____
bench	a	_____
bird	a flock of	_____
potato	four	_____
house	this	_____
wolf	a pack of	_____
man	that	_____
sheep	several	_____

Teacher: "In each blank space, write the plural form of the underlined word in the sentence."

Examples:

The <u>woman</u> had been speaking to the _____. (women)

There were many new _____ in the <u>dress</u> shop. (dresses)

1. The board was a <u>foot</u> wide and ten _____ long.

2. Put this <u>dish</u> in with the clean _____.

3. Many _____ claim to be the "most beautiful <u>city</u>."

4. The young <u>wolf</u> watched the older _____ hunt.

5. This <u>watch</u> is more expensive than the other _____.

6. The <u>spy</u> story was written by two _____.

7. There were many _____ in the <u>bus</u> station.

8. He asked the <u>boy</u> where the other _____ were playing.

9. That <u>lady</u> is president of the _____ group.

10. Put all of the smaller _____ in the largest <u>box.</u>

Teacher: "In each blank space, write the plural of the italicized word."

1. There was one *pony* in the pasture.

   There were two _____ in the pasture.

2. The police captured a *spy.*

   The police captured three _____.

3. Each *lady* bought a hat.

   All the _____ bought hats.

4. One *fly* flew away.

   Both _____ flew away.

5. John lost one *penny.*

   John lost several _____.

PREFIXES AND SUFFIXES

As children progress in reading, they will meet many words that contain prefixes and suffixes. Teaching aimed at making each child an independent reader will have to deal with structural analysis, phonic analysis, and syllabication. In addition, the teaching of reading will have to focus on the changes in meaning that result when affixes are added to root words.

   Many children develop the attitude that they will be unsuccessful in solving longer polysyllabic words, and they give up easily. Thus, their fears are self-fulfilling. One of the objectives of the following exercises is to provide hints that will help readers unlock such words. Children are led to see that English writing contains many prefabricated units (prefixes and suffixes). A number of clues are pointed out, namely that these affixes are spelled the same in thousands of different words and thus have the same visual pattern, have the same pronunciation in different words, consistently appear before or after a root word, and are usually syllables.

   The procedures and materials in example A focus on having children see and combine root words with prefixes and suffixes while pronouncing the words formed. Examples B and C stress syllabication.

A. Each line begins with a root word to which three prefixes are added. The children pronounce these words, noting the visual patterns resulting from the prefixes.

Root	+ *pre*	+ *re*	+ *un*
pack	prepack	repack	unpack
wind	prewind	rewind	unwind
paid	prepaid	repaid	unpaid

Root	+ dis	+ mis	+ re
place	displace	misplace	replace
use	disuse	misuse	reuse
count	discount	miscount	recount

B. The first word in each column is a root word; the second has a common prefix; the third, a common word ending.

Root	+ dis	+ ment
appoint	dis/appoint	dis/appoint/ment
agree	dis/agree	dis/agree/ment
place	dis/place	dis/place/ment

Root	+ re	+ able
clean	re/clean	re/clean/able
form	re/form	re/form/able
charge	re/charge	re/charge/able

Root	+ in	+ ness
complete	in/complete	in/complete/ness
direct	in/direct	in/direct/ness
visible	in/visible	in/visible/ness
human	in/human	in/human/ness

C. The first word in each column is a root word; a suffix has been added in the second; and another suffix in the third.

Root	+ less	+ ness
use	useless	uselessness
speech	speechless	speechlessness
sight	sightless	sightlessness

Root	+ ful	+ ness
watch	watchful	watchfulness
truth	truthful	truthfulness
play	playful	playfulness

D. This material stresses the structural (visual) changes resulting from adding affixes. It includes some inflected endings taught previously.
   1. Read each line of words in unison with the class.
   2. Have a volunteer read the same line of words.
   3. Have similar exercises available for individual practice.

agree	agrees	disagree	disagreement	agreeable
fill	refill	filled	refilled	refilling
place	placed	replaced	replacement	places
honor	honorable	dishonor	dishonorable	honored
hope	hopeless	hopeful	hopefully	hoping

E. For practice in building new words by writing common endings, form a new word by writing the ending shown above each group of words.

-ment
pay _____	agree _____
state _____	pave _____
move _____	treat _____
enjoy _____	punish _____
base _____	excite _____

-ness
blind _____	deaf _____
dry _____	clever _____
close _____	kind _____
bold _____	polite _____
calm _____	like _____

-ful
hope _____
cheer _____
doubt _____
grace _____
dread _____

-less
hope _____
cheer _____
doubt _____
cloud _____
sleep _____

-able
wash _____
honor _____
comfort _____
agree _____
change _____

USING CONTEXT

Teacher: "Note the underlined word in each clue. Add a prefix and suffix to that word so that the new word fits the clue."

Example:

to not deserve <u>trust</u>   (<u>un</u>)trust(<u>worthy</u>)

Helpers: | dis-   un- | | -ful   -able   -ment   -ness |

1. you can't <u>avoid</u> it   _____ avoid _____
2. a failure to <u>agree</u>   _____ agree _____
3. can't <u>depend</u> on him   _____ depend _____
4. the opposite of <u>happiness</u> is?   _____ happi _____
5. does not tell the <u>truth</u>   _____ truth _____
6. opposite of or lack of <u>honor</u>   _____ honor _____

Teacher: "Note the underlined word in each clue. Add an ending to that word so that the new word fits the clue."

Example:

Some <u>doubt</u> that it will happen.   doubt(<u>ful</u>)

Helpers: | -able   -ful   -less   -ness |

1. no <u>change</u> over the years   change _____
2. can <u>depend</u> on him   depend _____
3. always being <u>idle</u>   idle _____
4. has little or no <u>use</u>   use _____
5. results in <u>pain</u>   pain _____
6. shows <u>grace</u> in dancing   grace _____

To help children achieve mastery of root words plus affixes, use the following paragraphs for reading practice. Read one paragraph, then select a volunteer to read. Tell students, "As we read each paragraph, note the meaning of the underlined words:"

The Governor said, "I <u>doubt</u> that the bridge will be built. <u>Doubtless,</u> many of you would like to see it built. However, it is quite <u>doubtful</u> that funds will be available. Informed observers agree that this is <u>doubtlessly</u> true."

<u>Advertisers</u> spend money on <u>advertising</u> because <u>advertisements</u> help to <u>advertise</u> what they have to sell.

A towel will <u>absorb</u> water. This towel is <u>absorbing</u> water. Now it has <u>absorbed</u> about all it can. It <u>absorbs</u> because it is made of <u>absorbent</u> material.

A mountain climber must <u>care</u> about safety. Mountain climbers who <u>care</u> will be <u>careful,</u> not <u>careless.</u> <u>Carelessness</u> in the face of danger does not lead to a <u>carefree</u> climb. When plans are thought out <u>carefully,</u> one is not likely to act <u>carelessly.</u>

For writing practice, tell students to write a paragraph using all (or as many as possible) of the words on each line.

> beauty, beautiful, beautifully
> joy, joyful, joyfully, joyous, joyless, joylessly
> help, helpful, helpfulness, helpless, helplessness
> war, prewar, postwar, prowar, antiwar, warlike

Syllabication

A syllable is a vowel or a group of letters containing a vowel sound that together form a pronounceable unit. The ability to break words into syllables is an important word analysis skill that cuts across both phonic and structural analysis. Syllabication is an aid in pronouncing words not instantly recognized as sight words, arriving at the correct spelling of many words, and breaking words at the end of a line of writing.

Two major clues to syllabication are prefixes and suffixes, and certain vowel-consonant behavior in written words. Thus, the ability to solve the pronunciations represented by many longer printed words is built on the recognition of both structural and phonetic features.

Much of the material regarding prefixes and suffixes can be used for teaching syllabication, as well as visual recognition of word parts. This chapter section continues to build recognition of prefixes and suffixes but also stresses how these function as syllables. With practice, syllabication tends to become an automatic process. To illustrate, there will be considerable agreement among adult readers when they pronounce the following nonsense words: *dismorative, unmurly, interlate,* and *motoption.* The syllabication patterns arrived at would probably be *dis · mor · a · tive, un · mur · ly, in · ter · late,* and *mo · top · tion.* In addition, there would probably be relatively high agreement as to which syllable was to receive the primary accent: *dis · mor' · a · tive, un · mur' · ly, in' · ter · late,* and *mo · top' · tion.*

The reader's pronunciation of these nonsense words probably did not involve calling to mind rules that might apply, yet the responses were undoubtedly conditioned by previous learning and experiences that relate to principles of syllabication. Despite numerous exceptions to some generalizations dealing with syllabication, other generalizations may be useful to students aspiring to become independent readers.

Generalizations Relating to Syllabication

1. There are as many syllables in a word as there are vowel sounds. Syllables are determined by the vowel sounds heard, not by the number of vowels seen.

	Vowels Seen		Vowels Heard		Vowels Seen		Vowels Heard
measure	(4)	mezh'er	(2)	moment	(2)	mō'ment	(2)
phonics	(2)	fon iks	(2)	cheese	(3)	chēz	(1)
write	(2)	rīt	(1)	which	(1)	hwich	(1)
release	(4)	rē'lēs	(2)	precaution	(5)	prē'kô shun	(3)
skill	(1)	skill	(1)	receive	(4)	rē sēv'	(2)

2. Syllables divide between double consonants or between two consonants.

hap · pen	can · non	sud · den	ves · sel	vol · ley	com · mand
bas · ket	tar · get	cin · der	har · bor	tim · ber	wig · wam
don · key	pic · nic	gar · den	lad · der	let · ter	sup · per

3. A single consonant between vowels usually goes with the second vowel.

fa mous	ho tel	di rect	ti ger	ce ment	pu pil
ea ger	wa ter	po lice	lo cate	va cant	spi der
be gin	fi nal	be fore	pi lot	li bel	sto ry
pa rade	e lect	re ceive	lo cal	sta tion	be hind

The previous two generalizations are often combined: Divide between two consonants and in front of one.

4. As a general rule, do not divide consonant digraphs (*ch, th,* etc.) and consonant blends.

tea*ch* er	wea*th* er	ma *ch*ine	se *c*ret	a *gree*
bro*th* er	prea*ch* er	*ath* lete	coun *try*	cel e *brate*

5. The word endings *-ble, -cle, -dle, -gle, -kle, -ple, -tle,* and *-zle* form the final syllable.

mar ble	mus cle	han dle	sin gle	an kle	tem ple
ket tle	puz zle	no ble	pur ple	bat tle	bu gle

The following list of words can be used in building chalkboard or seatwork exercises. Instruct your students to practice these words so they can recognize and pronounce each one instantly. Point out how easy it is to learn to spell the words.

no ble	rat tle	sin gle	han dle	tem ple	an kle
mar ble	ket tle	wig gle	mid dle	ma ple	spar kle
sta ble	ti tle	jun gle	pad dle	ap ple	wrin kle
tum ble	bat tle	strug gle	bun dle	sam ple	sprin kle
trou ble	bot tle	gig gle	fid dle	pur ple	crin kle
fa ble	gen tle	bu gle	bri dle	stee ple	tin kle
dou ble	cat tle	ea gle	nee dle	sim ple	puz zle
rum ble	man tle	an gle	sad dle	un cle	fiz zle
peb ble	set tle	shin gle	kin dle	cir cle	muz zle
bub ble	lit tle	strag gle	pud dle	ve hi cle	daz zle

6. Usually, prefixes and suffixes form separate syllables.

re load ing	un fair	dis agree ment	pre heat ed
hope less	trans port ing	un like ly	ex cite ment

Affixes as Syllables

As we have noted, many prefixes and word endings constitute syllables that are highly consistent in regard to spelling and pronunciation. When children encounter difficulty in attacking and solving longer words, experiences should be provided that help them see the spelling and syllable patterns. The following lessons can help children recognize polysyllabic words that contain a prefix, suffix, or both.

SEEING SYLLABLES IN LONGER WORDS

A. Read down each column.

lo	con	dis
lo co	con ver	dis a
lo co mo	con ver sa	dis a gree
lo co mo tive	con ver sa tion	dis a gree ment

B. Read down each column.

lo	con	dis
lo co	con ver	dis a
lo co mo	con ver sa	dis a gree
lo co mo tive	con ver sa tion	dis a gree ment
lo co mo	con ver sa	dis a gree
lo co	con ver	dis a
lo	con	dis
locomotive	*conversation*	*disagreement*

C. Read across each line as quickly as you can.

locomotive	lo	lo co	lo co mo	locomotive
conversation	con	con ver	con ver sa	conversation
disagreement	dis	dis a	dis a gree	disagreement

D. Note the italicized parts of the first word in each column. The words in each column begin and end with the same prefix and suffix, which in every case are pronounced exactly the same. Reading down the columns, pronounce these words as quickly as you can. This practice will help you recognize and sound out words when you meet them in your reading.

*con*duc*tion*	*re*fill*able*	*dis*appoint*ment*
conformation	remarkable	disagreement
condensation	reclaimable	disarmament
conservation	recoverable	disarrangement
concentration	redeemable	displacement
conscription	recallable	disfigurement
contraction	respectable	discouragement

contribution	reliable	disenchantment
conviction	renewable	disengagement
consolidation	restrainable	discontentment

E. The following words contain prefixes and suffixes, but the words are in mixed order. Also, some prefixes and suffixes may be new to you. Practice pronouncing the words as quickly as you can.

dishonorable	resentment	discernment	remorseless
relentless	preoccupation	resistant	readjustment
premeditate	consolidation	distractible	configuration
reconstruction	distributive	preparatory	reelection
protective	recollection	consignment	disqualification
confederation	presumably	prohibitive	constructive
unseasonable	imperfection	automotive	protectorate
implication	discoloration	concealment	unwholesome

F. Each line consists of long words that contain the same prefix and word ending. The prefixes and suffixes are italicized and the words are broken into syllables. Read each line as quickly as you can, blending the syllables into the proper pronunciation of the word.

con ven *tion, con* sti tu *tion, con* ver sa *tion, con* tri bu *tion*

ex am i na *tion, ex* pe di *tion, ex* cep *tion, ex* hi bi *tion*

dis ap point *ment, dis* a gree *ment, dis* arm a *ment, dis* cour age *ment*

re fill a *ble, re* place a *ble, re* new a *ble, re* pay a *ble*

in ex act *ly, in* sane *ly, in* dis tinct *ly, in* stant *ly*

ABBREVIATIONS

Abbreviations represent a special instance of structural (visual) changes that are found in printed material. Children need to understand the following concepts about abbreviations.

1. They are a short form of writing that represents a longer word or phrase.
2. They are frequently followed by a period.
3. They are not pronounced, but the word the abbreviation stands for is pronounced.

We See	We Say	We See	We Say
Mr.	Mister	Pres.	President
Dr.	Doctor	Gov.	Governor
Ave.	Avenue	St.	Street

One approach for helping children learn and deal with abbreviations is to present a series of related terms, such as measures, language terms, state names, days of the week, names of months, titles, and so on.

Columns A and B illustrate series; column C presents mixed terms.

A		B		C	
Sunday	Sun.	inch	in.	abbreviated	abbr.
Monday	Mon.	pound	lb.	abbreviation	abbrev.
Tuesday	Tues.	mile	mi.	building	bldg.
Wednesday	Wed.	quart	qt.	plural	pl.
Thursday	Thurs.	square foot	sq. ft.	Northwest	N.W.
Friday	Fri.	yard	yd.	mountain	mt.
Saturday	Sat.	pint	pt.	Boulevard	Blvd.

Directions: Write a number of abbreviations on the chalkboard. Have volunteers give the words the abbreviations represent.

Examples:

Pres.	President
Dr.	Doctor
Ave.	_____
sq. yd.	_____
Gov.	_____
etc.	_____
St.	_____
U.S.	_____

Directions: Have the children write the abbreviations for the words listed. If they need help, they can choose from the abbreviations in the clue box.

Clue Box

D.C.	Gov.	Atty.	Prof.	Wk.
Dr.	Bldg.	Ave.	Chap.	Mr.

Mister	_____	Doctor	_____
Building	_____	Governor	_____
Professor	_____	Week	_____
District of Columbia	_____	Avenue	_____
Chapter	_____	Attorney	_____

Teacher: "In the blank space under each underlined word, write the abbreviation of that word."

1. Last <u>Monday</u> the <u>President</u> spoke to the <u>Governor.</u>
   _____   _____   _____

2. To write the <u>plural</u> of <u>pound</u> add an *s.*
   _____   _____

3. The <u>doctor</u> has an office on Elm <u>Avenue.</u>
   _____   _____

4. The words <u>mile,</u> <u>foot,</u> and <u>quart</u> are measures.
   ____ ____   _____

5. The <u>professor</u> lives on <u>Mountain</u> <u>Boulevard.</u>
   _____   _____   _____

RECOGNIZING CONTRACTIONS

In oral language, children both use and understand contractions. In reading, they need to learn the visual patterns involved, along with the following facts about contractions.

- A contraction is a single word that results from combining two or more words.
- A contraction omits one or more letters found in the combining words.
- A contraction contains an apostrophe where a letter or letters have been omitted.
- A contraction carries the same meaning as the long form it represents, but it has its own pronunciation.

Children need practice in seeing and saying the contracted forms so they can eventually master them as sight words. There are three steps in dealing with contractions: (a) seeing words and contractions together, (b) matching words and contractions, and (c) writing contractions.

1. Seeing Words and Contractions Together

Teacher: "Look at the two words in each line of the first column and see how they form a contraction when combined in the second column."

Words	Contractions	Words	Contractions
I am	I'm	do not	don't
you are	you're	does not	doesn't
it is	it's	was not	wasn't
I have	I've	would not	wouldn't
you have	you've	could not	couldn't
they have	they've	should not	shouldn't

2. Matching Words and Contractions

Teacher: "Draw a line from the two words in each row of column A to their contraction in column B."

A	B	A	B
does not	I've	let us	wouldn't
I have	doesn't	would not	let's
do not	can't	was not	I'd
I am	don't	could not	wasn't
cannot	I'm	I would	couldn't

3. Writing Contractions

Teacher: "Write the contraction for each of the following word pairs."

they are _____   I have _____

she is _____   should not _____

must not _____   here is _____

will not _____   they have _____

Teacher: "In the blank following each sentence, write the contraction for the italicized words."

Example:

Bill *cannot* go swimming. <u>can't</u>

1. *We will* be careful with our campfire. _____
2. Sue *did not* brush her teeth after breakfast. _____
3. *Let us* have a sack race. _____
4. They *could not* catch a fish. _____
5. *I have* eaten my lunch already. _____
6. Larry *does not* play in the street. _____
7. *I am* very happy to see you. _____
8. Karen and Jeff *were not* ready to sing. _____
9. This *is not* my house. _____
10. They *do not* seem very friendly. _____

FINDING LITTLE WORDS IN BIG WORDS

In the past, considerable confusion has arisen over a particular practice. It was once quite common, in materials prepared for teachers, to suggest that children be taught to look for little words in big words. The theory was that after children had learned to recognize smaller words, it would be useful to them as readers if they would see these smaller units when they were part of larger words. This, it was alleged, would help children solve or pronounce the larger words.

This practice, of course, has only limited utility or justification. It is justifiable when dealing with compound words or known root words to which prefixes or suffixes have been added. In general, however, the habit of seeing little words in big words will actually interfere with sounding out words in a great many cases. This is true even in beginning reading.

To illustrate, let us look at some of the more common "little words." In each of the following, if children see and pronounce the little word, they cannot arrive at the pronunciation of the word under attack.

at:	bo at	b at h	pl at e	o at	at e	at omic
	r at e	pot at o	co at	at hlete	he at	
as:	bo as t	ple as e	As ia	co as t	as hore	
on:	on e	t on e	d on e	h on ey	st on e	
he:	he at	he lp	c he st	bat he	the y	w he at
me:	me at	a me n	ca me	sa me	a me nd	

Hundreds of other examples could be added, using the previous list of little words and many others, such as *in, an, it, am, if, us, is, to, up, go, no, lid, are,* and *or.* Little words (or their spellings) occur frequently in larger polysyllabic words, but the pronounceable autonomy of the little words in big words is often lost. Therefore, teaching children to look for little words in big words has little justification from the standpoint of phonic or structural analysis.

ACCENT

Every syllable in polysyllabic words is not spoken with the same force or stress. These variations in stress are called *accent.* The syllable that receives the most stress is said to have the primary accent (*car′ pen ter*). Other syllables in a word may have a secondary accent, or syllables may be unaccented (*in′ vi ta′ tion*).

Teaching accent is usually reserved for the later stages of word analysis. The majority of words met in beginning reading consist of one or two syllables; longer words are those a child has probably heard or spoken hundreds of times (*yesterday, grandmother, afternoon, tomorrow, telephone*).

Accent is important in using a dictionary when the objective is to determine a word's pronunciation. It is important in reading when children meet words they do not know on sight, but have heard and whose meanings they know. For instance, if children have heard or used the words *celebration* and *appendicitis* but do not recognize the printed symbols, they may distort the pronunciation through improper syllabication: *cē leb′ ra tion* rather than *cēl e′ bra tion;* or improper accent: *ap′ pen di ci tis.*

Skills to be taught include the following.

1. How to read primary and secondary accent marks in the dictionary.
2. The habit of trying different soundings if the first attempt does not result in a known word.
3. The use of clues or rules of accent in attempting the pronunciation of words.

Such clues and rules include:

> In compound words, the primary accent usually falls on (or within) the first word (sail' boat, wolf' hound, fish' er man, door' way).
>
> In two-syllable words containing a double consonant, the accent usually falls on the first syllable (cop' per, mil' lion, pret' ty, val' ley, sud' den).
>
> When *ck* ends a syllable, that syllable is usually accented (chick' en, rock' et, pack' age, nick' el, mack' er el).
>
> Syllables comprised of a consonant plus *le* are usually not accented (*ble, cle, dle, gle, ple, tle*).
>
> Many of the instances covered by the preceding rules might be summarized under one inclusive generalization: In two-syllable root words, the accent usually falls on the first syllable, except when the second syllable contains two vowels (pa rade', sur prise', sus tain', ma chine', sup pose').
>
> Prefixes and suffixes are usually not accented (lone' ly, un hap' pi ly, re fresh' ment, dis re spect' ful, re tract' a ble).
>
> Two-syllable words ending with *y* are usually accented on the first syllable (cit' y, ear' ly, ba' by, can' dy, sto' ry, par' ty, fun' ny, mer' ry, tru' ly).

Shift in Accent

Adding suffixes to some longer words may cause a shift in the primary accent. The words in the left-hand column have the primary accent on the first or second syllables, but in the right-hand column, the accent has shifted.

u' ni verse	u ni ver' sal
mi' cro scope	mi cro scop' ic
vac' ci nate	vac ci na' tion
ac' ci dent	ac ci den' tal
con firm'	con fir ma' tion

We can thus generalize that in many longer words, the primary accent falls on the syllable before the suffix. Exception: In most cases, the primary accent falls two syllables before the suffix *-ate:* ag' gra vate, dom' i nate, ed' u cate, hes' i tate, med' i tate, and op' er ate.

Homographs and accent shift.   Homographs are words with identical spellings, different meanings, and, in some cases, different pronunciations. Note in the following sentences that usage or context determines the pronunciation. Changes may occur in accent or in both accent and syllabication. For example, present = pre/sent' or pres'/ent; content = con/tent' or con'/tent.

1. The mayor was *present* to *present* the awards.
2. The editor was not *content* with the *content* of the article.

3. Always be careful to *address* the letter to the correct *address*.

The following words can be used in exercises when context is provided.

protest—protest	annex—annex
perfect—perfect	rebel—rebel
convict—convict	object—object
permit—permit	contract—contract
excuse—excuse	produce—produce
subject—subject	conduct—conduct

STRESS ON WORDS WITHIN SENTENCES

When working on the accents of syllables within words, one might point out the parallel of stress on words within sentences. While this is not usually seen as a word analysis skill, it is a most important factor in mastering the reading process. Concomitant teaching of accent and stress may help children understand both concepts. Simple sentences might be placed on the board. Children should read the sentences, place added stress on each underlined word, and note the effect of the stress on the melody of the sentence.

<u>This</u> is very bad news.

This is very bad <u>news</u>.

This is <u>very</u> bad news.

This is very <u>bad</u> news.

USE OF THE DICTIONARY AS A WORD ATTACK SKILL

As children become independent readers, they are likely to meet a number of words that they do not know or use in their speaking vocabularies or they cannot easily solve by applying phonic generalizations.

Because the dictionary is a source for the pronunciation of words, certain dictionary skills are, in effect, word analysis skills. Effective use of the dictionary involves learning the speech equivalents of visual symbols, including primary and secondary accent marks and other diacritical marks, such as the macron (¯) (make = māk), the breve (˘) (ăt), and the schwa (ə) (ten dər).

Different dictionaries and glossaries in textbooks may use a variety of symbols, or phonetic spellings, all of which will have to be mastered. For example,

technique: tek nēk, tĕk nēk, tek neek

temperament: tem′ p ə r ə m ənt, tĕm pēr ment

(For a discussion of the schwa sound, see Chapter 6).

Children should be taught word attack skills using the same pronunciation key that is found in the dictionaries they use. The dictionary will be of little value in arriving at the correct pronunciation of words if these various symbols are not mastered.

 # SUMMARY

Teaching the decoding process involves more than just letter-sound relationships. Children must also learn to recognize and respond quickly to a number of frequently occurring visual patterns found in English writing. These include inflectional endings, plurals, contractions, abbreviations, prefixes, and suffixes.

After many experiences with affixes (which are also syllables), successful readers develop the ability to treat these word parts as units rather than decoding the same set of letters separately each time they encounter the letters. Thus, in teaching structural analysis skills, the goal is to provide experiences that lead children to this type of behavior. The structural changes that occur over and over in English writing must be instantly recognized. Fortunately, many of these high-frequency affixes have a high degree of consistency in both their visual patterns and sounds.

Bibliography

Adams, M. J. (1990). *Beginning to read: Thinking and learning about print*. Cambridge, MA: MIT Press.

The Reading Teacher. (1991). Beginning to read: A critique by literacy professionals and a response by Marilyn Jager Adams, *44*, 366–395.

Bailey, M. H. (1967). The utility of phonic generalizations in grades one through six. *The Reading Teacher, 20*, 413–418.

Bhat, P., Griffin, C. C., & Sindlelar, P. T. (2003). Phonological awareness instruction for middle school students with learning disabilities. *Learning Disability Quarterly*, *26*, 73.

Bishop, A. G. (2003). Prediction of first grade reading achievement: A comparison of fall and winter kindergarten screenings. *Learning Disability Quarterly*, *25*, 189–200.

Bloomfield, L., & Barnhart, C. (1961). *Let's read: A linguistic approach.* Detroit: MI: Wayne State University Press.

Bruner, J. S. (1972). Address to the International Reading Association Convention. Detroit.

Burmeister, L. E. (1968). Vowel pairs. *The Reading Teacher, 21, 445–452.*

Burrows, A., & Lourie, Z. (1963). When two vowels go walking. *The Reading Teacher, 17,* 79–82.

Clymer, T. (1963). The utility of phonic generalizations in the primary grades. *The Reading Teacher, 16,* 252–258.

Cunningham, J. W. (2001). The national reading panel report. *Reading Research Quarterly*, *36*, 326–334.

Cunningham, P. M. (1990). The names test: A quick assessment of decoding ability. *The Reading Teacher, 44*, 124–129.

Cunningham, P. M., & Cunningham, J. W. (1992). Making words: Enhancing the inverted spelling-decoding connection. *The Reading Teacher, 46*, 106–115.

Downing, J. A. (1963). *Experiments with Pitman's initial teaching alphabet in British schools*. New York: Initial Teaching Alphabet Publications.

Downing, J. A. (May, 1965). Common misconceptions about i.t.a. *Elementary English*, *42*, 492–501.

Downing, J. A. (December, 1967). Can i.t.a. be improved? *Elementary English*, *44*, 849–855.

Emans, R. (1967). The usefulness of phonic generalizations above the primary grades. *The Reading Teacher, 20*, 419–425.

Fink, R., & Keiserman, P. (1969). *ITA teacher training workbook and guide*. New York: Initial Teaching Alphabet Publications.

Flesch, R. (1955). *Why Johnny can't read*. New York: Harper.

Fries, C. C. (1963). *Linguistics and reading*. New York: Holt, Rinehart, & Winston.

Fry, E. (1988). The most common phonograms. *The Reading Teacher, 51*, 620–622.

Gattengo, C. (1962). *Words in color.* Chicago: Learning Materials.

Gentry, J. R. (2000). A retrospective on invented spelling and a look forward. *The Reading Teacher, 54*, 318–332.

Goodman, K. S. (1992). I didn't found whole language. *The Reading Teacher, 46,* 188–198.

Heilman, A. W. (1977). *Principles and practices of teaching reading.* (4th ed.) Columbus, OH: Merrill.

Hempenstall, K. (1997). The whole language-phonics controversy: A historical perspective. *Educational Psychology, 17,* 399–418.

Johnston, F. R. (1999). The timing and teaching of word families. *The Reading Teacher, 53,* 64–75.

Juel, C. M., & Cupp, C. (2000). Learning to read words: Linguistic units and instructional strategies. *Reading Research Quarterly, 35,* 458–492.

Lee, C. H., & Turvey, M. T. (2003). Silent letters and phonological priming. *Journal of Psycholinguistic Research, 32,* 313–333.

Mesmer, H. A. E. (2001). Decodable text: A review of what we know. *Reading Research and Instruction, 40,* 121–142.

Moustafa, M., & Maldonado, C. E. (1999). Whole-to-post phonics instruction: Building on what children know to help them know more. *The Reading Teacher, 52,* 448–458.

Norman, K. A., & Calfee, R. C. (2004). Tile test: A hands-on approach for assessing phonics in the early grades. *The Reading Teacher, 58,* 42–52.

Oaks, R. E. (1952). A study of the vowel situations in a primary vocabulary. *Education, 72,* 604–617.

Pollard, R. (1889). *Pollard's synthetic method.* Chicago: Western Publishing House.

Roberts, T. A. (2003). Effects of alphabet-letter instruction on young children's word recognition. *Journal of Education Psychology, 95,* 41–51.

Smith, F. (1973). *Psycholinguistics and reading.* New York: Holt, Rinehart, & Winston.

Smith, N. B. (1934). *American Reading Instruction.* New York: Silver Burdett.

Snider, V. E. (1997). The relationship between phonemic awareness and later reading achievement. *Journal of Education Research, 90,* 203–211.

Stahl, S. A. (1992). Saying the "P" word: Nine guidelines for exemplary phonics instruction. *The Reading Teacher, 45,* 618–625.

Stahl, S. A., Osborn, J., & Lehr, F. (1990). *Beginning to read: Thinking and learning about print—a summary.* Champaign, IL: University of Illinois.

Strickland, D. S. (1994). Reinventing our literacy programs. Books, basics, balance. *The Reading Teacher, 48,* 294–302.

Troia, G. A. (1999). Phonological awareness intervention research: A critical review of the experimental methodology. *Reading Research Quarterly, 34,* 28–52.

Wood, C., & Terrell, C. (1998). Pre-school phonological awareness and subsequent literacy development. *Educational Psychology, 18,* 253–274.

Yopp, H. K. (1995). A test for assessing phonemic awareness in young children. *The Reading Teacher, 49,* 20–28.

Yopp, H. K., & Yopp, R. H. (2001). Supporting phonemic awareness development in the classroom. *The Reading Teacher, 54,* 130–143.

Index